FLORIDA STATE
UNIVERSITY LIBRARIES

JAN 8 1998

TALLAHASSEE, FLORIDA

THE RACIAL DIMENSION OF AMERICAN OVERSEAS COLONIAL POLICY

Recent Titles in
Contributions in Comparative Colonial Studies

Black and White in Southern Zambia: The Tonga Plateau Economy and British Imperialism, 1890–1939
Kenneth P. Vickery

The Carrier Corps: Military Labor in the East African Campaign, 1914–1918
Geoffrey Hodges

Germans in the Tropics: Essays in German Colonial History
Arthur J. Knoll and Lewis H. Gann

War, Cooperation, and Conflict: The European Possessions in the Caribbean, 1939–1945
Fitzroy Andre Baptiste

No Country for a Gentleman: British Rule in Egypt, 1883–1907
William M. Welch, Jr.

Railway Imperialism
Clarence B. Davis and Kenneth E. Wilburn, editors, with Ronald E. Robinson

Countdown to Rebellion: British Policy in Cyprus, 1939–1955
George Horton Kelling

Science and Social Science Research in British India, 1780–1880: The Role of Anglo-Indian Associations and Government
Edward W. Ellsworth

Journalists for Empire: The Imperial Debate in the Edwardian Stately Press, 1903–1913
James D. Startt

Imperial Diplomacy in the Era of Decolonization: The Sudan and Anglo-Egyptian Relations, 1945–1956
W. Travis Hanes III

The Man on the Spot: Essays on British Empire History
Roger D. Long, editor

Imperialism and Colonialism: Essays on the History of European Expansion
H. L. Wesseling

THE RACIAL DIMENSION OF AMERICAN OVERSEAS COLONIAL POLICY

Hazel M. McFerson

Contributions in Comparative Colonial Studies, Number 33

GREENWOOD PRESS
Westport, Connecticut • London

Library of Congress Cataloging-in-Publication Data

McFerson, Hazel M.
　　The racial dimension of American overseas colonial policy / Hazel M. McFerson.
　　　　p.　cm.—(Contributions in comparative colonial studies,
　ISSN 0163–3813 ; no. 33)
　　Includes bibliographical references and index.
　　ISBN 0–313–28996–4 (alk. paper)
　　1. United States—Insular possessions—History.　2. United States—
Territorial expansion—History.　3. Racism—Political aspects—
United States—Insular possessions—History.　I. Title.
　II. Series.
F970.M39　 1997
973—dc21　　　　97–2233

British Library Cataloguing in Publication Data is available.

Copyright © 1997 by Hazel M. McFerson

All rights reserved. No portion of this book may be
reproduced, by any process or technique, without the
express written consent of the publisher.

Library of Congress Catalog Card Number: 97–2233
ISBN: 0–313–28996–4
ISSN: 0163–3813

First published in 1997

Greenwood Press, 88 Post Road West, Westport, CT 06881
An imprint of Greenwood Publishing Group, Inc.

Printed in the United States of America

The paper used in this book complies with the
Permanent Paper Standard issued by the National
Information Standards Organization (Z39.48–1984).

10　9　8　7　6　5　4　3　2　1

Copyright Acknowledgments

Grateful acknowledgment is given for permission to quote from the following source: Hazel M. McFerson, "Racial Tradition and Comparative Political Analysis: Notes Toward a Theoretical Framework," *Ethnic and Racial Studies* 2, no. 4 (October 1979).

Every reasonable effort has been made to trace the owners of copyright materials in this book, but in some instances this has proven impossible. The author and publisher will be glad to receive information leading to more complete acknowledgments in subsequent printings of the book and in the meantime extend their apologies for any omissions.

Contents

Tables		vii
Preface		ix
Introduction		1
1.	The Racial Tradition Approach	5
2.	The Evolution of the American Racial Tradition	23
3.	Race, the Law, and the Courts	51
4.	Race and American Territorial Expansion	79
5.	"For a Mess of Pottage": Pragmatic Materialism and American Colonial Policy	99
6.	The Case of Puerto Rico	117
7.	The Case of the U.S. Virgin Islands	139
8.	Back to the Future?	167
References		171
Index		183

Tables

4.1	Trends in Self-Government	89
4.2	Racial and Ethnic Composition of the U.S. Territories, 1994	91
7.1	Per Capita Income in Selected Caribbean Countries, 1970 and 1994	150
7.2	Racial Structure of the U.S. Virgin Islands, 1917–1990	151
7.3	Population of the U.S. Virgin Islands, 1917–1995	157

Preface

From Somalia to Bosnia to Zaire, American foreign policy—now deprived of the bright guiding light of cold war rivalry—has had to contend with the obvious importance of racial and ethnic variables in international conflict. Undoubtedly, this will continue to be the case for the foreseeable future. Yet, while much has been written on the impact of racial and ethnic factors in the conflicted countries themselves, little attention has been given to the influence on American policy of *American* racial attitudes. This book provides a test case of sorts: the complex interaction between racial attitudes and foreign policy that emerges from the American colonial experience in overseas territories acquired at the turn of the century. This interaction is the main focus of this book and is intended to suggest a useful perspective for the analysis of future foreign policy issues.

Toward this end, the book first defines the key elements of the American "racial tradition," as it evolved from early history through the period of continental territorial expansion. The ambivalent nature of the overseas colonial empire, which the United States backed into as a result of the Spanish-American War, is then described. Finally, the book traces the impact on American colonial policy of exporting to overseas territories the peculiar set of racial attitudes that had developed in America itself, and that shaped domestic policies toward nonwhites: people of mixed-race ancestry, Asians, Hispanics, Africans, and Native Americans. These patterns would also be duplicated—both in general overseas policies toward nonwhites and specifically in American overseas territories, represented here by the cases of Puerto Rico and the U.S. Virgin Islands. The book's specific focus on the interaction of racial ideology and territorial expansion is limited to domestic racial influences on overseas colonial policy and does not include either an exhaustive account of nineteenth-century race relations or a narrative of the detailed experience of all American overseas territories.

The key themes are two. First, the explanation of complex events must be approached through the interplay of history, politics, and sociology. The American racial tradition cannot be understood except in the historical and political context within which it evolved. Racial ideology, in turn, had a significant influence on the future course of American history and on the specific political decisions taken about the evolving political status of the predominantly nonwhite territories acquired after 1898. Second, although the interaction of ideas and events is well understood in the domestic arena, it is often forgotten that the ideas themselves were exported to influence events elsewhere. Thus, to paraphrase John Maynard Keynes, American overseas colonial policymakers viewed problems through the prism of their own racial attitudes, which were shaped in the context of domestic race relations.

Thus, the direct audience for this book consists of those concerned with contemporary American history, or with the makings of foreign policy, or with American race relations. This book should also be useful for anyone wishing to learn about the U.S. colonial experiment and should interest a more general readership as well.

Indirectly, this book has had a very long gestation. I have been concerned with the formation of racial traditions from the beginning of my academic life and interested in colonialism ever since residing and teaching in Puerto Rico in 1972–1973 and in Fiji in 1977–1978. My understanding of the importance of the *interaction* between ethnicity, history, and politics is more recent—but still goes back ten years, to residence and field work in Somalia in 1985–1987.

In this long voyage, I benefited greatly from the warm support and friendship of a number of outstanding intellectuals—former professors who became friends—whose influence spans several decades. These include the late Dr. Nathan I. Huggins, former director of the W.E.B. DuBois Institute, Harvard University, and Dr. Gene Sharp, founder, Albert Einstein Institution, Cambridge, Massachusetts, on whose board of directors I currently sit. Also a special thanks to Dr. Lawrence Fuchs and Dr. Ruth S. Morgenthau, both at Brandeis University, and Dr. Martin Kilson at Harvard University, all of whom provided constant encouragement and support. My frequent visits to Puerto Rico and the U.S. Virgin Islands were greatly enhanced by the hospitality and extensive contacts of Drs. Fuad Andic and Suphan Andic, formerly of the University of Puerto Rico at Rio Piedras.

Since joining the faculty at George Mason University, I have benefited from the warm support and intellectual guidance of my colleagues, particularly those without whose support the project probably would have died.

Among those who commented on various drafts, and provided invaluable advice, a special thanks goes to Dr. Charles ("Chip") Hauss, Dr. Melvin Friedlander, Dr. Barbara Knight, Dr. Nand Hart-Nibbrig, Dr. Julia Mahler, Dr. James Pfiffner, and Dr. Louise H. White, chair, Department of Public and International Affairs. Also thanks to Dr. John Stone, former chairman of Mason's Sociology-Anthropology Department; to Dr. Richard Rubenstein and Dr. Chris Mitchell, former chairmen, Mason's Institute for Conflict Analysis and Resolution (ICAR); and to my colleague Dr. Brack Brown for specific terminology that was helpful in documenting certain ideas. My editor and copyeditor, John Dan Eades and Arlene Belzer, respectively, at Greenwood Press, also merit a special thanks. Ms. Belzer's painstaking and perceptive editing significantly sharpened the manuscript.

Finally, I am grateful to my wonderful family for their constant support, patience, and love. My husband, Dr. Salvatore Schiavo-Campo, and our three children: Rino, Jr., Pia, and Mara, daughter-in-law Zara, and granddaughter Jianna Hazel.

Introduction

> It is from the results of colonial policy rather than from statements of its objectives that its true character may be ascertained.
> —J. S. Furnivall, 1948.

Until 1898, American territorial expansion focused on acquiring and consolidating contiguous territories in continental North America (except for Alaska, which was purchased from Russia in 1867). After 1898, largely as the result of victory in the Spanish-American War, America found itself in a phase of overseas territorial expansion. With the acquisition of territories in the Caribbean and the Pacific, the United States became the last Western power to join the Age of Imperialism.

The major territories acquired in 1898 were Cuba, Puerto Rico, Hawaii, Guam, and the Philippines. The Eastern Samoan Islands were acquired in 1899 by agreement with Britain and Germany. American colonial holdings increased in 1917 with the purchase of the former Danish Antilles, and the defeat of Japan in World War II added the newly created American Trust Territory of the Pacific Islands, consisting of the Northern Mariana Islands, Palau, Micronesia, and the Caroline Islands. The remaining American overseas territories include Midway Island (annexed earlier as a Pacific coaling station in 1867), Baker and Howland Islands, Jarvis Island, Johnston Atoll, Navassa Island, and Palmyra Atoll; except for Midway and Johnston (respectively with 453 and 1,375 residents—mostly military personnel) all are uninhabited.

A convenient starting point is William Franklyn Willoughby's taxonomy of American territorial expansion in three periods (Willoughby, 1905.) The first period, 1783–1853, began with the British recognition in the Treaty of 1783 of the claims of the original thirteen states to the territory to the west as far as the Mississippi River. The second period, 1853–1898, consisted of continental expansion beyond the Mississippi, predated by the acquisition of Texas and other territory following the war with Mexico. The third period, the period of overseas territorial expansion, began with the annexation of the Hawaiian Islands in 1898 and ended with the creation of the American Trust Territory of the Pacific Islands in 1947. While race was never totally absent from the ideology underpinning American territorial expansion, it was a key dimension of the phenomenon during the second and especially the third periods, with its overt colonial motives and manifestations. The focus of this book is on these latter periods of American territorial expansion, covering a span of about a century.

RACE AND AMERICAN TERRITORIAL EXPANSION

This book is about history, politics, and race. The key theme is that the relationship of the United States to its newly acquired territories has been shaped by prevailing "racial tradition" and the social structure in the United States itself. Prevailing racial attitudes have served as important justifiers of territorial expansion. (It is well known, for example, that attitudes of racial superiority contributed to justifying the expropriation of Native American lands.) Moreover, following territorial acquisition, the "racial tradition" was exported to the territories. That racial tradition largely determined policies toward the territories, the nature of social and racial conflict, and the direction and pace of political evolution.

As noted, the racial factor was not totally absent even in the first period of American expansion—to the Mississippi. It is, however, with the second period, from the mid–nineteenth century, that it became a major dimension of the phenomenon. The race of the predominantly white residents of the new territories in the southwest and northwest ("white men's territories") was a key factor in these territories' admission to statehood—as was the race of the politically dominant white minority in Hawaii. By contrast, the fact that the populations of the "flag territories" acquired after 1898 were predominantly nonwhite has led these territories along a path of political evolution different from that of the earlier acquisitions. From the very beginning of overseas colonial expansion (and at the very core of "Manifest Destiny" ideology), the nonwhite inhabitants of the flag territories were viewed as "alien" and "dissimilar"—as much the result of their race as of the distant locations and different natural conditions: people of "foreign blood" speaking foreign languages. In addition, the period of overseas acquisition followed the tightening of racial segregation in the United States resulting from the 1896 Supreme Court ruling in *Plessy v. Ferguson* (which institutionalized "separate but equal" Jim Crow laws and practices).

Race is a major reason—this book argues—why none of these territories have become states, nor are they ever likely to be. They are instead likely to settle onto one or another of the other three political options: (1) independence (e.g., the Philippines); (2) "commonwealth" or "free association" status, in one or another of its possible variants (e.g., Puerto Rico, the Northern Marianas and the Marshalls); or (3) "unincorporated territory" status (e.g., the U.S. Virgin Islands). Puerto Rico and the U.S. Virgin Islands are the major cases in point.

ORGANIZATION OF THE BOOK

The relationship between America's territorial expansion and its racial attitudes is examined through the concept of "racial tradition," discussed in chapter 1. Chapter 2 traces the historical development of the American racial tradition by examining the evolution of attitudes toward Native Americans, African Americans, and Asians, and chapter 3 recounts the role of the law and the courts in institutionalizing these attitudes. Chapter 4 reviews American territorial expansion of the second and third periods and the influence of racial attitudes on the policy adopted toward the new territories. Chapter 5 explains the differences between American and European colonialism; the genesis and nature of American colonial ideology (including the powerful but little-known influence of Booker T. Washington); the characteristics of colonial administration, and the "basic bargain" of American rule: provision of short-term material benefits in exchange for the abandonment of claims to rapid political advancement. These chapters show how the American racial tradition established by the latter half of the nineteenth century was superimposed onto the Caribbean and Pacific possessions—exporting attitudes toward the nonwhite inhabitants, defining the nature and practice of colonial policy, and determining the path of later political development.

Although data and illustrations are drawn from most of the present and former United States colonial possessions and are used throughout the book as appropriate, the two most pertinent current cases are Puerto Rico and the U.S. Virgin Islands. Chapters 6 and 7 accordingly present in detail the interaction among race, politics, and society in these two territories and their past political evolution and future prospects. These cases demonstrate the wide impact of the substitution of the flexible racial tradition of the Spaniards and the Danes with the much more rigid American variant. A brief concluding chapter looks at the recent elements of flexibility in the American racial tradition, their possible influence on American views of other-race and mixed-race people of the territories, and the likely prospects for the future of the remaining overseas possessions.

1 *The Racial Tradition Approach*

THE LIMITS OF A-RACIAL POLITICAL ANALYSIS

Two of the most widely used theoretical concepts to study political change and social conflict have been "modernization" and "plural society" theories (Apter, 1965; Furnivall, 1948; Stone, 1985). Although dated, both concepts still retain their validity in directing attention to underlying structural aspects of race relations in multiracial and multiethnic societies. Although modernization theories, in particular, have come under criticism for some basic assumptions about sociopolitical change and development (including a value-bias in the direction of westernization), both theories have directed attention to some important structural characteristics of colonial and post-colonial societies. The concept of modernization directs attention to the changes taking place in indigenous societies as the result of both external and internal factors. The plural society thesis facilitates comparative analysis of Western and non-Western societies and contributes to explaining consensus and conflict. Both, however, have by and large overlooked the interaction between racial ideology, racial formation, and sociopolitical variables. This is a serious weakness in view of the increased importance of racial and ethnic conflict in the post–Cold War world.

As noted by Ira Katznelson, despite considerable gains in methodological sophistication and despite a growing recognition that issues of race are of global significance, race relations scholars have operated within the relatively closed world of the traditional literature on race, while students of comparative politics remain largely uninformed by that literature. He continues:

"By themselves, the physical facts of race are of little or no analytical interest. Racial-physical characteristics assume meaning only when they become criteria of stratification. Thus studies of race inescapably put politics—which fundamentally, is about organized inequality—at the core of their concern" (Katznelson, 1973, p. 13).

The extensive literature of the 1940s and 1950s on psychological explanations of race relations is not helpful. On the contrary, "prejudice theories" may well have led away from an improved understanding of the interaction of race with social and political developments. As R. A. Schermerhorn puts it:

If we begin with the matter of prejudice, any approach to [race relations] from this viewpoint has a subtle tendency to psychologize group relations by seeing them as personality process writ large. . . . If research has confirmed anything in this area it is that prejudice is the product of situations, historical situations, economic situations, political situations; it is not a little demon that emerges in people because they are depraved. (1970, p. 6)

Among the very few early scholars to pay attention to the *interaction* of class and culture with the characteristics of racial ideology and structure are Christopher Bagley and Carl N. Degler. Bagley, in his study of Dutch pluralism (1973), examined the reasons for the differential incorporation of nonwhite former colonials into contemporary British and Dutch society. In his view, the greater racial tolerance of the Netherlands (relative to Britain) is the result of both institutional and ideological factors. He cites the influence of religion and the degree of consensus on social peace maintained in Dutch society by a number of institutionalized beliefs and modes of behavior. His conclusions highlight the relationship between cultural factors, national ideology, and racial attitudes. Degler's analysis of slavery and race relations in Brazil and the United States also points to the importance of national ideology, culture, and social variables as key elements in shaping a country's past and contemporary race relations (1971). In addition, Degler suggests that current race relations in multiracial societies are often rooted in historical legacies of institutionalized inequality such as slavery and colonialism that persist and are reinforced by power differentials of whites and nonwhites: "Upon power depends the ability to put into practice the perception . . . black or colored peoples have not been in a position to enforce their sense of difference upon the white man" (Degler, 1971, p. 245). Subordinate societies are vulnerable since the dominant segment often determines official policy in race relations in line with its own prevailing racial tradition and attitudes.

On balance, however, it is fair to say that a conceptual framework linking the structure and ideology of race with the more conventional variables of class and culture, is conspicuous for its absence. This chapter formulates

THE RACIAL TRADITION APPROACH

such a framework. We will see in the next chapter how the American variant of race relations developed and point out later in the book the practical application of these concepts to the policy and practice of American territorial expansion.

The spectrum of possible positions on the role of race in society can be summarized in the following three statements: (1) Race alone matters; (2) Race matters; and (3) Race doesn't matter. Many modernization and plural society theorists, having demonstrated that it is false that "race alone matters," proceed as if they had thereby established that race doesn't matter at all—a clear non sequitur. This book instead argues that conflict in the American plural society and the nature and policy of American territorial expansion have been to a major extent influenced by the American way of looking at race.

THE CONCEPT OF RACIAL TRADITION

The term "racial tradition" as used here refers to the complex of beliefs, attitudes, images, taxonomies, laws, and social customs that shape the structure of race relations and racial formation in multiracial societies. The racial tradition approach assumes that patterns of race relations (manifested among other things in the intensity of racial conflict and value dissonance about racial matters) are best understood by analyzing the historical evolution of racial thought.

Central to the concept of racial tradition are the following: (1) prevailing ideas about racial group superiority and inferiority as manifested in custom as well as in formal law; (2) the role of race relative to the more conventional variables of stratification, for example, class and culture; and (3) the criteria used to classify racial groups, the resultant hierarchy of race groups, and the centrality to this arrangement of the role of either genotypic or phenotypic definitions in racial formation of race. One basic implication is that the intensity of conflict in different systems is partly the result of sharp discontinuities in the socioracial status ranking of individuals belonging to different racial groups. (By socioracial status is meant the concordance between the ranking of individuals by race and the ranking by social and cultural standards.) When the ranking is more continuous, status mobility is perceived as possible and conflict tends to be less intense.

Racial traditions determine the mode of allocating or denying socioracial status. Socioracial status is allocated or withheld on the basis of a number of variables including: physical features, stereotypes, color, cultural orientation, past and present socioeconomic conditions, political power and past historical status in relation to institutionalized patterns of inequality (namely slavery, colonialism, and the subordinate or dominant position of the group in these structures). In the contemporary period, the opposite poles in the status continuum have been Europeans (dominant) and non-Western, non-white indigenous (dominated) peoples.

It is essential to note that racial traditions are dynamic—although only in the very long term. They can undergo modification as the result of a number of factors, including changes in the power situation. The ability to sustain or put into practice a particular racial tradition is dependent upon the power differentials of different racial groups and institutionalized systems of inequality including colonialism, neocolonialism, and slavery. In their absence, the characteristics of the prevailing racial tradition are likely to change over time. As we shall see in the next chapter, the American racial tradition has changed considerably through history since preindependence times, in response to economic changes and political ideology.

The concept of racial tradition is pertinent for several reasons. First, dominant or colonizing powers formulate policy in line with their own racial tradition, with profound consequences for the local society. (The reverse is, of course, also true, with the objectives of empire contributing to the shaping of racial ideologies.) Feelings of racial group superiority, reinforced by cultural and technological differences, are often translated into racial policy, as, for example, when the dominant group embarks upon internal or external imperialist expansion, or if a group, characterized by visible differences, is introduced into the territorial space claimed by the dominant group. Second, societies where institutionalized inequalities exist (such as slavery, "internal colonialism," colonial, and neocolonial systems) tend to absorb the racial mores of the dominant segment, which has the physical capacity to enforce racial stratification. Third, institutionalized inequalities have generally meant European control over people of non-European ancestry and thus have been concomitant with notions of racial superiority and inferiority. (This can also be applied to postindependence societies in which the national bourgeoisie incorporates the aesthetic and cultural values of the former dominant group into its own racial tradition.) Fourth, in multiracial societies, the prevailing definitions of race, values, and beliefs, have far-reaching structural implications and determine not only the structure of race relations but also, in part, the characteristics of political activity. Finally, the concept of racial tradition helps to define the role and weight of ascriptive criteria (such as genotype or color) relative to nonascriptive criteria (such as culture, income, or skills) in the determination of individual mobility, economic opportunity, social status, and access to power.

Consequently, a particular racial tradition can have an impact on a society similar to that of modernization, especially on criteria of stratification, elite formation, and characteristics of political activity. Both the concepts of modernization and of racial tradition are concerned with assessing the relative weight of ascriptive or nonascriptive criteria as primary determinants of group or individual status and mobility in multiracial societies.

In the racial tradition approach, a key consideration is the presence or

THE RACIAL TRADITION APPROACH

absence of a mixed-race group, the extent to which it is recognized as a separate socioracial category, and the consequences of this for political activity and social conflict. Neither plural society nor modernization theorists pursue this line of analysis, even though a mixed-race intermediate group exists in many of the societies that have attracted their attention. Wherever European powers maintained colonies or dominated indigenous societies, there developed a biologically mixed-race group. As is well known, countries maintaining colonial dominance sent representatives to the dominated areas to further imperial and commercial interests. These colonial and commercial representatives were usually males. Few European women were initially allowed to venture into the frontier regions. Thus, sexual contacts that did occur across racial lines were necessarily between European men and indigenous women.

The children of these relationships were treated as a separate racial group or as elite members of the indigenous and subordinate maternal group.[1] (Only in very few instances did they take the superior socioracial status of the paternal group.) Where the mixed-race children were treated as a separate group, a three-tiered socioracial structure emerged: Europeans, an intermediate mixed-race group, and the indigenous race. Where the mixed-race children were considered members of the indigenous group, socioracial distinctions that emphasized the European or non-European ancestry were more rigidly drawn and the socioracial structure was bipolar. The essential element for the structure of race relations is the status attributed to the intermediate mixed-race group. *The socioracial position of the mixed-race group is the key to an understanding of the dynamics of the prevailing racial tradition.*

Racial traditions may be broadly classified as "flexible" or "rigid" depending in large measure on the perceived existence, treatment, and status of the intermediate group(s). Flexible and rigid racial traditions are ideal-types in that neither type exists in a pure form; rather, racial traditions can contain both flexible *and* rigid characteristics simultaneously, but for different groups. Nevertheless, some (such as the American or the South African tradition under apartheid) are closer to the rigid model and others (e.g., the Spanish or the French) are closer to the flexible type.

CHARACTERISTICS OF A FLEXIBLE RACIAL TRADITION

Race by any definition is an ascriptive criterion. However, it makes a great deal of difference whether a genotypic or phenotypic rule is applied in racial formation. A system of racial classification based on phenotypic criteria (gradients of color and/or physical features) is flexible insofar as a greater number of racial categories exist and movement from one category to another is, over time and under certain conditions, permissible at least in principle.

This is because, unlike ancestry, phenotype is a visual continuum and inherently incapable of clear definition. Thus, the boundary between one group and another can shift over time and, for an individual, is amenable to policy manipulation on the basis of criteria other than racial phenotype itself.

The flexibility of phenotype-based racial traditions thus stems, in part, from the absence of strict adherence to rigid rules of ancestry in the attribution of socioracial status and racial formation. Indigenous group ancestry, per se, does not carry an absolute stigma, and mobility is not altogether denied on this account. Within a flexible racial tradition, status is awarded on the basis of a complex "package" including, in addition to racial phenotype, social achievement, economic class, and cultural orientation. The socioracial status of mixed-race individuals is intermediate between that of the European and that of the indigenous parent groups, and is potentially capable of moving from one racial group to another. Even further, the class-culture bias characteristic of flexible racial traditions (as in Latin America and parts of the Caribbean) often results in attributing relatively high status to mixed-race individuals of the requisite attainments, while withdrawing it from some Europeans who do not meet these requirements.[2]

Superficially similar to an intermediate mixed-race group, but quite different in reality, is what H. M. Blalock Jr. calls "middle-men minorities"—for example, the "overseas Indians" descendants of indentured workers in several former colonial societies.[3] Blalock sets four conditions for "middleman minority" status: (1) intermediate position; (2) small numerical size; (3) dependence on the goodwill or tolerance of the dominant power elite; and (4) high status and income relative to that of the subordinate masses (Blalock, 1967). In East Africa, the overseas Indians were outside the racial structure and served to reinforce its clarity. Elizabeth Hopkins has written:

By stressing their common identification as Asians and clearly differentiating them from the other subordinate group, the Africans, the British were able to manipulate more effectively minority group tensions and, by implication, to reinforce the dominance of the European's position. Unlike Great Britain where both groups are conventionally designated "Colored", Asians and Africans in East Africa were made aware of their disparate status through differential treatment in the political and economic as well as in the social sphere. By virtue of their dominant commercial role, the Asians tacitly assumed the position of the "middle class" in the pluralistic hierarchy, although they failed outside the economic sector to serve as either a buffer or intermediary between the European and African as did the half-caste in other colonial contexts.[4]

This was also true in preindependence Fiji, where the intermediate socioracial status was ascribed to part-Europeans, and the Fiji-Indians functioned only in an economic capacity (in the sugar industry and in retail trade.)

THE RACIAL TRADITION APPROACH   *11*

In general, the end of colonialism has brought about widespread changes in the status of the intermediate mixed-race groups, who have seen their superior position vis-à-vis the indigenous population abruptly abolished by the new independence governments.[5] In some countries (e.g., Western Samoa) the part-European group has even been officially abolished by fiat of the new state. It is not surprising, therefore, that part-Europeans have, in the postcolonial period, played down their mixed-race heritage, partly as the result of the changing power situation and partly to reduce residual hostilities toward them on the part of the indigenous groups. The important point here is that political events can bring about a major change in the prevailing racial tradition—and in arbitrary racial formations—*when the underlying power situation changes and informal attitudes and majority views are consistent with the change.* On the contrary, as discussed in chapter 3, status differences between racial groups can persist even after legal changes intended to abolish them change, if the informal racial customs are inconsistent with the formal change. (The failure of Reconstruction after the American Civil War is a case in point.)

In contemporary societies that feature a flexible racial tradition, as in parts of Latin America, the Caribbean, and the South Pacific before independence, the status of lower-class members of the dominant racial group (usually Europeans) can be low on economic and cultural grounds, but high in socioracial status terms. Their socioracial status thus may be higher than that of upper-class members of the subordinate (usually nonwhite) groups who meet the requisite socioeconomic and cultural criteria.[6] It follows that a flexible racial tradition has as a probable consequence a lower level of conflict among racial groups, and thus (*other things being equal*) somewhat greater racial stability. (Of course, *other sources* of conflict can give rise to severe social instability even within a highly flexible racial tradition.)

This lower level of racial conflict results in part from a greater degree of ambivalence about racial identity on the part of members of the favored segments of the subordinate groups. In turn, this ambivalence is the result of the existence of a greater number of recognized racial categories and the concomitant greater potential for individual mobility through a "mulatto escape hatch" (Banton, 1988). Potential tension and conflict are therefore typically subsumed in efforts to acquire membership in a higher-status category. It matters little that successful reclassification into a higher-status category is, even in highly flexible racial traditions, very much the exception rather than the rule. The belief that individual mobility is possible appears to be shared by all elements of society—even those at the lowest level. For this group, raising the socioracial status is perceived to be possible through interracial marriage or concubinage with individuals from higher groups.

To rephrase this crucial point: The social and psychological mechanisms that operate in a flexible racial tradition tend to defuse group conflict and lead to greater stability in race relations. It is also important to emphasize that this racial stability can coexist with social instability from *other* sources. The two are not mutually incompatible. The important distinction is that socioracial mobility is perceived as possible; but the probability of successful upward movement is directly related to the acceptability of the individual's social behavior. The tendency is therefore strong to sublimate antisocial attitudes and to conform to the cultural norms of the dominant group. This has been noted by observers of Latin American societies. In Brazil, for example, Florestan Fernandes (1969) early on identified a "pathology of normality," which curtails behavior damaging to one's social status. (As chapter 5 discusses, this self-regulation of behavior has also been noted by Thomas G. Mathews in his analysis of the role of color in Puerto Rico.)

A related feature of a flexible racial tradition, and of its multiple socioracial taxonomies, is the ambivalence often exhibited by members of the intermediate racial groupings about their affinity with members of the subordinate group, to whom they are biologically related. This is often manifested in "passing" or in otherwise identifying with the dominant group. Identification within the dominant group is on the basis of a perceived community of economic and social interests and a system of maintaining social behavior. The commonality of interests may be quite real, and this perception is the result of a realistic assessment by the intermediate groups that they also would stand to lose some privileges if there were changes in the structural arrangement of society. Indeed, unless such changes were of a very radical nature, any gains of the lowest group would most probably occur at the expense of the status of the intermediate groups and *not* of the status and privileges of the dominant group.

As noted earlier, the prevailing ethos of socioracial mobility in a flexible racial tradition is embraced even by members of the lowest-ranking group. In some societies, it is precisely members of that group who exhibit the strongest "conservatism" in racial matters and an almost pathological avoidance of any open identification with movements whose aim is to raise the socio-racial status of the very group to which they belong. Many black American visitors to Latin America and the Spanish Caribbean have been shaken to find that often it is the darkest-skinned individuals who go to the most extreme lengths to emphasize their differences (whatever these are) from their American counterparts. But what these visitors often fail to understand is the psychological mechanism with which this avoidance is bound. For it is precisely among the lowest-ranking socioracial group that the need for a myth to explain away or rationalize the disabilities imposed by the structure of society is strongest.

Ambivalence toward racial identity among the members of the intermediate groups can seriously inhibit their *collective* social and political advancement. In the relatively flexible racial traditions, typified by Brazil, Paraguay, and Colombia, the racial tradition (with its degrees of mulatto mobility) is detrimental to people of African phenotype who, until recently, have not organized for collective purposes. The ambiguity of the color-class line has also left clearly identifiable blacks without cohesion, racial organization, or leaders. The tendency has been for the rising mulattoes and educated blacks to be drawn off from the broader group. The overall result, as noted earlier, is that race relations tend to exhibit a low degree of polarization.[7] The emphasis on *individual* rather than group mobility clearly has important implications for the direction and pace of political and social change, as well as leadership styles. As long as the individual is led to believe that his/her success or failure is the result of personal efforts or shortcomings, attention is directed away from group activities and from the structural basis of inequalities. In addition, the intermediate group often becomes the target of violence and antisocial behavior of the lower segment. Such behavior is not threatening to the stability of the social system as the intermediate group is not the repository of real power and authority. Thus, conflict between the intermediate and lowest-ranking groups may provide an additional safety valve important for the maintenance of the system.

An additional important characteristic of a flexible racial tradition is its tolerance of sociosexual contact between individuals from different racial groups; sociosexual relations involve more than simply sexual relationships. Concubinage, for example, involves a well-defined system of roles, rights, and obligations and is often viewed as a "second marriage" for the male partner. In such a situation, resourceful and attractive women from the subordinate and intermediate groups experience some upward shift in status and increased indirect access to opportunity. Furthermore, children born of these relationships are often treated as legitimate. In essence, sociosexual relationships in a flexible racial tradition are not viewed with opprobrium. Conversely, relatively unaccomplished women from the dominant group often trade their "superior" socioracial status for the superior socioeconomic status of the successful male partner from the subordinate group.

Sociosexual relationships most often involved European men and intermediate or subordinate group women. Rarely is the reverse found—even in the most flexible of racial tradition, particularly in the Western Hemisphere.[8] (It should be noted, however, that this does not apply in many Melanesian and Polynesian societies. The numbers of mixed marriages involving South Pacific Island women and European men is almost equal to that involving South Pacific men and European women.) This pattern originated in part due to the shortage of European women in frontier societies. But even where no such shortage exists, white women are rarely partners in socially condoned sociosexual relations such as interracial concubinage, although this is becoming less so for marriage. Generally, however, societies with a flexible racial tradition do have a relatively more tolerant view toward sociosexual relationships involving individuals from different socioracial groups. Equally important is the fact that the offspring of such unions, as noted earlier, are accorded distinct socioracial status, different from that of either progenitor. Often, transgroup sexual relationships function as a socially recognized mode of mobility and status for the women and as extralegal, informal subsystems of power. This is of obvious importance where the dominant male has access to power and privileges denied to the intermediate and subordinate groups as a whole. In such situations, it is acceptable and customary for a client-patron relationship to exist.

Finally, a feature of many flexible racial traditions is the phenomenon of arbitrarily manipulating individual membership in statutory or sociocracial status categories. Owing to the diversity of individual phenotypes within the intermediate group(s) and the absence of a rigid rule of hypodescent, individuals who are physically and culturally similar to the dominant group may sometimes be legally transferred from one sociocracial category to a higher one. This happened in societies colonized or administered by Danes, Italians, Dutch, French, Germans, Portuguese, Australians, and New Zealanders. This has not happened in societies colonized by the United States, as discussed in the next section of this chapter. (The manipulation of sociocracial status in the Danish Antilles is further discussed in detail in chapter 7.) In the Danish Antilles, before it passed to the United States, in 1917, King Frederick VI issued a series of decrees from Copenhagen in 1831 and 1834, which were intended to equalize the sociocracial status of a small segment of mixed-race individuals with that of upper-class whites.

A similar policy was followed in Western Samoa, which was a German protectorate until World War I and was then administered by New Zealand in what became their Mandated Territory after 1919. Under the Germans most of the European community of traders, castaways, and consuls who came and lived in Samoa in the mid–nineteenth century were single men, and many took Samoan wives (Pitt, 1970). By the end of the nineteenth century a part-European community emerged. There were two distinct groups within this community: an elite group of part-Europeans descended from German traders or planters and a part-Chinese group descended from indentured plantation workers. These distinctions were continued by New Zealand. Under this administration all inhabitants of the territory were classified as either European or Samoan. The European category included mostly individuals of part-European and Samoan ancestry (*Afkasi*), some part-Chinese, and a few white foreigners. Membership in the European category was granted to the descendant of a European man legally married to a Samoan woman, *or to any part-European or part-Chinese who successfully petitioned the court to be included in the registry of Europeans*, thus creating through the legal system a mulatto escape hatch. The distinction continued until independence in 1961. After independence, the practice of classifying part-Samoans, or part-Chinese as Europeans was ended. The 1971 census further abolished these distinctions by omitting the question of race entirely, substituting, instead, nationality. A number of high-ranking government officials of part-European ancestry have, since independence, tended to emphasize their Samoan ancestry. This includes, on occasion, eschewing European-style dress, particularly for state ceremonies in which the preferred outfit is the cloth kilt (the traditional *lavalava*). Other aspects of tradition are also being revived.[9] These examples illustrate the ease of racial classifications and cultural adaptations in a flexible racial tradition, at least for a small group of the nonwhite population.

CHARACTERISTICS OF A RIGID RACIAL TRADITION

A rigid racial tradition entails: (1) the definition and formation of racial groups on the basis of genotype; (2) the relative unimportance of phenotypic appearance; and (3) in the perception of the dominant socioracial group, the virtual absence of socioracial distinctions within the subordinate group on the basis of nonascriptive criteria such as class and culture. A rigid racial tradition may, or may not, result in the perception of fewer racial groups than a flexible racial tradition. The key consideration is that racial ancestry—rather than socioeconomic and cultural criteria—is the dominant element of socioracial status. In predemocratic South Africa, as in Nazi Germany, officially, only two racial groups existed: whites and nonwhites, Aryans and non-Aryans. Instead, as discussed further in chapter 2, in the case of the American racial tradition, founded on the rule of hypodescent, *any* degree of subordinate-race ancestry suffices to place the entire group fully within the subordinate racial category. Hence, only two racial groups exist.

While the number of recognized socioracial categories is important, the crux of the difference between flexible and rigid traditions is the use of genotype (ancestry) as *the* basis of racial classification. Ancestry—unlike appearance—is often capable of precise definition and legal proof. The socioracial status of individuals is virtually fixed at birth; the boundary between groups is incapable of gradual shifts over time; movement from one to another racial category is ruled out, as is the manipulation of socioracial placement to reward social and cultural conformity as occurs in a flexible racial tradition. The consequences for social and political activity are far-reaching. The status of whites, is of course, higher—as in a flexible racial tradition. However, subordinate group ancestry—African or other non-European—is both necessary and sufficient for bestowing negative socioracial status. (This applies to the racial tradition of the dominant group; the value of non-European ancestry among the subordinate group has increasingly become central to current "black consciousness" movements.) In these particular types of rigid racial traditions where groups are defined on a basis of a strict rule of racial descent (the "one drop rule"), as in the United States, a two-tiered socioracial structure has emerged, white and nonwhite, and socioracial status is either granted or withheld on this basis. In such two-tiered structures a mixed-race group does not exist as a separate entity; both legally and in the view of the dominant group, mixed-race individuals are considered members of the lower group. Also, other groups, such as Asians and Native Americans are subsumed within the nonwhite category.

Adherence to the rigid, ancestry-based definition of race cuts across other indicators of status and is not significantly modified by either class or cultural achievements. Rigid racial traditions thus create groups of "genes prisoners." Individual achievement is secondary to group position. As noted by Heribert Adam in his analysis of predemocracy South Africa:

> Class or status structures within each group seem to be of secondary importance, since the ascriptive criteria of race determines overall life chances. The achievement principle, however, does apply within the racial segments, although with a greater significance among nonwhites. Since they face greater obstacles in acquiring a higher education or a comparable white income level, the prestige attached to this rare achievement is also relatively higher. In the case of those few who reach the top of their respective racial group, the discriminatory limitations are particularly felt when compared with the privileged whites of lower educational status. This status incongruity is a primary source of tensions. (1971, p. 2)

Arthur A. Fletcher, former U.S. assistant secretary of labor during the Nixon administration, and a candidate for the Republican presidential nomination in 1995, recounts his early experience in graphic terms: "The same whites I had gone to college with were beginning to move into middle-management positions and I was still washing windows—when I could find the work. I couldn't change my color. Education couldn't change my color. The same thing was happening to me that happened to my mother. A college degree . . . didn't help her."[10]

Cynthia Enloe has noted that in a vertical system social stratification is synonymous with ethnicity. Upward mobility requires a change in ethnic identity. When ethnic differentiations overlap with genotypic race criteria, upward mobility is virtually impossible except from generation to generation through intermarriage (Enloe, 1973, p. 28). She does not specify with whom intermarriage takes place, but she does seem to suggest that "passing" or "bleaching" is an alternative to the rigidities of this type of social system. The phenomenon of "passing" in the United States is circumscribed by local custom and appears to be a less attractive alternative to many since the "internationalization" of the black identity movement. The rigidities of the structure preclude individual mobility out of the assigned socioracial group and this forces greater cohesion at the political level, within the group defined as subordinate. Thus, in a rigid racial tradition, the root cause of tension and conflict across racial lines is the striving for group, rather than individual status and recognition.

In a rigid racial tradition, therefore, socioracial status within both the dominant and the subordinate group is "leveled" upward or downward, along the lines of the color caste. Individuals belonging to the subordinate group uniformly share low group socioracial status. Conversely, the group socioracial status of members of the dominant group is higher, regardless of class and culture. In sharp contrast with the outcome of a flexible tradition, in a rigid racial tradition the socioracial status of the poorest, least educated white is higher than that of the richest, most educated black. (There is a clear parallel here between the American tradition and the caste system in India.)[11] Class and culture are of course important criteria of social differentiation, but generally only *within* each racial group.

One further consequence is that a rigid racial tradition, such as the American tradition, increases the numerical size of the subordinate group, and this is important for political development.[12] Unlike the flexible racial tradition, the subordinate group is not politically fragmented and tends to perceive political and social realities from a collective perspective. This also means that communication of political issues is made in terms of the widest appeal and is heavily reliant upon the symbolisms inherent in the division between racial groups. In addition, the earlier reluctance of many light-skinned blacks to identify with the mass of black people significantly has diminished since the "black revolution" of the sixties. The part-white ancestry of many current black American leaders is no longer a source of pride and may even be viewed negatively within the subordinate group.

It is important not to confuse the formal regulations concerning race with the overall racial tradition, which has a heavy informal, customary component. In the United States, for example, notwithstanding civil rights legislation, there still remains a gap between removing the customary basis of racial divisions and changes in public sentiment and social custom. It was not until the mid-1960s that the legal prohibition against interracial marriages was removed throughout the country. Yet, in many areas, even though legal, mixed-race marriages are still viewed with opprobrium rooted in some customs. The antimiscegenation doctrine, a crucial element of American social custom, is only slowly eroding.

RACIAL TRADITION AND POLITICAL ACTIVITY

The prevailing racial tradition has an important influence on the nature of political activity and styles of leadership among the subordinate racial group(s). In a flexible tradition, politics can be ideology-based, and political organizations usually include a racial cross-section of members. As noted, the role of achievement criteria and of phenotype (rather than genotype per se) leads individuals into striving for an improvement in socioracial status for themselves and members of the immediate family. Group cohesion is low. The probability of success on an individual basis is high and positively correlated with acceptable social behavior. Consequently, the potential for *individual* mobility in flexible traditions implies the political expression of *individual* views and interests in *mainstream* political language.

By contrast, in a rigid racial tradition, the leveling of socioracial status places a premium on group political cohesion. Talented and articulate individuals from the subordinate group are forced to become advocates of the entire group, for the only chance for individual status improvement is through the improvement of the socioracial status of the group as a whole. The rigidity of the socioracial structure precludes individual mobility out of the group and thus forces greater cohesion within it. Political organizations are often race-based rather than ideology-based. (In a system where the subordinate racial group is a minority, as in the United States, group advancement *is* the only realistic ideology.) Political activity therefore makes frequent use of race-based imagery and symbolism, intended to strengthen the cohesion of subordinate group members. Naturally, this also reinforces society's view of the subordinate group as an undifferentiated mass. In this vicious circle, the nature of subordinate group politics in a rigid racial tradition serves to reinforce the racial paradigm itself.

In general, three types of political leaders emerge in a rigid racial tradition. First, there is the emissary *integrationist* leader, whose goal is the raising of the socioracial and economic status of the group, through greater interaction between the races, and who functions as an emissary and diplomat to the majority dominated system, appealing for political support, participation, and resources. (This type is exemplified by the late Roy Wilkins of the National Association for the Advancement of Colored People [NAACP], or an Allan Boesak in South Africa.) Second, there is the *separatist* leader (in the tradition of Marcus Garvey, Malcolm X, and Louis Farrakhan), who emphasizes racial solidarity and economic empowerment on a separate basis. All forms of integration with members of the dominant group, particularly intermarriage, are scorned and participation in the political system is rejected until there is economic empowerment of the subordinate group. (Of course, there is intense political activity *within* the group.) Before unifying overtures can be made to external groups, internal unity must be achieved. Thus, separation is both an end and a means to that end.

Finally, and most relevant for the American colonial experience, there is the *accommodationist* type of leader (historically exemplified by Booker T. Washington), whose goal is to raise the economic status of the group, but not its socioracial status per se.[13] This type of leader eschews political action and all forms of confrontation. He fully accepts social and political subordination *in exchange for* short-term material benefits and support to improve group members' skills in the lower levels and to open access to the skilled ("industrial arts") occupations. Economic cooperation, based on complementarity, not competition, is a key goal but social integration is not, and neither is political advancement. (However, the accommodationist sometimes cooperates with the emissary-integrationist, depending on the context and the ends being sought.) As discussed in chapter 5, it is precisely this style of local leadership that prevailed in many of the U.S. colonial territories, where the influence of Booker T. Washington was pervasive.

CONCLUSION

The assumption of the racial tradition approach employed in this book is that although race always "matters" in a colonial context, for the explanation of political and social phenomena, the specific form and strength of its influence differs. This is undoubtedly a major reason why observers conditioned to thinking in terms of a *specific* form of racial interaction often, and erroneously, conclude that race is not an independent criterion of stratification in societies where such interaction assumes a different form. In order to understand the role of race in contemporary societies and in the arbitrary construction of racial groups in domestic and colonial settings, it is essential to take into account the significance of race relative to class and culture in the attribution of socioracial status. As shown in the next chapters, society, politics, and colonial policy and administration are greatly influenced by the characteristics of the prevailing racial tradition and the method of racial formation, whether bureaucratic, legal, or customary. The next chapter examines the relationship between racial formation and racial tradition and the subsequent influence on territorial expansion within North America and the overseas territories.

NOTES

An earlier and longer version of this chapter was originally published as "Racial Tradition and Comparative Political Analysis: Notes Toward a Theoretical Framework," *Ethnic and Racial Studies* 2, no. 4 (October 1979).

1. The biological characteristics of the mixed-race groups varied, depending on geographical area and the dominant and subordinate groups in question. In Asia there emerged an "Eurasian" minority, in the South Pacific the mixed-race group is "Euronesian" or part-European, although the former term is rarely used. In Fiji the group is called *Kai Loma*, meaning intermediate group of "entente" between Fijians and Europeans, or part-Europeans. In the Caribbean, the historical term is coloreds, Mestizos in Latin and Hispanic America. In colonial Ceylon, they were called Burghers, in Burma Anglo-Burmese, Anglo-Indians in India, and in South Africa Coloreds. All have resulted from sexual relations across racial lines. Many of these categories have been formally abolished in the postindependence period, as in Western Samoa, for example.

2. See, for example, Albert A. Campbell, *St. Thomas Negroes* (Evanston, Ill.: American Psychological Association, 1946), and chapter 7 of this book, for a discussion of the status of poor whites in the Danish Antilles before 1917. Also see Jill Sheppard, *The Redlegs of Barbados* (Millwood, N.Y.: Kraus-Thompson Organization Ltd., 1977) for an historical study of poor whites in Barbados.

3. H. M. Blalock Jr., *Toward a Theory of Minority Group Relations* (New York: Capricorn Books, 1967).

4. Elizabeth Hopkins, "Racial Minorities in British East Africa," in *The Transformation of East Africa: Studies in Political Anthropology*, ed. Stanley Diamond and Fred G. Burke (New York: Basic Books, 1966), pp. 95–96.

5. One of few exceptions is Fiji, where, because of the presence of a large Indian population, part-Europeans have been brought into the postindependence structure and share power with the dominant Fijian group.

6. The late Walter White, executive secretary of the National Association for the Advancement of Colored People (NAACP) from 1929 to 1955, wrote:

I am a Negro. My skin is white, my eyes are blue, my hair is blonde. The traits of my race are nowhere visible upon me. . . . I knew . . . who I was. I was a Negro, a human being with an invisible pigmentation which marked me a person to be hunted, hanged, abused, discriminated against, kept in poverty and ignorance, in order that those whose skin was white would have readily at hand a proof of their superiority, a proof patent and inclusive, accessible to the moron and the idiot as well as to the wise man and the genius. No matter how low a white man fell, he could always hold fast to the smug conviction that he was superior to two-thirds of the world's population, for those two-thirds were not white.

Cf. *A Man Called White* (New York: The Viking Press, 1948; reprint, New York: Arno Press and the New York Times, 1969), p. 11.

7. This is not to imply that Africans have not played important roles in all of these countries, which they have. In Brazil, for example, the African role in the evolution of society was, as noted by José Honório Rodrigues, "like Cuba, more Africanized than any of the American states except Haiti, which is the most purely African" (p. xiv). He also notes that ethnic miscegenation was in Brazil a factor in easing race relations and played a role in making Brazilian history less bloody. Negatively, however, through what he terms the "whitewash complex, its effect has been to hold mestizo and black elements of the population subservient to white elements." Cf. Rodrigues, *Brazil and Africa* (Berkeley: University of California Press, 1965). He also commends Brazil's "racial democracy." In recent years this has been discredited by a number of revisionist scholarship works. See, for example: David J. Hellwig, *African-American Reflections on Brazil's Racial Paradise* (Philadelphia: Temple University Press, 1992; Robert M. Levine, *Race and Ethnic Relations in Latin America and the Caribbean: A Historical Dictionary and Bibliography* (Metuchen, N.J.: Scarecrow Press, 1980); Benjamin Nunez, *Dictionary of Afro-Latin America* (Westport, Conn.: Greenwood Press, 1980); Thomas Skidmore, *Black into White: Race and Nationality in Brazilian Thought* (New York: Oxford University Press, 1974); Richard Graham, ed., *The Idea of Race in Latin America, 1870–1940* (Austin: University of Texas Press, 1990).

8. Andre Beteille has written: "Closely associated with the rules regulating marriage are certain attitudes towards women. . . . A very high value is placed on the purity of women belonging to the upper strata and they are protected from sexual contamination by men of the lower strata by sanctions of the most stringent kind. On the other hand, there is a strong element of 'sexual exploitation' in the relations between men of the upper strata and women in the lower." Andre Beteille, "Race, Caste and Ethnic Identity," *International Encyclopedia of Social Sciences* 23, no. 4 (1971), p. 530.

9. For a contrasting view of the process in New Guinea under German and Australian control, see Stephen Winsor Reed, *The Making of Modern New Guinea* (Philadelphia: The American Philosophical Society, 1943).

10. Quoted in Cynthia Enloe, *Ethnic Conflict and Political Development* (Boston: Little, Brown and Company, 1973), p. 28.

11. Andrew Beteille (1971) notes similarities between the American system of racial classification and caste in India. He writes:

The fact of hereditary membership is of great importance. It fixes the social status of the individual at birth and prevents his movement from one group category to another. In spite of many exceptions, these factors combine to fit the social divisions in a caste society into an uncommonly rigid mould [*sic*]. . . . Caste systems may be described as systems of cumulative inequality. Advantages of status tend to be combined with advantages of wealth and power, and those who are socially under-privileged also tend to be at the bottom of the economic and political scales. There are many exceptions to this in the colour-caste system where poor whites co-exist with well-to-do Negroes. (pp. 530–31)

12. For this reason many black lawmakers oppose movements to create a category of "other" or "multiracial." State Representative Ed Vaughn (D–Mich.) notes: "The reason it has tremendous political overtones is because it will greatly destroy our [Blacks] numbers. That would decrease our revenue sharing and what affirmative action and quotas are left for us." Quoted in *Jet*, June 16, 1995, p. 46.

13. Contemporary black neoconservatives are omitted from this analysis. They are without organizational resources and support, and unlike the other types, they do not represent segments of the subordinate group. Rather, they are extremely individualistic, represent only themselves, and they serve as supplicants to those members of the majority community with whom they establish personal relations. They rely on their own individual personalities in their dealings with powerful members of the dominant group, who serve as their mentors. Individuals of this type include Supreme Court Justice Clarence Thomas and his relationship first with President George Bush, and later with Justice Anton Scalia, and Armstrong Williams who was mentored by Senator Strom Thurmond (R–S.C.). Neoconservatives also share some of the characteristics of the accommodationists and can be considered the contemporary incarnation of this type.

2 The Evolution of the American Racial Tradition

Based on the concepts explained previously, this chapter traces the evolution of the American racial tradition—from relatively flexible to highly rigid—beginning from the first contacts of English settlers with Native Americans and through the complex relations with Chinese and other Asian immigrants. Because Native Americans were the first to be encountered by the English settlers, their experience is fundamental to delineating the development of the American racial tradition. Next in shaping American racial attitudes was the interaction with African Americans. The remaining components of the American racial tradition were cast by the experience with Asian immigrants and particularly the Chinese.

Thus, by the time overseas expansion began, the American racial tradition was fully formed. External policy tends to follow domestic policy, even if at a distance. Liberty, social justice, and democracy, "if approved as sauce for the domestic goose, are served up a little later with the colonial gander" (Furnivall, 1948, p. 7). As shown later in this book: The American racial tradition, as fully defined at the turn of the century, set the tone for colonial practice and relations with people of color in the territories.

ASSIMILATION IN AMERICAN HISTORY: MYTH AND REALITY

Beginning with the publication of *Letters from an American Farmer* in 1782, written by French immigrant J. Hector St. John de Crevecoeur, assimilation has featured prominently in the historiography of American domestic racial and ethnic politics. The assimilation doctrine assumes that people of different cultures and ethnic backgrounds can be molded through education and other means into a homogeneous group. Group incorporation into the national society will result from the absorption of commonly attainable objective criteria, such as speaking English, gaining American citizenship, absorbing American ways, and conforming to Anglo-cultural patterns. In America, however, assimilation has also been a function of ascriptive criteria, that is, somatic characteristics and/or genetic ancestry. Consequently, assimilation has been largely a myth as far as African Americans are concerned, and partial and selective as far as Native Americans and, to some extent, Asians, are concerned.

Thus, the perpetual debate between those who view American society as a "melting pot" and those who view it as a "salad" is simplistic. Both visions are true, but for different segments of the American plural society. For people of European ancestry, America has indeed proven to be a kind of melting pot—albeit only after two or three generations in the case of immigrants from poorer European countries (mainly Ireland and Italy). To be sure, several distinct ethnic and cultural characteristics have persisted, but in many respects the Americanization process affected all European immigrants—*including* their absorption of racial prejudice. But for people of non-European ancestry—people of color—assimilation has not occurred, and, as long as the American racial tradition retains its rigid criteria of hypodescent, it will not occur. However, at the beginning of the interface between English settlers and people of other races, racial attitudes were relatively fluid and much more flexible.

NATIVE AMERICANS AND THE ROOTS OF THE AMERICAN RACIAL TRADITION

The American racial tradition is partly grounded in the attitudes which the English settlers evolved toward the Native Americans whom they encountered upon their arrival in the New World. Race was not an issue at first in Native American–white relations; it was not until the middle of the eighteenth century that most Anglo-Americans viewed Native Americans as significantly different in color from themselves and not until the nineteenth century did they perceive them as "red."[1] Thus, while attitudes were largely shaped by supremacist views about race and culture, some early views toward Native Americans were positive. English explorers such as Francis Drake and Walter Raleigh considered Native Americans as almost godlike creatures, handsome in form and civil in manner. Contrast this view with the opinion widely held in the second half of the nineteenth century that—in the words of General Philip Sheridan—"the only good Indian is a dead Indian."[2] It was only after centuries of contact, and for the purpose of justifying the expropriation of Indian lands, that the conquest myth was formulated:

> The basic conquest myth postulates that America was virgin land, or wilderness, inhabited by non-people called savages; that these savages were creatures sometimes defined as demons, sometimes as beasts "in the shape of men"; that their mode of existence and cast of mind were such as to make them incapable of civilization and therefore of full humanity; that civilization was required by divine sanction or the imperative of progress to conquer the wilderness and make it a garden. (Jennings, 1976, p. 15)

The early conflicting views generated ambiguous and shifting policies. Were Native Americans to be considered on a par with Europeans? Or were they different? If so, were they better or worse? The debate can best be understood through the prism of attitudes toward intermarriage—the hot policy issue of the day.

The Question of Intermarriage

The antiamalgamation doctrine of the American racial tradition evolved during this period. Interracial marriage was rare, although interracial sexual liaisons were common, particularly between Native American women and Englishmen (as can easily be expected from the largely male settler population). In contrast to the French in North America, who, in Jennings' words, "were not slow in forming connections with the daughters of the natives," the reluctance of the English to intermarry with Native Americans foreshadowed the development of antimiscegenation sentiments, which have shaped the American racial tradition to this day. Nineteenth-century American historians regarded the reluctance to marry Native Americans as the "proud self-consciousness of a superior Anglo-Saxon race" (Gossett, 1963).

On the positive side, marriage between whites and Native Americans was sometimes viewed in a benign manner, as indicated in records from a 1757 Massachusetts Bay Colony legislative session:

> we ought to have intermarried with [Indians], which would have incorporated them with us effectively, and made them stanch friends . . . but this our wise politicians at home put an effectual stop to at the beginning of our settlement here, for when they heard that Rolfe had married Pocahontas, it was deliberated in council, whether he had not committed high treason in so doing, that is, marrying an Indian princess; and had some troubles not intervened which put a stop to the enquiry the poor man might have been hanged up for having done the most just, the most natural, the most generous and polite action that was ever done on this side of the water. This put an effectual stop to all intermarriage afterward. Our traders have indeed their squaws, alias whores, at the Indian towns where they trade, but they leave their

offspring like bulls or bears to be provided for at random by their mothers. (Quoted in Henriques, 1975, p. 56)[3]

More concretely, the American patriot, Patrick Henry presented a bill in 1784 advocating that:

every white man who married an Indian woman should be paid ten pounds, and five for each child born of such a marriage; and that if any white woman married an Indian she should be entitled to ten pounds with which the county court should buy them livestock; that once each year the Indian husband of this woman should be entitled to three pounds with which the county court should buy clothes for him; that every child born to the Indian man and white woman should be educated by the state between the ages of ten and twenty-one years. (Quoted in Henriques, 1975)

A bill was also presented to the Virginia Legislature to provide for payments and cattle to white men and women who married Native Americans. These efforts were generally unsuccessful. A perceptive quotation of the day illustrates the missed opportunity:

Had the English consulted their own security and the good of the colony, had they intended either to civilize or convert these gentiles, they would have brought their stomachs to embrace this prudent alliance. The Indians are usually tall and well proportioned, which makes full amends for the darkness of their complexions. Added to this, they are healthy and strong with constitutions untainted with lewdness . . . and not enfeebled with luxury. Besides morals and all . . . I can't think the Indians were very much greater heathen than the first adventurers, who, had they been very good Christians, would have had the Charity to take this only method of converting the Natives to Christianity. For, after all that can be said, a sprightly lover is the most prevailing missionary that can be sent among these or any other infidels. Besides, the poor Indian would have had less reason to complain that the English took their Lands, if they received it by way of a marriage with their daughters. Had such affinities been contracted in the beginning, how much bloodshed would have been prevented, and how populous would the country have been, and consequently, how considerable. Nor would the shade of the skin have been any reproach at this day; for if the Moor may be washed in three generations, surely the Indian might be blanched in two."[4]

Unfortunately, as we know, the antimiscegenation attitude prevailed. Yet, real ambivalence remained. Even the symbolism of the union of Pocahontas and John Rolfe is mired in racial ambiguities. Despite the antiamalgamation bias, Pocahontas became a symbol of the unity of whites and Native Americans, and her marriage was used to give ancestral legitimacy to early white Americans—a phenomenon termed by Werner Sollors as establishing "a new fictional line of noble Native American ancestry" (Sollors, 1986, p. 79). (The objections of King James I to the marriage were ostensibly not for racial reasons, but from his concern that Rolfe or his descendants might lay claim to the colony of Virginia because of Pocahontas' royal blood [Gossett, 1963, p. 19].)

The Question of Power

Any examination of official American policy vis-à-vis Native Americans must start by a reference to the Northwest Ordinance of 1787, which contained the first full declaration of policy toward Native Americans:

The utmost good faith shall always be observed towards the Native Americans, their lands and property shall never be taken from them without their consent; and in their property, rights, and liberty, they shall never be invaded or disturbed, unless in just and lawful wars authorized by Congress; but laws founded in justice and humanity shall from time to time be made, for preventing wrongs done to them, and for preserving peace and friendship with them.

Thus, the newly organized United States of America, in need of support from Native Americans and unsure of its feelings toward them, proclaimed a policy of peaceful coexistence. It was not much later that the doctrine fell by the wayside, pushed by economic and territorial interests and the ordinance's promise of good faith was never fulfilled.

This shift from coexistence to domination was supported by eminent American statesmen such as John Quincy Adams, James Monroe, and Supreme Court Chief Justice John Marshall, as we shall see in chapter 3, reviewing the role of law and the courts on the formation of the American racial tradition.

With phase two of territorial expansion (west of the Mississippi), the promise of the Northwest Ordinance was abandoned altogether. As a Native American chief remarked sadly, the white man broke all his promises to the Indian except the promise of taking away his land.

The status of the overseas territories obtained in 1898 closely parallels the status of Native Americans. Just four years earlier, a U.S. commission to investigate matters pertaining to the five civilized tribes of Indian nations, noted: "They have demonstrated their incapacity to govern themselves." The same sentiment would be expressed about the territories after 1898.

The Question of Culture and the Policy of "Coercive Assimilation"

Counterpoised to the paradigm of raw conquest and domination of inherently inferior people was the view that, with "proper" education, Native Americans could be brought into the mainstream of American life. So to speak, having lost their land to the whites, they could perhaps be compensated by being given the whites' culture.

Even a cursory review of writings about "Indians" by explorers and commentators, from the days of the *Mayflower* through the beginning of the nineteenth century shows a continuous increase in the frequency of use of terms such as "uncivilized," "primitive," "wild," and "savage." (As we shall see later, these very terms used to describe unfamiliar races and peoples in the continental territories were later applied to inhabitants of the overseas colonial possessions.)

Interestingly, English settler attitudes toward Native Americans had an early parallel in fourteenth-century Europe in relation to the Irish, whom the English regarded as "wild" and politically and culturally inferior to themselves—even though cultural levels of both countries were similar in many respects.[5] The political basis of the assertion of superiority was the "fact" that, as with Native Americans and Africans, Ireland was a loose confederation of independent tribes and clans instead of a strong central government with vassal lords. Nicholas P. Canny suggests that for the English, "their years in Ireland were years of apprenticeship" for future dealings with Native Americans. They went to Ireland with "a preconceived idea of a barbaric society and they merely tailored the Irishman to fit this ideological straight jacket" ([1973] 1976, p. 46).[6] But the English were of the view that the Irish could experience upward ethnic mobility, status change, and assimilation, thereby transcending their "barbaric" state by adopting the English language, dress, religion, and world-view, that is, by cultural assimilation. This was to be facilitated by national schools in which the Gaelic language and Irish history would be excluded from the curriculum. Instead, English values and culture would be emphasized.

This policy of "coercive assimilation" was later to be mirrored in federal government policies toward Native Americans. If Christian Caucasians of Europe such as the Irish were perceived as inferior largely because of culture and a different political organization, it was only a short leap toward viewing the "pigmented heathens of distant lands as not only dark, idolatrous but *savage* on racial, political *and cultural* grounds (Jennings, 1976, emphasis added).

The desire to transform culturally Native Americans into whites was the guiding force behind the federal government's fifty-year policy of coercive assimilation (1880s–1930s). The goal was to culturally "whiten" Native Americans by breaking down Native American traditional ways and forcing the adoption of white cultural values. Native Americans were encouraged to identify as white—provided they renounced their Native American culture and identity.

The policy of coercive assimilation was advocated by white Christian missionaries, who worked among the Native Americans. Curiously, Booker T. Washington, the ubiquitous black leader, was instrumental in its implementation. He was supported by friends of the Negro, such as Samuel Chapman Armstrong, an architect of social policy in the reconstruction era and founder of Hampton Normal and Agricultural Institute, and by Richard Henry Pratt, the Founder of Carlisle Indian Industrial School. Indian children were to be removed from the influence of their parents and communities by placing them in boarding schools—run practically like military camps—and to force their assimilation by any means possible, including physical punishment for speaking their tribal language and withholding food rations from reluctant parents to force them to relinquish their children to whites. Many parents did resist, but the success of the forced assimilation policy was evident in the fact that participating boarding schools had full enrollments for nearly fifty years. During school vacations, the children were placed in white households in a determined effort to keep them in contact with white culture and out of contact with Native American culture (Spicer, 1980, p. 117).[7]

Because—with respect to Native Americans—the American racial tradition was in effect flexible, children attended either black or white boarding schools *depending on appearance.* (It will be recalled that a rigid racial tradition is based solely on genetics and not on appearance.) Not all Native Americans were placed in a white environment. Some, who were phenotypically Negro and regarded as "half-Negro mongrels" were placed with blacks and taught by Negro educators.[8] *Plessy v. Ferguson,* discussed in the next chapter, was by then the law of the land, and the school policy fostered divisions among Native Americans on somatic grounds.

A unique chapter in American racial history unfolded at Hampton Institute between 1878 and 1923. Booker T. Washington, who wrote of his experiences in Indian education in *Up From Slavery*, started an unprecedented biracial education program for Native American children at the Hampton Institute. The Hampton Normal and Agricultural Institute had been founded in 1868, during the Reconstruction Era, in response to the demand by newly freed African Americans for educational opportunities. Ten years after its founding, Hampton opened its doors to American Indian students. At the turn of the century, Hampton Institute's Native American Program had almost one thousand students. Native American boys at Hampton lived in a brick dormitory called The Wigwam, presided over by Principal Booker T. Washington, in which sixty-five tribes were represented. This program would also become the model for educational policy in the overseas territories, in which Hampton and Washington's influence played key roles.

The program was fashioned after the program developed for African Americans. Hampton sought to provide the students with an "education for life," through a program structured to train "the head, the hand, and the heart" (Green, cited in Hultgren and Molin, 1989). Academic course work, manual training, and Christian education were combined with service to the community. Education was seen as the main key to civilization, which meant teaching Native Americans to read, write, and speak English. Their assimilation policy is described as follows:

The policy added white skills to native skills in some instances, but it was more often designed to banish native skills and practices forever. It forbade, whether in school or on reservation, tribal singing and dancing, along with the wearing of ceremonial and "savage" clothes, the practice of native religions, the speaking of tribal languages, the acting out of traditional gender roles. It was ironic, indeed, that a society that declared the education of blacks and slaves illegal insisted on teaching Indians to read and write, often even sending military units to separate them from their parents and homes. If native children could not actually become white, they would at least attain the trappings of white society. (Green, cited in Hultgren and Molin, 1989, p. 11)

The program of coercive assimilation was terminated by the Indian Reorganization Act (IRA) of 1934.

The Flexible Element of the American Racial Tradition

The history of Native Americans is too rich and complex for an attempt at further summary. Their experience does demonstrate, however, that the American racial tradition has been "flexible" with respect to Native Americans—in contrast to African Americans. The classificatory ambivalence toward Native Americans never disappeared. In the 1920s, for example, a provision of the Virginia State Bureau of Vital Statistics recognized "as an integral and honored part of the white race the descendants of John Rolfe and Pocahontas" (Smith, 1993).

The American racial tradition has proven relatively flexible in bestowing socioracial status upon Native Americans. It has been emphasized in chapter 1 that the nature of the prevailing racial tradition has powerful implications for group identity, group membership, and group political action. A flexible racial tradition has the effect, among other things, of diluting the political strength of groups defined within this tradition. Despite the lumping together of very different Native American tribes as "Indians,"[9] the flexibility had operational value: As long as Native Americans preserved their tribal identity and kept a minimum distance from the whites, they would keep a degree of independence and remain a potential threat. To the extent that *individuals* could be reclassified as white on the basis of physical appearance and acquired culture, their tribal identity was diluted and so was their potential threat. In chapter 3 we will review the legal and judicial evolution of the definition of Native Americans.

THE EVOLUTION OF ATTITUDES TOWARD AFRICAN AMERICANS

It is not possible to summarize here all salient aspects of "the American dilemma." Below, we touch only on those aspects that are directly relevant to the themes of this book.

The Formative Years

After the arrival of "twenty negars" as indentured servants in Virginia in 1619, negative racial attitudes quickly developed toward Africans as well. Africans, more so than Native Americans, personified for whites the opposite end of the physical and cultural spectrums. Negative views of blackness derived from Elizabethan times (the Othello myths notwithstanding) and provided a convenient rationale for racial biases against Africans, perceived as the "moral antithesis" of whiteness and civilization.

Alexis de Tocqueville, in his impressions of America, described Africans and Native Americans as "two unlucky races," whose misfortunes were alike. In part, the low status was attributed to the traditional tribal structures of both groups, which were considered antithetical to civilization. It was said that neither group produced an alphabet, a written language, metal works, or organized governments. De Tocqueville, however, envisioned a special role for Native American–white "half-castes," whom he saw as inheriting their white father's cultural enlightenment without entirely giving up the "savage customs of the race on the mother's side" ([1848] 1966, p. 329). In contrast, he believed of Africans: "The Negro has no family; for him a woman is no more than the passing companion of his pleasures, and from their birth his sons are his equals." He did underline the key economic difference correctly, however. While the Native Americans died as they lived, in isolation, the fate of Negroes was in a sense linked with that of the Europeans, bound one to the other without mingling, making it equally difficult to separate completely or to unite ([1848] 1966, p. 321).

The treatment of African Americans varied in significant ways from that of Native Americans, starting from the early application of the rigid racial tradition to the former. This is evident in early legislative attempts to define a rule to "fix" the status of black slaves, freedmen, and other ancestors in perpetuity. There were no comparable attempts to force cultural assimilation on blacks compatible to those with Native Americans. Indeed, *exclusion* of blacks was the constant of American social policy. The racial definition that finally emerged was, if extreme, at least clear: *Any* degree of African ancestry would suffice to define the individual as *fully Negro*.

There was, of course, nothing inherent or unique in the Africans' condition to automatically qualify them for slavery, and *slavery was not present at the start of the colonization of America*. When the first "twenty negars" arrived in Virginia in 1619, their socioracial status was relatively fluid. There was not yet a rigid definition of their race on a hereditary and perpetual basis. As Africans came into the colonies over the next half century of economic expansion, the white ruling class concentrated on fixing their socioracial status (all the while trying to decide the status of Native Americans). By the eighteenth century, slavery acquired clear legal status, distinguished from the status of villeinage, indenture, or bondage resulting from a debt owed because of poverty, crime, or mischance. After the fixing of a racial rule, slavery and low status became hereditary.

The legal restrictions of slavery are well documented (Higginbotham, 1978; Hoetink, 1973; Patterson, 1967; Van den Berghe, 1967; Du Bois, [1896] 1970; Gossett, 1963; Foster, 1970; Klein, 1989). Whether racial prejudice preceded slavery is not the point; the issue is that slavery required an ideology of sharp racial inferiority and its existence, in turn, justified and reinforced the rigid racial classification. The objective condition of slavery put the Negro apart from all other races. Any evolution of the definition of African Americans stopped with the *Plessy v. Ferguson* decision, which will be discussed in the next chapter.

It is interesting to note that, in contrast with settler ignorance of African political structures, the English political establishment in London recognized and approved of African governments. The British political elite were inclined to see the structures of African societies as analogous to their own, complete with kings, counselors, gentlemen, and "people of the baser sort."[10] Such a recognition was absent in the New World. In any event, it would have been psychologically impossible while continuing to justify slavery. Blackness was linked with evil and sexual debauchery. It was variously explained by references to: (1) a curse by God; (2) fitness for servitude; (3) a biblically indelible badge of sin; (4) the resulting punishment for the sin; (5) lack of restraint over sexual impulse; (6) childlike behavior and defiance of paternal authority; and (7) similarity to the devil and other negative images (Schwartz and Disch, 1970, pp. 9–10). The dehumanizing effect (and intent) of the "ignoble Savage" myth served of course to rationalize slavery and the slave trade.

Images and Stereotyping

Images of racial groups presented in the media and in the visual arts provide additional insight into the nature of the American racial tradition and convey messages to the polity about who is worthy of assimilation and who is not. Naturally, the group that controls image-formation is in a powerful position to determine the future evolution of the racial tradition as well.[11] During the period 1590 to 1900, images of Native Americans far outnumbered representations of blacks in American art, suggesting, Parry (1974) writes, that the former were much more in the minds of white Americans. The image of Native Americans shifted, from object of curiosity to romantic "noble savage" to fearsome enemy and finally settled into a representation of a sad, nonthreatening disappearing race.

Conversely, images of African Americans were relatively rare until the late nineteenth century. In the seventeenth century pictures of blacks in America were virtually nonexistent, except for a minor figure or two who often occupied the lower corner of a decorative European map of the New

World. Subsequently, Native American and African images converged, as in the evolution of the cigar store Indian or Negro, a popular nineteenth-century American artifact originating with the English in London (Parry, 1974, p. 68). This convergence was reflected in portraits of Native Americans as producers and consumers of tobacco and of African slaves as tenders of tobacco plantations. As a result, the wooden figure of a "Black Boy" or "Virginian" wearing a headdress and kilt of tobacco leaves became a standard storefront emblem for London tobacco shops. Until the 1800s, the portrait of African Americans reflected changes in the American racial tradition. Images of blacks before the Civil War were greatly influenced by sympathetic white abolitionist writers, such as Harriet Beecher Stowe, whose 1851 *Uncle Tom's Cabin* popularized abolitionist sentiment in the North, made her a pariah to Southerners, and was credited by President Lincoln with having contributed to the outbreak of the American Civil War.[12] The primary impact of the cruelty of slavery was based on sympathetic images of kindly Uncle Tom, and the mixed-race Eliza, and reached worldwide. Nevertheless, the image of blacks, although sympathetic, still reflected the view of childlike behavior and rootlessness expressed earlier by de Tocqueville.[13]

At the turn of the century, in parallel with the institutionalization of segregation from *Plessy v. Ferguson*, came a very different set of images. African Americans were lampooned while glorifying the plantation and rationalizing lynchings in early American movies and as the minstrel in popular literature. In minstrel shows—white performers appeared with faces blackened by burnt cork, and they portrayed blacks as shiftless, dirty buffoons.

Thomas Nelson Page, a famous Southern writer, idealized antebellum plantation life and the Civil War years, and he portrayed blacks with patronizing affection. In 1904, the title of a nonfiction work by Page revealed the changing American tone: *The Negro: The Southerner's Problem* (Ely, 1991). Another classic of the period, *The Clansman*, became the basis for D. W. Griffith's film *The Birth of a Nation* (1915), which presented blacks not only as inferior, but as bestial savages and a serious menace to society unless their rapacious nature was checked by valorous white forces such as the Ku Klux Klan.

The notion that blacks would degenerate into their natural savagery, if not held in check by whites, was spread throughout the country. One way to perpetuate these views was to tightly control the publication of images that did not support the stereotyped views of African Americans. In 1910, when the black heavyweight champion, Jack Johnson—who was also married to a white woman—beat the former white titleholder, Jim Jeffries, Congress passed a law barring from interstate commerce "any film or other pictorial representation of any prizefight" intended for showing to the public. Even though moral indignation against prizefighting existed for some time, it was only when a black fighter had beat a white boxer that Congress acted to prevent dissemination of the images (Ely, 1991; Kennedy, 1997). Many argued at the time that exhibition of the films might lead to racial conflict, and the films were banned outside the United States, but *The Birth of a Nation* was not. By 1905, African Americans were routinely depicted as chicken thieves, crapshooters, and the proverbial shiftless "darkey." It is not surprising then, that these images were readily transposed onto the colored people of the overseas territories acquired in 1898 and thereafter.

The definite "fixing" of both the rigid aspect of the American racial tradition and of popular images of African Americans is well reflected in Woodrow Wilson's views expressed ten years before he became president:

An extraordinary and *very perilous* state of affairs had been created in the South by the sudden and absolute emancipation of the Negroes, and it was not strange that the Southern legislatures should deem it necessary to take extraordinary steps to guard against the *manifest pressing dangers* which it entailed. Here was a vast laboring, landless, homeless class, once slaves; now free; *unpracticed* in liberty, *unschooled* in self-control; *never sobered* by the discipline of self-support; never established in any habit of prudence; *excited* by a freedom they do not understand, *exalted* by false hopes, *bewildered* and without leaders, *and yet insolent and aggressive; sick of work, covetous of pleasure* a host of dusky children untimely put out of school. (Wilson, 1901, p. 376)

RACIAL ATTITUDES TOWARD ASIANS

By the time mass immigration began in the latter half of the nineteenth century, the flexible and rigid features of the American racial tradition were already well established, and its schemes were easily superimposed on the immigrants. (As we shall see, they were later to be exported to the newly acquired territories.) Not all immigrants were considered equal. Some groups, such as the Chinese and Japanese, were deemed quite unsuitable for assimilation into the American national union. Asians were subjected to exclusion, congressional and executive hostility, and social and legal discrimination. Southern Europeans were suspect. The only desirable immigrants, the "kindred races," were immigrants from Northern and Western Europe. The distinction was also summarized in the categories of "old" versus "new" immigrants.

The American racial tradition influenced official views of Asian immigration, especially the Chinese, since they comprised the first group of Asian immigrants. Other Asians followed in the late nineteenth and early twentieth centuries. All were deemed inassimilable because of the differences in their national institutions, race, and culture. (In any event, the extant legislation forbade naturalization of nonwhites.) A cultural rationale for barring Asians was presented by an otherwise sympathetic observer, J. H. Oldham, secretary of the American-Based International Missionary Council:

The wide differences between the civilizations of the West and those of Asia must be recognized as a fact to be objectively considered and allowed for independently of any question of superiority or inferiority. The molding influence of centuries of history cannot be treated as if it did not exist. *Diversity of tradition gives rise to a multitude of differences in ways of thinking, feeling and acting.* The preservation of its tradition unimpaired, save in so far as it voluntarily assimilates from outside what meets its needs, is a vital interest of a people. (1926, p. 136, emphasis added)

In the main, however, the "cultural difference" rationale was a cover for racial exclusion: The Naturalization Act of 1790 reserved citizenship for whites only. The law provided that "any alien being a free white person," might on fulfilling the necessary conditions become a citizen; and the same words were retained in subsequent naturalization laws. Citizenship was extended to African Americans in 1866 by the Fourteenth Amendment, which was ratified in 1868, at the end of the Civil War. The Fifteenth Amendment removed race, color, or previous condition of servitude as barriers to citizenship in 1869 (ratified in 1870). Yet, when Chinese immigration came to be regarded as an economic threat to white immigrant laborers, such as the Irish, the Chinese Exclusion Act was passed by Congress in 1882, suspending Chinese immigration for ten years. In 1892, the Geary Act extended the immigration ban for another ten years and required that Chinese already living in the United States obtain certificates of residence to prove that they were legal residents. In 1902 the Chinese immigration ban was extended indefinitely (Takaki, 1989, p. 111).

For example, as with blacks, whites viewed the Chinese as especially interested in white women, and in California, these views led to the enactment of antimiscegenation laws aimed at the Chinese."[14] And for good measure, Asians were officially forbidden from bringing their wives, who were classified as "aliens ineligible to citizenship," to the United States with them (Takaki, 1989, p. 14). Asians were prohibited from marrying whites, and white women who did marry Asian men stood to lose their citizenship if they remained in the United States. As a result, Chinese men were mainly limited to prostitutes or black women. Of the former, Takaki writes that the overwhelming numbers of Chinese women in the early years were prostitutes (p. 121). He notes that in the 1870 census manuscripts, 61 percent of the 3,536 Chinese women in California had their occupation listed as "prostitute."

Anti-Chinese Racism

The Chinese were the first Asian immigrants to arrive in the United States beginning as early as 1571, with the arrival of an occasional worker (Johns, 1981).[15] It was not until the nineteenth century that Chinese sojourners came in numbers, expecting to stay for a fixed period, and then return to

China. The Chinese went to the West Coast, particularly during the mid-1800s, where they worked on building the transcontinental railroads, in gold and back-breaking borax mines. Their experiences in the United States frequently mirrored that of African Americans and Native Americans. The experiences of the Chinese also established the model that determined the treatment of other Asians in the United States and in the overseas territories. The Chinese were a politically proscribed group, handicapped by a uniform of color (Takaki, 1989, p. 99). Almost from the beginning, the Chinese, particularly in California, provoked widespread concerns about the relationship between race and national identity.

In particular, the Chinese were associated with blacks in the racial imagination of whites. Shortly after the Civil War, the *New York Times* issued a warning that depicted the newly freed blacks and the newly arrived Chinese as threats to the American political system. Ronald Takaki writes that the newspaper noted:

We have four millions of degraded negroes in the South . . . and if there were to be a flood-tide of Chinese population—a population befouled with all the social vices, with no knowledge or appreciation of free institutions or constitutional liberty, with heathenish souls and heathenish propensities . . . we should be prepared to bid farewell to republicanism. (Takaki, 1989, p. 101)

The *San Francisco Chronicle* compared the Chinese "coolie" to the black slave and condemned both as antagonistic to free (white) labor.

Interestingly, the extension of the American racial tradition to the Chinese meant that the racial qualities assigned to blacks quickly became "Chinese" characteristics (Takaki, 1989, p. 101). The Chinese were alleged to suffer from presumed racial inferiorities, and they were described as of low character, lacking moral sense, and having criminal instincts. In common with African Americans, Chinese were also denigrated as "heathen, morally inferior, savage, childlike, and lustful." Anti-Chinese rage also conditioned the absurd view that the depravity of the Chinese was associated with their physical appearance and that they were "but a slight removal from the African race." Thus, the Chinese were depicted as "nagurs," with dark skin and thick lips (Takaki, 1989, p. 101).

These racist sentiments were soon enacted into public policy. California, in particular, was a hotbed of anti-Chinese sentiment and contrasted with Hawaii, where conditions were more favorable. In 1862, the California state legislature passed a law "to protect Free White Labor against competition with Chinese Coolie Labor, and to Discourage the Immigration of the Chinese into the State of California." An 1870 San Francisco city ordinance prohibited the use of sidewalks to those carrying loads on a pole, a law aimed at the traditional Chinese method of carrying heavy objects. Anti-Chinese sentiment was often violent. In 1871, a riot in Los Angeles resulted in the murder of nineteen Chinese, and in 1885, mob violence at Rock Springs, Wyoming, left twenty-eight Chinese dead. Just as the ideology of racial conquest of the Indians rationalized the confiscation of their land, and the ideology of racial inferiority of the African was used to justify the economic institution of slavery, the ideology and imagery of racial and cultural alienness of the Chinese was used to underpin the economic position of lower-class whites.

The Chinese Exclusion Act of 1882 singled out the Chinese ostensibly because they were of an "amazingly low standard of living."[16] But it was also feared that their "amazing industriousness" would enable them to displace American workmen. The *Reports of the U.S. Industrial Commission*, described the Chinese: "[As] a distinct race and religion, unacquainted with representative institutions, not bringing their families, expecting to return to their native land, and while temporarily here resorting to low practices and filthy abodes" (Quoted in Abbott, [1924] 1969, p. 187). After the acquisition of the overseas territories, stateside exclusion laws were also extended to all U.S. possessions by the 1904 Deficiency Act, which barred Chinese laborers from entering the American overseas territories.

Because many Chinese came as temporary sojourners, they were viewed, in official circles, as ideal for exclusion, as noted in "Brief Statement of the Investigations of the Immigration Commission, with Conclusions and Recommendations and Views of the Minority," *Reports of the U.S. Immigration Commission* 1 (1911):

As far as possible, the aliens excluded should be those who come to this country with no intention to become American citizens or even to maintain a permanent residence here, but merely to save enough, by the adoption if necessary, of low standards of living, to return permanently to their home country. Such persons are usually men unaccompanied by wives or children. (Quoted in Abbott, [1924] 1969, p. 210)

The report of the U.S. Immigration Commission continued that "as far as possible, the aliens excluded should be those who, by reason of their personal qualities or habits, would least readily be assimilated or would make the least desirable citizens." This description, of course, was not limited to the Chinese, but also applied, albeit to a lesser extent, to immigrants from Eastern and Southern Europe. But, in common with blacks, Asians were especially targeted for racism and discrimination, and their opportunities were limited by restrictive covenants and other racist legislation. In this, the Chinese were but the latest victims in a process that started with Native Americans and African Americans.[17]

In 1854, the California Supreme Court ruled in *People v. Hall* that Chinese could not testify against whites in court—a status also shared by blacks. (The case presaged the *Dred Scott* decision of 1857, in which Justice Taney declared that blacks had no rights that whites were bound to respect.) The court ruling had the effect of overturning the conviction of a white man who was convicted of murdering a Chinese man on the basis of testimony offered by one white and three Chinese witnesses. The utterly illogical decision highlighted the distorted view of the racist judge. But his view also illustrates that the American racial tradition was at the core of the decision:

Indian, as commonly used, refers only to the North American Indian, yet in the days of Columbus all shores washed by Chinese waters were called the Indies. In the second place the word "white" necessarily excludes all other races than Caucasian; and in the third place, even if this were not so, I would decide against the testimony of Chinese on grounds of public policy. (Quoted in Daniels, 1988, p. 54)

Chinese Socioracial Status in a Rigid Racial Tradition

The prohibition of bringing Chinese wives or other women to the United States, which remained in force until around the end of World War II, provides a window through which to analyze Chinese socioracial status in the rigid American racial tradition. As has been mentioned earlier, intermarriages between Chinese men and white women were forbidden during the early days of the mostly male immigration from China. But intermarriage among the various nonwhite groups perceived as inferior was not prohibited. Many Chinese men, therefore, established legal and extralegal relations with African American women, particularly from 1920 to 1950. (These relationships, which have not been sufficiently studied within the context of either black or Chinese intermarriage, merit further examination, particularly as the offspring of these liaisons often passed into the African American group.)

The low socioracial status of the Chinese was evidenced by segregated residential patterns, often in Chinatowns or in areas contiguous to black communities, or actually within African American communities. The low status of the Chinese was also evident in their exclusion from white schools in many areas of the country. In 1906, the San Francisco Board of Education ordered all schools to segregate Oriental and non-Oriental students. In 1907 President Theodore Roosevelt issued an executive order directing that Japanese or Korean laborers, skilled or not, who had received passports to go to Mexico, Hawaii, or Canada be refused permission to enter the continental territory of the United States. This resulted from conflict with Japan sparked by the school board's order segregating Orientals. The Chinese were excluded unless they could prove they were not laborers. Although phenotypically distinct from blacks, in the polarized biracial American classification of whites and nonwhites, the Chinese could only be classified as nonwhite, as there was no intermediate position for them to occupy. From a social and legal perspective, the nonwhite classification of the Chinese put them on a similar status level with African Americans.[18]

James W. Loewen's description of *The Mississippi Chinese: Between Black and White* (1971) documents the *socioracial* position of a group of first-generation Chinese immigrants living in the Mississippi Delta before 1940, and it provides a background for understanding the subsequent upward status change experienced by the Chinese—especially after the opening of U.S.–China political relations in 1972. Caste relations in Mississippi had profound consequences for the Chinese in several ways.

First, the social system embraced a rigid code of etiquette—characterized by white dominance and nonwhite subservience. Second, dating from their arrival in Mississippi, the Chinese were defined as status equals of blacks. This was reinforced by their residence in black neighborhoods and their occupations as small retail grocers living above their shops. Their trade was limited to blacks, and they offered black products. William Alexander Percy, a Greenville, Mississippi, planter, wrote in 1941 (*Lanterns on the Levee*):

Small Chinese storekeepers are almost as ubiquitous as in the South Seas. Barred from social intercourse with the whites, they smuggle through wives from China or, more frequently, breed lawfully or otherwise with the Negro. They are not numerous enough to present a problem—except to the small white storekeeper—but in so far as I can judge, they serve no useful purpose in community life. (Quoted in Loewen, 1971, p. 55)

Third, the Jim Crow legal restrictions enacted against blacks also applied to the Chinese, whose political power was as limited as that of blacks.

As usual, the most telling indication of the downward leveling of socioracial status in the rigid American racial tradition is to be found in interracial sexual relations. As noted, until about 1943, U.S. immigration laws made the importation of Chinese females almost impossible. Black women were accessible, and there were no legal barriers to black-Chinese intercourse. Thus, if a Chinese man did have a woman, it had to be a Negro or a prostitute. Loewen further notes: "White Mississippi, having placed Chinese in the social position of the Negro, didn't care if the two races 'fornicated' amongst themselves" (1971, p. 207). A Supreme Court decision confirmed that no section in the Mississippi legal code "prohibits any marriage or social relations between the negro [*sic*] and Mongolian races, and they are left free to maintain such social, including marriage, relations as they see proper to enter into" (*Rice v. Gong Lum* [1925]).

Another indicator of the low socioracial status of the Chinese was the exclusion of Chinese children from white public schools. By the mid-1920s, even the small group of merchants who managed to bring their families from China faced the problem of providing an education for their children.[19]

The Mississippi Supreme Court cited an 1890 decision from the Mississippi constitution, which stipulated that "separate schools shall be maintained for children of the white and colored races" and asserted that Chinese are not "white," but fall under the "colored races." Later, the U.S. Supreme

Court said: "It has been at all times the policy of the lawmakers of Mississippi to preserve the white schools for members of the Caucasian race alone." The majority decision, delivered by Chief Justice Taft, stated the rationale in terms of *Plessy v. Ferguson* (see chapter 3), which was by then the law of the land: "A child of Chinese blood, born in, and a citizen of, the United States, is not denied the equal protection of the laws by being classed by the State among the colored races who are assigned to public school separate from those provided for the whites, when equal facilities for education are afforded to both classes" (Loewen, 1971, p. 68).

The Chinese were not admitted to white public schools until the 1950s. And, in common with blacks, Mississippi Chinese were not overly optimistic about the legal system: "The Chinese were . . . afraid of the law, even though they themselves had little contact with it, because they saw the way it operated with the Negro" (Loewen, 1971).

By the late 1950s, the socioracial status of the Chinese in Mississippi began to change for the better. Today, they are among those considered by the larger society to be "model Asians"—a status that they share with Japanese and, more recently, Vietnamese, and other Asian newcomers. The "model minority" image has the convenient effect of separating Chinese and other Asians from other nonwhite minorities, with whom they might otherwise find common ground for political coalitions, and it diverts attention from poor Asians, who might benefit from social programs. This depiction also directs attention away from the racism and discrimination endured by the Chinese and the Japanese in America in the past.

Link to Colonial Policy: The Filipino Experience

In spite of the large nationality differences, the American racial tradition indiscriminately lumped together all Asians and deemed them incapable of assimilation (Abbott, [1924] 1969.) This included the Filipinos, who had come under American domination in 1898. In spite of the policy of "Benevolent Assimilation" in the Philippines (Miller, 1982), they were not exempted from racist treatment in America. In 1934, for example, the Tydings-McDuffie Act restricted Filipino immigration to the United States to fifty persons a year (Takaki, 1989, p. 332).[20]

The Philippines did not escape racist censure from members of Congress. U.S. Senator MacLaurin, during the debate on the Paris Peace Treaty of 1898, expressed fears that the possible annexation of the Philippines would mean the "incorporation of a mongrel and semi-barbarous population into our body politics" (Constantino, 1966). In MacLaurin's view, Filipinos were "inferior to, but akin to the Negro in moral and intellectual qualities and in [a lack of] capacity for self-government" (Constantino, 1966). Two years later, Senator Alfred J. Beveridge, in his maiden speech to the Senate, said of the Filipinos:

It will be hard for Americans who have not studied them to understand the people. They are a barbarous race, modified by three centuries of contact with a decadent race. It is barely possible that 1,000 men in all the archipelago are capable of self-government in the Anglo-Saxon sense. . . . They are not capable of self-government. How could they be? They are not of a self-governing race. They are Orientals, Malays, instructed by Spaniards in the latter's worse estate. (Quoted in Schirmer and Shalom, 1987, p. 25)

Filipino immigration to the United States was also opposed and was flamed by anti-Filipino race riots that occurred on the West Coast in the late 1920s and early 1930s. The most publicized of these riots occurred in Watsonville, California, in January 1930, and were investigated by the eminent sociologist Emory S. Bogardus. (For a full description, see Schirmer and Shalom, 1987, pp. 58–62.) The root causes of the riots included economics ("the new immigrants . . . increase the labor supply and hold down wages"); health concerns ("some Filipinos bring in meningitis, and other dangerous diseases"); and, fear of miscegenation: "a few have married white girls. Others will. If the present state of affairs continues there will be 40,000 half-breed in California before ten years have passed."[21]

MIXED-RACE PEOPLE AND THE AMERICAN RACIAL TRADITION

Several references were made earlier to the treatment of mixed-race individuals. Because the question is so central to the difference between flexible and rigid racial traditions and to understanding the nature of the American racial tradition, it is time to take a more organized look at it.

Hypodescent: The "One Drop" Rule

Generally, racial classification in America has been determined on the basis of hypodescent, that is, that any degree of African ancestry is sufficient to classify the person as "Negro" or "black." Less extreme definitions have surfaced from time to time. Thus, a few states (e.g., Mississippi, Missouri) adopted at some time the criterion of one-eighth of Negro blood (Davis, 1991, p. 9); Virginia changed its definition from one-fourth to one-eighth black blood in 1910, then in 1930 forbade a white designation to a person of any black ancestry. The inanity and hypocrisy of these variants, however, is most evident in the case of Louisiana's rule defining a black person as someone whose ancestry was more than one "thirty-second" black: One black great-great-great-grandparent out of eighteen was enough to make one black—a standard requiring 125 years of accurate recordkeeping or an elephantine communal memory. Later attempts to define with precision degrees of racial intermixture was expressed through terms in common use until the 1940s—mulatto (one-half black), quadroon (one-fourth), octoroon (one-eighth), mustee (one-sixteenth)—all of which carry a strong derogatory, "bastard" flavor. Indeed, it has been estimated that at least three-fourths of all people defined as American blacks have some white ancestry. Conversely, by other estimates up to one-fifth of all whites have a black ancestor.[22] Nevertheless, hypodescent has been the prevailing classificatory rule in the American racial tradition—and constitutes its most rigid single feature.

A stratification system in which as little as "one drop" of "X" ancestry qualifies one to be classified as a 100 percent member of the "X" racial group is socially absurd. (The very notion of "racial group" is biologically absurd, in any event.) What explains the persistence of this absurdity in America? There are the well-known economic and political advantages of the hypodescent rule for the ruling group. During slavery, in particular, the rule had the practical benefit of maximizing the number of useful slaves and minimizing the number of citizens entitled to economic benefits and legal protection.

In addition to economic and political reasons, however, a major explanation of the durability of the one drop rule is psychological and sexual. There is a powerful myth of the genetic power of blackness, or "power hematology" by which black blood is perceived as potent enough to obliterate white blood. Fear of racial contamination and fascination with black sexuality have both been at work. Thus, the immediate and key corollary of the rule was the universal prohibition of interracial intermarriage. The antimiscegenation laws in America typically prohibited interracial *marriage* and not interracial sexual relations with black women which—albeit officially frowned on—were widespread and received with a wink by fellow white men and with both eyes closed by white women. By contrast, in apartheid South Africa, the legal prohibition was against interracial *sex*. This shows that in the American racial tradition it was the legal, social, and political consequences of interracial sexual liaisons, and not the liaisons themselves, which were of concern. In addition, of course, there was the pathological complexity of feelings and attitudes toward white women—which made white liaisons with black women permissible and liaisons with white women a crime, with an automatic death penalty in the South less than two generations ago.

The absurdity of the rigid genotypic classification is brought home by a recent article by an African American woman: "I began with the knowledge that my mother came from a background that included Irish, Italian, Native American, and African strains. . . . There were virtually no traces of color or physical traits that have traditionally been thought of as Negroid. All of her family looked like white people. They had fair skin, straight hair in shades ranging from blond to red, and eyes also of every imaginable hue. [My grandmother's] eyes were said to have been gray" (Haizlip, 1994, p. 46).

EVOLUTION OF THE AMERICAN RACIAL TRADITION

Her other ancestors included "English aristocrats, Scottish poets and Virginia gentry." The woman is light-skinned and Latin in appearance. But this is not sufficient to qualify her, as it did not Homer Plessy over one hundred years ago, to be classified as white. *She is regarded by others, and therefore is obliged to regard herself,* as African American. This extreme rigidity is peculiar to the American racial tradition.

Racial Classification in Bureaucratic Practice

The reader must have noticed the absence of a discussion of Hispanics in our review of the evolution of the American racial tradition. This is because the Hispanic classification is geographic and cultural, not racial. With their diverse appearance and ancestry—from "white" to "black" to "Indian" and every gradation in between—Hispanics are emblematic of the mixed-race classification problem and of the arbitrary nature of the notion of race. This is, of course, also true in Latin America itself. As Chilean sociologist Hernan Godoy notes, "Chileans feel that Argentines are whiter, blonder and more secure, but on the other hand, the Chileans feel blonder and whiter than Peru or Bolivia."[23]

Bureaucratic classificatory practice, as expressed in the U.S. Census categories, has historically wavered: (1) between the polar white-nonwhite model and a more flexible classification including intermediate categories; and (2) between prescriptive classification by official authorities and permissive self-classification by the individuals themselves.

For 150 years, the U.S. Census has reflected the official ambivalence vis-à-vis mixed-race people, particularly those of black/white ancestry. Mixed-race people have usually been statistically collapsed into the "Negro" group, or, more rarely, counted as a separate intermediate group. As noted earlier, in the censuses of 1850, 1870, and 1910 a mixed-race "mulatto" group was recognized: The term was applied to all persons having any perceptible trace of Negro blood, except those of exclusively African ancestry.

Before emancipation, mulattoes (as defined above) were estimated to account for over 12 percent of the Negro population of the United States— 40 percent free and 60 percent slaves. As can be expected, a higher percentage of mulattoes were free than in the Negro population as a whole. Half of the Negroes in the North were mixed race as opposed to 11 percent in the slave-holding states; but, because of the preponderance of numbers in the South, over two-thirds of the free mulattoes lived in the slave states.[24]

In 1890, the classification evolved further, with blacks of mixed-race ancestry classified variously as mulattoes, quadroons, and octoroons. Interestingly, there was a time lag between the institutionalization of segregation and the official federal semantics, and the mulatto classification continued to appear until 1920, when the census included the categories white, black, mulatto (defined as less than three-fourths of African ancestry), Chinese,

Japanese, Indian, and "other." Thereafter, with Jim Crow taking a firm hold over federal definitions as well, the racial classification returned to its rigid formulation. The next census of 1930 dropped the mixed-race designations; enumerators were instructed to list people as "Negro" if they had *any* degree of African ancestry.

In contemporary times, the prescriptive criterion has given way to self-classification by the mixed-race individuals concerned. This was both a convenient way to sidestep the issue and a practical consequence of the shift from personal canvassing to mailed questionnaires. Nevertheless, the polar dichotomy still applies to mixed-race individuals, and no intermediate census category exists.

The instructions for recording race in the 1970 census required that people identifying themselves as "African, colored, Creole (in Louisiana), Dominican, Ethiopian, Haitian, Jamaican, mulatto, nonwhite, Trinidadian or West Indian" be listed as "blacks."[25] This category (formerly "nonwhite"), included Negroes and all other nonwhite races, such as American Indians, Japanese, Chinese, Filipinos, and so forth. In 1980, 6.8 million Americans who designated themselves as "other race" were reassigned by the census administration to one of four categories: white, black, American Indian or Asian/Pacific Islander.[26] Nor did the 1990 census include a category apart from black or Negro for people of mixed black-white ancestry.[27] It must be admitted that the practice is convenient for the African American leadership as well, for it enlarges the group as a whole and contributes to its influence. Be that as it may, mixed-race Americans are still faced with the surreal alternative of either abandoning some of their roots, or accepting the strangeness and stresses of living as "white black people" in a race-conscious society.

As America moves into the twenty-first century, the document that determines the American racial classification system is "Race and Ethnic Standards for Federal Statistics and Administrative Reporting" from the Office of Management and Budget (OMB) Statistical Policy Directive 15. The purpose of the directive is to provide standard classifications for recordkeeping, collection, and presentation of data on race and ethnicity in federal program administrative reporting and statistical activities.

A disclaimer emphasizes that the classifications should not be viewed as scientific or anthropological in nature, nor as determinants of eligibility for participation in any federal program—but are only meant to provide compatible, nonduplicated, exchangeable racial and ethnic data. Despite the disclaimer, the practical importance of Directive 15 as the ultimate reference for resolving statistical issues of numbers and "racial demography" is enormous. The implications of such statistical categories are concrete and far-reaching, and the question of classification is anything but academic (as the contemporary debate on affirmative action demonstrated). As spelled out in Directive 15, the racial classification that will underpin, directly or indirectly, all debates on racial questions in the foreseeable future in America consists of the following mutually exclusive categories, and does not have any mixed-race category (not even "other"):

a. American Indian or Alaskan Native. A person having origins in any of the original peoples of North America, and who maintains cultural identification through tribal affiliations or community recognition.

b. Asian or Pacific Islander. A person having origins in any of the original peoples of the Far East, Southeast Asia, the Indian subcontinent, or the Pacific Islands. This area includes, for example, China, India, Japan, Korea, the Philippine Islands, and Samoa.

c. Black. A person having origins in any of the black racial groups of Africa.

d. Hispanic. A person of Mexican, Puerto Rican, Cuban, Central, South American, or other Spanish culture or origin, regardless of race.

e. White. A person having origins in any of the original peoples of Europe, North Africa, or the Middle East.[28]

The courts have been instrumental in the American process of racial construction and definition. Their key role, heavily negative until the Warren Supreme Court of the 1950s, is discussed next.

NOTES

1. Peter Charles Hoffer, ed., "From White Man to Redskin," in *Indians and Europeans: Selected Articles on Indian-White Relations in Colonial North America* (New York: Garland, 1988), p. 288.

2. General Philip Sheridan made the comment to Tochoway, a Comanche chief, who entered Fort Cobb and introduced himself to Sheridan as a "good Indian," to which Sheridan replied: "The only good Indian is a dead Indian." John W. Kirshon and Ralph Berens, eds., *Chronicle of America* (Liberty, Mo.: J. L. Publications, 1993), p. 50.

3. The term "squaw" is derived from a vulgar French word for female genitalia.

4. J. S. Bassett, ed., *The Writings of Colonel William Byrd* (New York: N.p., 1901), pp. 8–9, quoted in Henriques, 1975, p. 57.

5. Both societies were fully agricultural, with flocks and herds as well as tillage. Both were haphazardly literate, and had their own alphabet as well as literature. Both had metals and masonry and weaving, lived in towns, built ships and engaged in commerce with other countries (Jennings, 1976, p. 6). The rationales for the view that the Irish were primitive were political and cultural.

6. Nicholas P. Canny, "The Ideology of English Colonization: From Ireland to America," *William and Mary Quarterly* 30 (1973), quoted in Jennings, 1976, p. 46.

7. This policy was also followed in Australia until the early 1970s. Mixed-race children were forcibly removed from their Aborigine households and placed in institutions. The purpose was to separate them from Aborigine culture.

8. Rayna Green, "Kill the Indian and Save the Man: Indian Education in the United States," in *To Lead and to Serve: American Indian Education at Hampton Institute, 1878–1923*, ed. Mary Lou Hultgren and Paulette Fairbanks Molin (Virginia Foundation for the Humanities and Public Policy, 1989), p. 9.

9. An extreme racist sentiment was that of General Philip Sheridan. See note 2, above.

10. This also resulted in a favorable British opinion of traditional Fijian society in the South Pacific island nation of Fiji, which the British saw as similar to their own. Cf. Hazel M. McFerson, "Unstable Equilibrium: The Roots of the 1987 Fiji Coups," in *Race and Ethnic TV Annual Report*, ed. Rutledge Dennis, (Westport, Conn.: Greenwood Press, 1994).

11. As Ellwood Parry stated: "In the continuing search for what is truly 'American' in American art . . . from the time of John Foster or John Hasselius to the era of Winslow Homer and Thomas Eakins, serious involvement with black and Native American themes seem to be one of the major characteristics that can be used to define the distinctive nature of American art" (1974, p. 173).

12. The book was a fictional work about a good and devoted slave, Uncle Tom, who flees after his kind master dies because of harsh treatment by the cruel overseer Simon Legree. It is based on accounts by Josiah Henson, an escapee from Maryland whose autobiography was published in 1858 and republished in 1962 (Low and Clift, [1981] 1984, p. 57).

13. Among the images immortalized in *Uncle Tom's Cabin* was that of Topsy, who, when asked: " 'Who was your mother?', replied 'Never had none!' with a grin. 'Never had any mother? What do you mean? Where were you born?', to which Topsy replied: 'Never was born!' 'Do you know who made you?' 'Nobody, as I knows on,' said the child, with a short laugh. . . . 'I spect I just grow'd' " (Stowe, *Uncle Tom's Cabin*, [1852] 1966, ch. 10).

14. For a story of such a marriage, see Katherine Anne Porter, *Mae Franking's My Chinese Marriage* (Austin: University of Texas Press, 1991).

15. Husishen, a Buddhist priest, is believed to have sailed across the Pacific to North America in the fifth century.

16. "Early Difficulties with Contract Labor Legislation," extract from *Reports of the U.S. Industrial Commission* 15 (1901), pp. 647–48, quoted in Edith Abbott, ed., *Immigration: Select Documents and Case Records* (Chicago: The University of Chicago Press, 1924; reprint, Arno Press, 1969), p. 187.

17. In common with African American civil rights activists, the Chinese did not passively accept discriminatory exclusion laws. Individuals and Chinese civil rights organizations, such as the Native Sons of the Gold State (NSGS), founded in 1895 in San Francisco, and renamed the Chinese-American Citizens Alliance (CACA) in 1915, pursued civil rights. H. M. Lai (1980) describes the movement:

> Chinatown leaders frequently petitioned for more equitable treatment. Diplomats such as Wu Tingfang (1842–1922) and Liang Ching (1864–1917), and prominent Chinese Americans such as Ng Poon Chew (1866–1931) . . . protested in numerous speeches and writings the draconian enforcement of the immigration laws. . . . In 1905 China and a number of overseas Chinese communities boycotted U.S. goods.

Law suits were also employed to gain Chinese civil rights. *United States v. Gue Lim* (1900) ruled that Chinese merchants had treaty rights to bring wives and minor children into the country. The right of an American-born Chinese to citizenship and hence to admission to the United States was affirmed by the court in *Kim Ark Wong v. United States* (1898).

18. The author recalls Chinese living in the predominantly black Roxbury neighborhood of Boston during the 1940s–1950s. The Chinese were not considered white by blacks, nor were they considered black; they were considered as colored, or as members of the yellow race. Marriage or cohabitation with black women was not uncommon, and the offspring of these relationships were considered part-black/Chinese by blacks in the community.

19. An example of the white exclusion of Chinese children was a case brought by Gong Lum, a Chinese merchant of considerable social status among whites in Rosedale, Mississippi. Lum was unable to educate his two daughters at the public school for whites, although "Martha, the oldest, had been admitted to the public school for whites along with others of her race. At the noon recess on opening day in October 1924, she was notified by the superintendent that she would not be allowed to return." Lum sued and the argument advanced by Martha's lawyers claimed: "She is not a member of the colored race nor is she of mixed blood, but . . . she is pure Chinese" (Loewen, 1971, pp. 66–67). Furthermore, they argued, separate and equal facilities were not provided for her, nor was she allowed to utilize white facilities. Their arguments were accepted and the Mississippi Circuit Court for the First Judicial District of Bolivar County decided in her favor—a decision which was appealed to the Mississippi Supreme Court.

20. Negative American attitudes even toward Asians in the Pacific Territories reveals a shameful past. Congressman Robert A. Underwood (Guam), shared the story of the unique experiences of the Chamorro people of Guam in World War II, who suffered wartime atrocities as the result of abandonment by the United States (see U.S. House Subcommittee on Native American and Insular Affairs, 1995, p. 95).

Guam was the only American territory occupied in World War II by the Japanese for thirty-two months, "The only American soil with American nationals occupied by an enemy . . . something that had not happened on American soil since the War of 1812." Japanese occupation of Guam was brutal for two reasons—one, the presence of American nationals on American territory whose loyalty to the United States would not "bend"; two, the Chamorros "dared to defy the occupiers by assisting American sailors who had evaded initial capture" by providing food and shelter. In the final months of the occupation, the brutalities against the Chamorros increased. Thousands were forced to perform labor for the Japanese. Others were put to work in race paddies. Forty-six in the southern village of Malesso were herded into caves and summarily executed by Japanese throwing hand grenades into caves and spraying the caves with rifle and machine gun fire. Congressman Underwood continued:

> One elderly woman called on me during my campaign for Congress and asked me to never let this country forget what happened on Guam and to promise that I would do everything I could to bring justice and recognition to the people of Guam. She survived the massacre in Malesso, and bore the scars of that massacre in the shrapnel in her back and in her feet, so that everytime she walked, with every step, she was reminded of that nightmarish occurrence on Guam.

In the capital city of Agana, another group was rounded up, executed by being beheaded, and mutilated by swords. Others were similarly tortured. Thousands were forced to march from their villages in northern and central Guam to internment camps in southern Guam. The Treaty of Peace with Japan, signed on September 8,

1951, by the United States and the Allied powers, precluded the provision of war reparations for the people of Guam. In the treaty, the United States waived all claims of reparations against Japan by Chamarrons who had, just one year earlier in 1950, by virtue of the Organic Act of Guam, become American citizens.

Today, the people of Guam are seeking reparations through revised 1945 Guam Meritorious Claims, which allowed only one year for claimants to file with the Claims Commission. Many Chamorrans were unable to file because of language barriers, displacement from their homes, and misunderstanding of the procedures. In addition, the navy employed cumbersome procedures that delayed the process of seeking claims.

The act did not allow compensation for the forced march and allowed death and injury claims only as a basis for property claims. In addition, Chamorrans were encouraged to settle claims for lesser amounts due to the time delay in having claims over $5,000 sent to Washington for congressional approval. Congressman Eni F. H. Faleomavaega (American Samoa) summarized the effect of the war in 1995 hearings before the U.S. House Subcommittee on Native American and Insular Affairs of the Committee on Resources, 104th Congress, January 1995:

> The devastation wreaked on the Chamorro people in World War II was unforgivable . . . our government shares some of the blame for the past. As the Japanese forces advanced, the decision was made by our government to evacuate only U.S. citizens from the island of Guam, but the Chamorros, who were U.S. nationals, were left in place for the Japanese invaders. [They endured] summary executions, rape, torture, and internment. . . . Congress addressed these injuries with the Guam Meritorious Claims Act of 1945. But for a variety of reasons, this was not a satisfactory resolution. The debt the Chamorro people paid to the United States could never be forgiven. (P. 95)

21. Also cited was the charge that Filipinos living in the Watsonville district drove recklessly. But the most important cause was white racism and antimiscegenation sentiments. In his investigation of the race riots Emory S. Bogardus cited a set of resolutions (the *Pajaro* Resolutions) by Judge D. W. Rohrback, which began:

> Coming out square-toed and flat-footed in an expression on the Filipino question, the Northern Monterey Chamber of Commerce adopted a resolution Wednesday night (January 8) designating the Filipino population of this district with being undesirable and of possessing unhealthy habits and destructive of the wage scale of other nationalities in agricultural and industrial pursuits. . . . When interviewed this morning Judge Rohrback said the move of the Monterey Chamber of Commerce was but the beginning of an investigation of a situation that will eventually lead to the exclusion of the Filipinos or the deterioration of the white race in the State of California.

Apparently, the commingling of Filipino men and white women in a specially leased dance hall five miles west of Watsonville, incensed many whites and was cited by a white resident of Watsonville in conversation with Bogardus: "Taxi dance halls where white girls dance with Orientals may be all right in San Francisco or Los Angeles but not in our community. We are a small city and have had nothing of the kind before. We won't stand for anything of the kind."

Bogardus wrote in his report that the ensuing anti-Filipino demonstrations involved "possibly 200 Americans [who] formed Filipino hunting parties, running in groups from 25 to over 100 persons." A mob of white men and boys arrived "at eleven o'clock [in] thirty full machines, filled with flaming youth." The mob was turned back by the sheriff, deputies, and constables. The next night, however, the anti-Filipino action resumed, and violence developed into the destruction of property, the beating of Filipinos, and murder:

> Forty-six terror-stricken Filipinos beaten and bruised, cowered in the City Council room . . . after being rescued from a mob of 500 infuriated men and boys who, being robbed of their prey, shattered windows and wrecked the interior of the brown men's dwellings. . . . The most serious rioting occurred on the San Juan road in Pajaro . . . when a mob estimated at 250 men entered several Filipino dwellings and clubbed the occupants. (Schirmer and Shalom, 1987, pp. 58–62)

22. In the United States, the experiences of "white" black people have historically been regarded as the "tragic mulatto" syndrome. Consider the experiences of individuals such as the eighteenth-century escaping slave Ellen Craft, who disguised herself as the white owner of her black husband. Rev. Patrick Healy, the son of an Irish immigrant and an African slave, was phenotypically white, but his racial classification was black. Healy was the first president of Georgetown University, Washington, D.C., from 1873–1882, and he was considered black. Other examples of white "blacks" include bibliophile Jesse E. Moreland, for whom the Spingarn-Moreland library at Howard University is named; National Association for the Advancement of Colored People (NAACP) executive secretary, the late Walter White who, during the 1920s escaped a southern white lynch mob looking for a "nigger agitator" from the North because of his white phenotype. In contemporary America, examples include the late Congressman Adam Clayton Powell and pop singer Mariah Carey. Thus, the status of these and others of similar phenotype, in being regarded as black, is unique in comparative race relations. Even in the Western Hemisphere, most Latin American countries would have classified all these individuals as white or mixed race, but never as black.

23. Quoted in Calvin Sims, "The South American Art of Name-Calling," *New York Times*, July 30, 1995.

24. Census Report of 1850.

25. "Black Americans," *Directory of Data Sources on Racial and Ethnic Minorities* (Washington, D.C.: U.S. Department of Labor, Bureau of Labor Statistics, 1975), p. 5.

26. Barbara Vobedja, "Categorizing the Nation's Millions of 'Other Race,' " *Washington Post*, April 29, 1991, p. A9.

27. Cf. *Your Guide for the 1990 Census Form*, no. 4 (Washington, D.C.: U.S. Department of Commerce, 1990). The Census hotline reported that many callers were confused about racial classification, especially how to identify people of mixed-race ancestry. Kenneth Riccini, assistant chief for the 1990 Census Processing Office advised: "It's really self-determination. It's what you feel you are. A person in doubt about the race of a child should use the race of the mother" (Vobedja, 1991). Riccini's response does not reflect the reality of racial classification and race in America. For example, many Hispanics, who consider themselves a mixed-race people of neither exclusive black nor white ancestry, checked "other race" only to be reassigned to one of the four standard categories.

28. The Office of Management and Budget (OMB) began hearings in 1994, to review existing racial and ethnic categories of Directive 15, with an eye to possibly adding a biracial category and a Middle Easterner category, both of which are intended to reflect more adequately the increasing diversity of America.

3 Race, the Law, and the Courts

WHO IS AN AMERICAN?

This chapter reviews some of the key judicial and administrative decisions that codified and institutionalized racial attitudes toward Native Americans, African Americans, and Asian Americans, reviewed in the previous chapter. A combination of American case law, bureaucratic fiat, and legislative statutes played a key role in defining the socioracial status, rights, privileges, and claims to citizenship of nonwhites in the American racial tradition. Common law is incremental and personal, and judges often drew upon their own experiences and prejudices in establishing precedents in cases involving race. As noted by Oliver Wendell Holmes: "The life of the law has not been logic; it has been experiences, based on the felt necessities of the time, the prevalent moral and political theories, intuitions of public policy, and the prejudices, avowed or unconscious, which judges share with their fellow men" (1881, quoted in Commager, 1940).

American case law was instrumental in codifying the characteristics of the American racial tradition, as described earlier. It would be a mistake, however, to interpret American jurisprudence in racial matters as merely a collage of individual prejudices and perceptions of justice. Underlying many of the court rulings, as shall be shown, was often an objective *purpose*, that is, furthering the economic and political interests of the dominant white groups.

As noted in chapter 2, whether one views the Americanization process as a melting pot, or a salad (where ingredients are mixed but retain their separate identities), the overwhelming evidence is that people of color were not included in the polity from the very early days of the Republic. The result of imposing by law arbitrary socioracial classifications was the solidification of Anglo-Saxonism and white supremacy and served to withhold or grant privileges of citizenship and status to different groups. Purpose, as an underlying theme of the American racial tradition, has been utilized in both negative and positive ways, depending on the racial and ethnic groups involved and the material interests at stake. (We mentioned earlier how John Marshall's ruling of 1823 rationalized the white confiscation of Indian lands.)

In 1782, the French immigrant J. Hector St. John de Crevecoeur (1735–1813), a petty Norman nobleman, raised a question in his popular *Letters from an American Farmer* which continues to have meaning in contemporary America: "What then is the American, this new man?" Crevecoeur replied:

> He is either an European, or the descendant of an European, hence that strange mixture of blood, which you will find in no other country. I could point out to you a family whose grandfather was an Englishman, whose wife was Dutch, whose son married a French woman, and whose present four sons have now four wives of different nations. *He* is an American, who, leaving behind him all his ancient prejudices and manners, receives new ones from the new mode of life he has embraced, the new government he obeys, and the new rank he holds. He becomes an American by being received in the broad lap of our great *Alma Mater*. Here individuals of all nations are melted into a new race of men, whose labours and posterity will one day cause great changes in the world. (Crevecoeur, [1782] 1968, p. 39)

Interestingly, while American-hood was viewed as adhesion to a common set of values, and hence in principle independent of race, neither de Crevecoeur nor most of the founders even *conceived* of the notion that any non-European could ever be "received in the broad lap of our great Alma Mater."

Out of such views, Americans fashioned an image of themselves as an inclusive group, at once diverse and homogeneous, ever improving as it assimilated many types of people into a unified and distinct nationality. John Higham notes: "According to this long and widely respected view, the Americans derived some of their very distinctiveness as a nationality from the process of amalgamation."[1]

The trouble, of course, was that 144 years later a prominent American "Anglo-Saxonist," President Theodore Roosevelt, *still* had no doubt about who did and did not belong in the American family. (Theodore Roosevelt's racial views are discussed in chapter 5.) Although stressing that all "Americans" stood on equal footing once they renounced all allegiance to the lands from which they or their forefathers came, he said of those participating in the "assimilative process":

> ... some are Protestants, some are Catholics, some are Jews. Most of us were born in this country of parents born in various countries of the Old World—in Germany, France, England, Ireland, Italy, the Slavonic and the Scandinavian lands; some of us were born abroad; some of us are of Revolutionary stock. All of us are Americans, and nothing but Americans (September 11, 1917). (Roosevelt, 1918, pp. 314–16)

There was no mention of Native Americans, Africans, or Asians.

Attempts to answer de Crevecoeur's penetrating question from a racial standpoint have been central in the jurisprudence defining race and the criteria of membership in the National Union. The principal groups affected by the imposition through the judicial system of arbitrary racial classifications to decide who would and would not be permitted to assimilate into the American family are Native Americans, Africans, and Asians. The legal construction of race would eventually also become important for deciding who would and who would not be permitted to migrate to the United States.

THE JUDICIAL DEFINITION OF "NATIVE AMERICANS"

The Articles of Confederation vested in Congress the exclusive power to regulate the affairs of Indians who were not residents of any states. In the process, Congress was also able to manipulate the socioracial classification of Native Americans. (Chapter 5 will discuss how the policy of congressional supremacy later became the cornerstone of American policy in the Caribbean and Pacific territories, as it was in the continental territories.) Thus, the U.S. Congress has the power to define who is, or is not, a Native American. This special relationship between Native Americans and the federal government is established in the Constitution of the United States, which grants to Congress the power "to regulate Commerce with foreign nations among the states and with the Indian tribes."

While there has never been a general definition of the term "Indian" that could be used by the courts, a working definition evolved through a variety of judicial precedents for general understanding of the legal status of Native Americans. A "Native American" came to be defined as a person, some of whose ancestors lived in America before the arrival of whites, who is generally considered to be an Indian by the community in which he lives or from which he comes, and who holds himself to be an Indian (Baca, [1978] 1990). Some of the court cases that have tried to determine who is and who is not a Native American, include Suquamish Tribe of Indians (*Oliphant v. Suquamish Tribe of Indians* (1978); and *Williams v. Lee* (1959), in which the Supreme Court held that the Arizona courts had no authority to hear a debt collection case by a non-Indian where the action arose on the Navajo Reservation; and recently, in 1974, *Morton v. Mancari* upheld an employment preference for Indians in the Bureau of Indian Affairs.

The contributions to American jurisprudence of the "Great Chief Justice," John Marshall, are well known: the doctrine of judicial review, the supremacy of the federal Constitution, the sanctity of contracts, the liberal construction of grants of constitutional authority to the federal government, and the limitation of state power when in conflict with valid federal power. Less well known is his role vis-à-vis Native American rights. Based on Marshall's 1823 decision that Indians did not have sovereignty over their territories because of the colonists' "right of discovery," the state of Georgia nullified in 1829 all Cherokee laws including those restricting land alienation. When the Cherokee appealed to the federal authorities, Marshall ruled in *The Cherokee Nation v. The State of Georgia* that the Cherokee Nation was a "domestic dependent nation," and thus outside federal jurisdiction (Steinberg, [1981] 1989, p. 17). With such utter disregard of the facts as could only have been willful, Marshall noted that their "occupation was war, and [their] subsistence was drawn chiefly from the forest." (On the contrary, the Cherokee were largely, by that time, settled farmers.) Therefore, "that law which regulates, and ought to regulate in general, the relations between the conqueror and conquered was incapable of application to a people under such circumstances." In plain English, Native Americans were uncivilized heathens outside the bounds of morality and protection of the law. Most telling for our story, it was only in *1979*, 160 years after the fact, that the state of Georgia repealed the Cherokee laws and posthumously pardoned the two missionaries sentenced in 1831 for trying to help the Cherokee.[2]

The General Allotment Act (1887), also known as the Dawes Act or the Dawes Severalty Act was the next important step in the direction of differentiating between the various Native American groups, in the tacit objective of regulating and facilitating the unilateral intervention of the federal government in the internal affairs of native nations.[3] Native Americans were legally defined for the first time on the basis of a "blood quantum" code that was employed for identification purposes by the federal government. The blood quantum code divided Native Americans into two groups, each with different rights and claims to land, and each regarded as having attained different levels of civilization.

"Full Blood Indians" were deeded with "trust patents," over which the federal government exercised complete control for a minimum of twenty-five years. The assumption was that full-blood Indians were less civilized and therefore less competent to handle their own affairs. In contrast, Native Americans with white ancestry—"Mixed Blood Indians"—were perceived as on the way to attaining civilized status, and thus were permitted to exercise rights over their lands, through "patents in fee simple." Once each "federally recognized Indian" received his or her allotment of land, the

RACE, THE LAW, AND THE COURTS 55

balance of reserved Indian land was opened up to non-Indian homesteading, corporate utilization, or incorporation into national parks and forests.[4] The division of Native Americans into "full" and "mixed" blood groups was at bottom a legislative device to permit the carving up of Indian lands. Earlier, the Indian Removal Act (1830) had the same intent, later reinforced by the Indian Citizenship Act (1924), the Indian Reorganization Act (1934), and the Indian Claims Commission Act (1946).

The rights and status of Native Americans thus depended on how they were racially and culturally defined and how much "white" blood flowed through their veins. A ruling from a Circuit Court in 1912 held that persons of one-eighth Indian blood were "of sufficient Indian blood to substantially handicap them in the struggle for existence" and therefore were Indians (Cohen, [1942] 1982, quoted in Baca, [1978] 1990). The arbitrariness of such distinctions was inevitable and evident. Because the hypodescent rule (see chapter 2) was applied to Negroes but not to Indians, the racial definitions were of dizzying complexity. The Virginia Code of the 1920s considered as white persons those with no more than one-fourth Indian blood and *no* other "non-Caucasic" blood. Symmetrically, "every person in whom there is any ascertainable Negro blood shall be deemed and taken to be a colored person, and every person not a colored person having one-fourth or more of American Indian blood shall be deemed an American Indian; except that members of Indian tribes existing in this Commonwealth having one-fourth or more of Indian blood and less than one-sixteenth of Negro blood shall be deemed tribal Indians" (Code 1–14, quoted in Sickles, 1972, p. 65).

There is the notion of purpose underlying these definitions. The objective of facilitating appropriation of Indian land overlapped with the separate objective to encourage Native Americans to intermingle with whites. The legal and administrative posture vacillated between assimilation and exclusion (with the occasional advocacy of extermination). As noted by Bieder: "The suggestion that the mingling of races in 'blessed unions' was preferable to war—and less expensive—caught the fancy and drew the support of many philanthropists, despite a lingering concern over the differences in color and intellectual capacity of the two peoples."[5]

Thus, there came into existence a group that claimed its descent from both Native Americans and Europeans, viewed as a potential vanguard for Europeanizing Native Americans and furthering the cause of white "civilization."

In later years, the rigidity and arbitrariness of the definitions of Native Americans gradually loosened, partly in keeping with changing political and economic motivations of the whites. The "bridge" was provided in the Indian Reorganization Act of 1934, which defined "Indian" in bureaucratic fashion as:

All persons of Indian descent who are members of any recognized Indian tribe now under Federal jurisdiction, and all persons who are descendants of such members who were, on June 1, 1934, residing within the present boundaries of any Indian reservation, and shall further include all other persons of one-half Indian blood. For the purposes of this Act, Eskimos and other aboriginal people of Alaska shall be considered Indians. (Quoted in Cohen, [1942] 1982).

A few years later, the 1942 *Handbook of Federal Indian Law* noted a further step toward common sense: "If a person is three-fourths Caucasian and one-fourth Indian, it is absurd from the ethnological standpoint to assign him to the Indian race. Yet legally such a person may be an Indian. From a legal standpoint, then, the biological question of race is generally pertinent, but not conclusive" (Cohen, [1942] 1982, quoted in Baca, [1978] 1990).[6]

And a later edition of the *Handbook* went further:

Racial composition is not always dispositive in determining who are Indians for the purposes of Indian law. In dealing with Indians, the federal government is dealing with *members or descendants of political entities, that is, Indian tribes, not with persons of a particular race* [emphasis added]. Tribal membership as determined by the Indian tribe or community itself is often an essential element. In fact, a person of complete Indian ancestry who has never had relations with any Indian tribe may be considered a non-Indian for some legal purposes. (Cohen, [1942] 1982).

The flexibility of the definition is shown by the numbers of people who claim varying degrees of Native American ancestry. In recent years an increasing number of whites have emerged claiming Native American ancestry. In 1948, the U.S. government recognized approximately 400,000 people in the then–forty-eight states as Native Americans, along with an additional 35,000 in Alaska. By 1960 the number had increased to 523,600 people in the fifty states, and the 1990 census counted those claiming Native American ancestry at 1.8 million. Furthermore, surveys show that up to 10 million Americans claim some degree of Native American ancestry, a far, far greater number than at any previous time.[7]

A corollary of the flexible racial definition, therefore, is the possibility to move in and out of the group, depending on situation and phenotype. Indeed, some Native Americans argue that the increase in whites claiming Native American ancestry has a cynical reason, such as the desire to qualify for federal benefits allotted to Native Americans, and to gain access to land, with no intention of advancing the social well-being of the group.[8]

And so, who is an Indian may depend on the situational context—the very essence of a flexible racial tradition. Not so, of course, for blacks.

THE DEFINITION OF AFRICAN AMERICANS IN LAW

The Early Days

The rigidity of the American racial tradition vis-à-vis African ancestry has been evident at all levels of case law since the founding of the Republic. As repeatedly noted (because it is such a hallmark of the American racial tradition), the rule of hypodescent meant that *any* discernible degree of African blood sufficed to define the person as *fully* Negro. Thus, down to this day, the group of mixed Indian-African parentage—although in all probability much larger than that of Indian-Caucasian parentage—lies submerged within the African American group. The historical evolution of the term "mulatto" is instructive.[9] A Virginia statute in 1705 prohibited any "negro, mulatto, or Indian" from holding any public office and further stated: "the child of an Indian, and the child, grandchild, or great grandchild of a Negro shall be deemed, accounted, held, and taken to be a mulatto."[10]

In 1866, as noted earlier, the Virginia Act of 1705 was modified: "Every person having one-fourth or more Negro blood shall be deemed a colored person, and every person not a colored person having one-fourth or more Indian blood shall be deemed an Indian."[11] Jane Purcell Guild (1936) comments:

> ... from 1705 until 1866 the only legal definition applying to mixed Native Americans (excepting those having one-fourth or more African ancestry) was that of 1705. Thus we might at first glance construe that a mixed American-European was legally a mulatto, if of one-half or more American blood *until* that statute of 1866 making such persons 'Indians'. All [African] American mixed-bloods remained mulattoes throughout the period, unless having less than one-eighth African ancestry (1705–85) or less than one-quarter African ancestry (1785–1910). After 1910 Virginia reclassified large numbers of persons by extending the "colored" category to include people with minute amounts of African ancestry. (Quoted in Forbes, 1993, p. 195)

Among the myriad of judicial decisions on this issue two stand out: the *Dred Scott* case and *Plessy v. Ferguson*. Between the end of the Civil War and the *Plessy* case lay some twenty years of judicial ambivalence—which conceivably could have produced a resolution on the saner side of the racial issue, but did not.

Dred Scott and Related Cases

One of the most important court cases in the racial construction of African Americans was *Dred Scott v. Sandford* (1857). In 1834, as is well known, the slave Dred Scott was taken by his master from Missouri, a slave state, to Illinois, a free state, then to present-day Minnesota (Fort Snelling) where slavery was forbidden by the Missouri Compromise of 1820, and then back to Missouri. In 1846 Scott initiated a suit to obtain his freedom, on the ground that he had become free when taken into free territory. The case was eventually brought to the Supreme Court. Three major legal issues were involved: (1) whether Scott was a citizen of the State of Missouri, so as to give the federal courts jurisdiction; if so, (2) whether he had been set free by his travels to the Free Territory of Wisconsin, and (3) whether the Missouri Compromise was constitutional.[12] The Court ruled that Scott was not a citizen of the United States or of the State of Missouri and therefore not competent to sue in the federal courts.[13] Having thus refused jurisdiction, the judges gave separate opinions on the other issues.

In the view of Chief Justice Roger Brooke Taney, the racial aspect of the case was critical to the issue of citizenship:

The question is simply this: Can a negro, whose ancestors were imported into this country, and sold as slaves, become a member of the political community formed and brought into existence by the Constitution of the United States, and as such become entitled to all the rights, and privileges, and immunities, guaranteed by that instrument to the citizen? We think they are not, and that they are not included, and were not intended to be included, under the word "citizens" in the Constitution, and can, therefore, claim none of the rights and privileges which that instrument provides for and secures to citizens of the United States. On the contrary, *they were at that time considered as a subordinate and inferior class of beings*, who had been subjugated by the dominant race, and whether emancipated or not, yet remained subject to their authority, and had no rights or privileges but such as those who held the power and the government might choose to grant them. . . . In the opinion of the court, the legislation and histories of the times, and the language used in the Declaration of Independence, show, that neither the class of persons who had been imported as slaves, nor their descendants, whether they had become free or not, were then acknowledged as a part of the people, nor intended to be included in the general words used in that memorable instrument. (*Dred Scott v. Sandford* [1857])

Whatever one thinks and feels about the obscene impact of the decision, Taney's argument was correct on its own merits; not de Crevecoeur, nor the Founding Fathers, nor any influential American when the Constitution was drafted really intended it at the time to apply to anyone other than white people and Anglo-Saxons at that. (Of course, tragically, the Court missed a historic opportunity to use its interpretive powers to remove from the Constitution the taint of implicit racism and exclusion.)

Some of the other more egregious cases involving slaves deserve brief mention for what they indicate about white racial privilege, American common law, and the complicity of the Courts. *State v. Mann* (1869) involved Lydia, the slave of Elizabeth Jones, whom she rented to John Mann. When Mann attempted to chastise Lydia for some offense, she started running, and Mann shot her in the back. There was no allegation that Lydia was attempting to escape, only that she was attempting to avoid a beating (Hall, Weicek, and Finkelman, 1991, p. 192). But Judge Thomas Ruffin, considered one of the "finest antebellum southern jurists," noted that

... while slavery exists amongst us in its present state, or until it shall seem fit to the Legislature to interpose express enactments to the contrary, it will be the imperative duty of the Judges to recognize the full domination of the owner over the slave, except where forbidden by statute. And this we do upon the ground that this domination is essential to the value of slaves as property, to the security of the master, and the public tranquility. (Hall, Weicek, and Finkelman, 1991, p. 207)

In another case, *Souther v. Commonwealth* (1851), Simeon Souther was indicted for murdering his slave. The charge was that he:

tied his negro slave Sam, with ropes about his wrists, neck, body, legs, and ankles to a tree. That whilst so tied, the prisoner first whipped the slave with switches. That he next beat and cobbed the slave with a shingle, and compelled two of his slaves, a man and a woman, also to cob the deceased with a shingle. That whilst the deceased was so tied to the tree, the prisoner did strike, knock, kick, stamp, and beat him, upon various parts of his head, face and body; that he applied fire to his body, back, sides, belly, groin and privy parts; that he then washed his body, & c., with warm water in which pods of red pepper had been put and steeped and he compelled his two slaves also to wash him with the same preparation ... that the prisoner then had Sam untied from the tree and carried into a shed and his feet put in stocks and a rope tied about the neck and fastened it to a bedpost there by strangling, choking and suffocating, and did kick, knock, etc. and again compelled his two slaves to apply fire to the body ... and the slave Sam then and there died. It appeared that the prisoner commenced the punishment of the deceased in the morning, and that it was continued throughout the day.

Souther was convicted of murder in the second degree. The reasoning, however, is revealing:

The owner of a slave, for the malicious, cruel and excessive beating of his own slave, cannot be indicted. ... It is the policy of the law in respect to the relation of master and slave, and for the sake of securing proper subordination and obedience on the part of the slave, to protect the master from prosecution in all such cases, even if the whipping and punishment be malicious, cruel and excessive. But in so inflicting punishment for the sake of punishment, the owner of the slave acts at his peril; and if death ensues ... the relation of master and slave affords no ground of excuse. (Quoted in Hall, Weicek, and Finkelman, 1991, p. 196).

Legal status and the right to citizenship for Negroes was not favorably adjudicated until the Civil Rights Act of 1866 and passage of Section 1 of the Fourteenth Amendment, adopted in 1868, which held that all *persons* born or naturalized in the United States, and subject to the jurisdiction thereof, were citizens of the United States and of the state wherein they resided. Finding that Negroes were "persons," thus automatically defined them as citizens, and thus entitled them to all constitutional protections.

On the Seesaw to 1896

While some subsequent court rulings affirmed fourteenth Amendment protections, others abridged them by establishing that blacks were separate and inferior. Most questioned the socioracial status of mixed-race Africans in the context of public accommodations and, most notably, transportation law. Until the 1896 ruling in *Plessy v. Ferguson* (discussed in the next section) the courts wavered back and forth between a forthright affirmation of the rights of Negroes and a variety of cavils designed to rationalize inferior status.

Among judicial limitations of the rights of Negroes in the post-Reconstruction period, one of the most damaging stemmed from the ruling in the *Slaughterhouse* cases (1873), which severely restricted the application of the Fourteenth Amendment, by not extending it to protect citizens of a state of the union against the legislative power of *the state*. The implications for blacks were enormous:

> Herein lay a terrible irony for blacks. After having construed the "pervading purpose" of the Civil War amendments to be the freedom of black people [Justice Miller] relegated freedmen, for the effective protection of their new freedom, to precisely those governments—the southern states—least likely to respect either their rights or their freedom should the Republican regimes fall from power. The federal government could protect only the privileges and immunities of federal citizenship. As enumerated by Miller, these included the right of access to Washington, D.C., and the coastal seaports; the right to protection on the high seas and abroad; the right to use navigable waters of the United States; the right of assembly and petition; the privilege of habeas corpus. Of these, only the last two would be significant for most blacks. (Hall, Weicek, and Finkelman, 1991, p. 241)

Until 1896, the courts tiptoed around the issue of separate racial accommodations for twenty years. In 1877, just prior to the end of the Reconstruction period, *Hall v. DeCuir* challenged an 1869 Louisiana law giving common carriers the power to make rules and regulations regarding passenger service within the state, "provided said rules make no discrimination on account of race or color." Mrs. DeCuir, a Negro woman, tried to buy a first-class ticket on an interstate boat operating between New Orleans and another Louisiana city. Refused first-class accommodations, she bought a second-class ticket and promptly took possession of a first-class cabin set apart for whites. She was ejected and sued for damages. A Louisiana jury awarded her damages in the sum of $1,000, and the Louisiana courts upheld the verdict. (Court records do not indicate whether Mrs. DeCuir was a mulatto.)

In the post-Reconstruction period, a number of states passed racially restrictive transportation laws. Tennessee was the first Southern state to enact such a law in 1881—stemming from an 1875 law adopted expressly to subvert the Civil Rights Act. Other restrictive transportation laws were enacted in Florida (1887), Mississippi (1888), Texas (1889 and 1891), Louisiana (1890 and 1894), Alabama (1891), Arkansas (1891 and 1893), Georgia (1891), and Kentucky (1892). (After the *Plessy* ruling, a second wave of laws were passed between 1898 and 1901, in South Carolina, North Carolina, and Virginia; in 1904 and 1907, Maryland and Oklahoma followed suit.)

The separate-car law also sustained the slave regime's practice of separating husbands and wives in mixed marriages, as well as the white parent and his or her mulatto children. This was a significant practice for what it revealed about the Louisiana socioracial tradition that emphasized non–Anglo Saxon laws in permitting interracial sociosexual relationships.

In the North, cases in the genre included *Roberts v. The City of Boston* (1849) which, preceding Emancipation, considered that the continuance of separate schools for colored children was not only legal and just, but best adapted to promote the instruction of that class of the population. In *Anderson v. Millikin et al.* (1859), the Ohio Supreme Court declared that the constitutional prohibition on black suffrage was limited to persons who were more than half-black. The decision declared mulattos white, and it made Ohio one of the two states to reject the hypodescent doctrine.

The judicial ambivalence of the post–Civil War period came to an end in 1896, when the Supreme Court ruling in *Plessy v. Ferguson* reaffirmed the "one-drop" rule of hypodescent and institutionalized racial segregation.

Recast in Concrete: *Plessy v. Ferguson*

As is well known, *Plessy v. Ferguson* was a Supreme Court test case in 1896 culminating from several cases challenging post-Reconstruction transportation segregation laws in Louisiana. The Supreme Court ruling in the *Plessy* case legitimized racial segregation and the doctrine of "separate but equal." Charles A. Lofgren describes the prevailing constitutional climate at the time of the *Plessy* case as ominous: "The judiciary's application of the 13th and 14th Amendments to issues of Negro rights was timid or lacking: the origins of the Amendments had been forgotten."[14]

Homer Plessy was of mixed black-white ancestry, a Louisiana "Creole of color," with seven white great-grandparents, and white in physical appearance, who was prosecuted for sitting in the "whites only" section of a New Orleans railroad car. He argued in his law suit that he should be permitted to sit in the white section. Plessy's legal challenge was rejected by the Criminal Court for New Orleans, and the case was appealed to the U.S. Supreme Court.

The litigation was organized by seventeen black citizens of Louisiana, members of the recently formed American Citizens' Equal Rights Association who were opposed to the Louisiana Separate Car Act. The group brought the suit through the "Citizens' Committee To Test The Constitutionality Of The Separate Car Law," whose members were blacks and Creoles. (The tester in an earlier case *Abbott v. Hicks* [1892], which tested segregated transportation laws was also a Creole of color, Daniel F. Desdunes, an octoroon and the twenty-one-year-old son of one of the principal organizers of *Plessy*. He was arrested for taking a seat in a white car on the L&N, having purchased a first-class ticket for a trip from New Orleans to Mobile, Alabama.)

The preparation of the test case was subtle and highly sophisticated. The racial makeup of Homer Plessy was important to test the segregated transportation laws, and the decision to utilize such an individual is as illuminating of the American racial tradition as are the specifics of the case itself. In Louisiana, mulattoes were recognized as a separate socioracial group of "Creoles of color." The black and colored organizers wanted to challenge the law in a manner that would take account of both railway practices and existing legal doctrines (Lofgren, 1987, p. 31). The choice of a near-white person to test the Louisiana law was deliberate and intended to strike at the heart of the case. The choice of a white lead attorney in the case, Albion W. Tourgee of Mayville, New York, was equally calculated. Charles A. Lofgren writes:

> . . . by setting up the case around a light-complexioned Negro, the *arbitrariness of the classification would be accentuated*, which . . . was a point of importance under developing Fourteenth Amendment jurisprudence . . . a nearly white Negro might not be refused entrance to a white car, at least in the New Orleans area, for "people of tolerably fair complexion, even if unmistakable colored, enjoy[s] here a large degree of immunity from the accursed prejudice." (P. 31, emphasis added)

Furthermore, a person of unmistakable black phenotype could book a seat from out of state and be forced into a Jim Crow car on entry into Louisiana. To use such a person for the test case would create an interstate commerce issue, which the organizers did not want. Since 1891, all the surrounding states had similar legislation, which meant the person would probably be assigned a separate car from the beginning of the journey. Another possibility was to have a black man try to buy a sleeper ticket and be refused after a white person received one. However, the organizers feared that by using a black the employees and perhaps the white passengers, too, would simply beat him up and throw him out, and there would be no arrest and thus no test case. The person would have to be refused admission into the "white" car before the train started. A phenotypically white octoroon could do so in the New Orleans area without personal danger. Homer Plessy's violation of the law was reported by the white conductor. He was arrested and taken to jail.

Arguments for Plessy were based on the Thirteenth and Fourteenth Amendments and challenged the rigid nature of the American racial tradition:

> What else but a badge of servitude is imposed and perpetuated . . . when a person, seven-eighths white and one-eighth of colored blood, or a person fifteen-sixteen parts white and one-sixteenth part of colored blood, is subjected to fine or imprisonment by authority of State law, for insisting [contrary to a conductor's judgment] that he or she, as the case may be, should be classed as a white person . . . although color be not discernible in their complexion? (*Plessy v. Ferguson* [1896])

Based on the fact that Plessy was seven-eighths white and that his colored background was not discernible, the petition argued that he was "entitled to every recognition, right, privilege, and immunity secured to citizens of the United States of the white race by the Constitution and laws of the United States." And the brief before the State Supreme Court noted that: "The statute leaves uncertain and indefinite who are among those classed as persons of the colored race," noting that Louisiana law and judicial precedent were similarly silent. (However, the issue of the racial classification of a mulatto had already been raised unsuccessfully in the previous *Abbott* case.)

Furthermore, Judge Ferguson had never addressed the question of what guided the conductor in determining Plessy's race. It was never clear how the conductor knew that Plessy was violating Louisiana's Jim Crow law by taking a seat in the "white" railroad coach. As Loren Miller writes: "All we know is that he ordered Mr. Plessy, who held a first-class ticket, to ride in the 'colored' coach and that Mr. Plessy staged a nineteenth-century sit down. He refused to budge. The conductor summoned police officers, who removed the obstinate passenger and filed a criminal complaint, as required by Louisiana's 1890 status."[15]

In its ruling rejecting Plessy's challenge, the U.S. Supreme Court held that a state law that "implies merely a legal distinction" between the two races did not conflict with the thirteenth Amendment forbidding slavery, nor did it tend to reestablish such a condition (Foner and Garraty, 1991). The Court also rejected the argument that segregation stigmatized African Americans. The purpose of the fourteenth Amendment, the Court said, was "to enforce the absolute equality of the two races before the law. . . . Laws requiring their separation . . . do not necessarily imply the inferiority of either race." With extraordinary hypocrisy, the Court further rejected the argument that segregation "stamps the colored race with a badge of inferiority. If this be so, it is . . . solely because the colored race chooses to put that construction upon it." Furthermore, "[if] the colored race should become the dominant power in the state legislature, and should enact a law in precisely similar terms, it would thereby relegate the white race to an inferior position. We imagine that the white race, at least, would not acquiesce in this assumption." In a ringing dissent, John Marshall Harlan wrote: "Our Constitution is color-blind and neither knows nor tolerates classes among citizens. . . . In respect of civil rights, all citizens are equal before the law." (Above quotes are from *Plessy v. Ferguson* [1896].)

Finally, the argument doubted that "social" prejudices could be overcome by legislation, nor could equal rights be secured to the Negro except by an enforced commingling of the two races. The Court noted: "We cannot accept this proposition. If the two races are to meet upon terms of social equality, it must be the result of natural affinities, a mutual appreciation of each other's merits and a voluntary consent of individuals. . . ." This argument ignored the obvious reality that Homer Plessy himself and millions of people of black-white ancestry were proof that commingling had occurred in the United States since the arrival of the first Africans. Ironically, it was precisely in New Orleans that these relationships were institutionalized. Beautiful young mixed-race women in New Orleans entered into arrangements of concubinage with wealthy white men. The city maintained a "fancy-girl" market for wealthy planters, where concubines sold for as much as $5,000 (Genovese, 1974). The women were chosen at quadroon balls, presided over by the watchful eyes of their mothers. Mostly of mixed African and Spanish or French heritage, some women were of such light complexions that a law required them to wear kerchiefs or chignons to identify them as colored. For the most part, of course, the relationships were unofficial, although some did function as power relationships for the women involved.

The problem facing the Court was, at bottom, the perennial one of racial classification of mixed-race individuals. In 1896, the Supreme Court had the power to change the rule of hypodescent—to open the door to the creation of a mixed-race group, thus nuancing the crude criterion of racial ancestry with considerations of phenotype, culture, or economic class. The positive implications for race relations in America would have been incalculable. Instead, prisoners of Oliver Wendell Holmes' "prejudices, avowed or unconscious, which judges share with their fellow men," the justices of the Taney Supreme Court acted to confirm and reinforce them.

Seventy years were to pass before the Civil Rights Act of 1964 put an end to de jure segregation. But in the meantime, as we shall see, the full force of custom and judicial precedent for racial segregation fell upon the overseas territories inhabited by "colored" and nonwhite people, territories acquired just two years after the *Plessy* ruling.

ASIANS AND THE AMERICAN LEGAL SYSTEM

The 1790 Naturalization Act limited naturalization only to "free white persons." Almost from the beginning of their arrival in the United States, Asians reacted strongly to attempts to pigeonhole them into racial categories in order to limit their participation in American life. In particular, through a series of legal cases challenging racist naturalization and immigration laws, the Chinese emerged as stalwarts. Their role in advancing immigration and naturalization laws has been akin to that of black activists in advancing civil rights legislation.

Interestingly, among the many lawsuits brought by Chinese, in particular, were those challenging their initial classification as black. Ronald Takaki writes, "The Chinese migrants found that racial qualities previously assigned to blacks quickly became 'Chinese' characteristics.... White workers referred to the Chinese as 'nagurs' " (quoted in Haney Lopez, 1996, p. 51). (The social context of this classification was examined in chapter 2.)

During the course of challenging the racist restrictions dating from the 1790 naturalization law, the Chinese also forced the American legal system to reveal important aspects of racial formation and assimilation pertaining to nonwhites. Asian legal challenges, although often unsuccessful, also had major implications for socioracial status, rights, privileges, and claims to citizenship of Filipinos, Puerto Ricans, Virgin Islanders, Samoans, and Micronesians in the overseas American territories, as elaborated in the next chapter.

Throughout the history of the United States, Native Americans, Africans, Asians, and, by implication, the inhabitants of U.S. territories were granted or denied citizenship on the basis of complicated and often contradictory laws that had race at their center. The underlying motivations for imposing arbitrary socioracial constructions remained rooted in Anglo-Saxon needs to create permanent unassimilable groups in America, whose exclusion was justified on pseudoscientific racial grounds. But, as has been shown, unlike blacks, the socioracial status of other nonwhite groups was not rigidly fixed and permanent. Asians in particular have experienced fluctuations in their socioracial stereotype, from "coolie" and "chink" to that of "model Asians" in the contemporary period. Among the legal cases challenging racist naturalization laws, two are key to an understanding of American racial attitudes toward Asians: *Ozawa v. United States* and *Toyota v. United States*.

Ozawa v. United States (1922)

The landmark case of *Ozawa v. United States* sought to establish Japanese eligibility for citizenship and settle the issue of whether Japanese were white. This case specifically raised the issue of race, whereas other cases had raised other constitutional issues, such as common law, due process, the Burlingame Treaty, etc. The point-counterpoint between petition and judgment summarizes all the key issues.

The arguments presented in the brief for Ozawa provided insight into the implications of racial formation for people of nonwhite ancestry, and, by extension, for the inhabitants of the overseas territories. The brief noted:

The policy of the United States has been to include into its citizenship by annexation vast numbers of members of races not Caucasian, including many Mongolians. The annexation of Hawaii converted thousands of Japanese, not to mention other nationalities, into American citizens. The most recent is the Porto Rico Act, which makes the Porto Ricans, who are as dark as the Japanese, American citizens. (*Ozawa v. United States*)

Ozawa argued that nothing in the words "free white persons," in their "common and popular meaning, nor in their scientific definition, defined a race or races, or prescribed a nativity or locus of origin." Rather "they deal with personalities and the qualities of personalities, and are only susceptible of meaning those persons fit for citizenship and of the kind admitted to citizenship by the policy of the United States. The words deal with individuals, not with races, nor with natives of any country or of any particular descent." Furthermore, the provisions of the Fourteenth Amendment in reference to persons "are universal in the application to all persons within the territorial jurisdiction without regard to any difference of race, or color, or nationality." (Two other cases, *Yick Wo v. Hopkins* (1886) and *Wong Wing v. United States* (1896), had applied the same rule to include aliens under the Fifth and Sixth Amendments.)

Mr. Justice Sutherland delivered the opinion of the Court. It was noted that the appellant was a person of the Japanese race born in Japan, whose application to the U.S. District Court for the Territory of Hawaii to be admitted as a citizen of the United States was opposed by the U.S. District Attorney. The "model" status of the appellant was recognized: He was a graduate of the Berkeley, California, High School, had been a student for nearly three years in the University of California system, had educated his children in American schools, his family had attended American churches, and he had maintained the use of the English language in his home. Thus, the Court conceded that he was well qualified by character and education for citizenship. Echoing de Crevecoeur, however, the Court's question was "who are comprehended within the phrase 'free white persons'?"

The Court considered that the mere color of the skin is impractical as color differs greatly among persons of the same race, even among Anglo-Saxons. Hence, to adopt the color test alone would result in a confused overlapping of races and a gradual merging of one into the other, without any practical line of separation. However, instead of accepting the logical conclusion from this obvious fact, the Court hid behind previous court decisions (beginning with the 1878 decision of Circuit Judge Sawyer, in *re Ah Yup v. Sawyer* [1878]), by which the words "white person" were meant to indicate only a person of what is popularly known as the Caucasian race. The Court thus concluded that the appellant was clearly of a race that is not Caucasian and therefore belonged entirely outside the zone on the negative side and was ineligible for citizenship. In effect, while implicitly recognizing the utterly unscientific nature of the notion of race, nevertheless the Court gave judicial cover to the naked reality of a political power relationship.

Toyota v. United States (1924)

Although *Toyota* involved a Japanese native, the Court opinion had a major influence on prospects for naturalization (and, indirectly, statehood) of other Asians, particularly Filipinos. Mr. Toyota served in the U.S. Coast Guard from 1913 to 1923, and on May 14, 1921, filed a petition for naturalization in the U.S. District Court for Massachusetts. His petition was approved and a certificate of naturalization was issued. However, the federal government wanted it cancelled, ostensibly because the certificate was illegally obtained, but in reality because of the precedent this action might set for naturalization of other Asians.

The federal government was especially concerned about the Filipinos. Unlike the Chinese, Japanese, and Koreans, Filipinos came from a territory then held by the United States. They came by the tens and tens of thousands after the United States received the Philippines from Spain—traveling first to the territory of Hawaii in the early 1900s and then to the mainland in the 1920s (Takaki, 1989, p. 56). They were American in their language and outlook, as many had been educated in schools established by Americans. Nevertheless, in *Toyota*, the Court held that the Filipinos could not be naturalized under the Act of June 29, 1906, and ruled that Filipinos would not be eligible for naturalization until the special passage of legislation to eliminate color and race as qualifications for naturalization.

At issue was whether the racially and culturally distinct peoples of the overseas territories, brought under American sovereignty without the promise of citizenship or statehood, could be held indefinitely as subject peoples, permanently excluded from the American political community and deprived of equal rights, without doing violence to American values.[16] As will be discussed in the next chapter, Congress succeeded in resolving the citizenship question only after several years of debate. In the view of Congressman Thomas Spight of Mississippi: "The Philippine inhabitants are of wholly different races of people from ours—Asiatics, Malays, negroes and mixed-blood. They have nothing in common with us and centuries cannot assimilate them.... They can never be clothed with the rights of American citizenship nor their territory admitted as a State of the American union" (quoted in Cabranes, 1979, p. 425).

In an earlier debate in 1900, Congressmen Newlands and Dalzell had been forthright about the economic reason for ruling out assimilation of Filipinos. Respectively:

It can be easily imagined what will be the effect of putting inside of our governmental and industrial system 9,000,000 people possessing a high degree of industrial aptitude and accustomed to a scale of wages and mode of living appropriate to Asiatics.

I am unwilling to see the wage-earner of the United States, the farmer of the United States, put upon a level and brought into competition with the cheap half-slave labor, savage labor, of the Philippine Archipelago. (Cabranes, 1979, p. 421)

These words were greeted by loud applause in the House.

INTERRACIAL MARRIAGE, ASSIMILATION, AND THE LAW

Gunnar Myrdal noted that the centerpiece of the American racial tradition is its deep antipathy toward miscegenation and race mixing between blacks and whites,[17] and, as previewed in chapter 2, the existence of the mixed-race group has long stood as confirmation of the realities of interracial sex. Visitors to colonial America wrote of plantation slaves as light as their masters, whom they often resembled. Going back another one hundred years, it is interesting to speculate how the American racial tradition might have developed had the suggestion of Patrick Henry been taken that the State of Virginia encourage intermarriage (albeit between whites and Native Americans), through the use of cash incentives. Even more ironic, when the suspected "miscegenator" Thomas Jefferson supervised the original census in 1790, he had the power to institutionalize an intermediate census category for people of mixed black/white ancestry. (See chapter 2 for a discussion of the racial taxonomy in official U.S. statistics.)

As in other aspects of race relations, the law and the courts here too exerted a strong negative influence. The law was utilized to punish as a crime interracial marriages until *1967*. A primary concern of the American legal system had been to prevent intermarriage between blacks and whites, and, less so, among whites and other nonwhites. Among the earliest of statutes promulgated in colonial America were prohibitions that condemned as a crime miscegenation between black men and white women. In 1664, for example, the colony of Maryland enacted a law decreeing that free born white women marrying Negro slaves would be doomed to serve the master of such slaves during their husband's lifetimes and that all children of such unions would be slaves.

Virginia was always in the forefront of promulgating punitive racial laws.[18] The mercenary meanness of a 1691 Virginia statute is remarkable:

Whatsoever English or other white man or woman, bond or free, shall intermarry with a Negro, mulatto, or Indian man or woman, bond or free, he shall within three months be banished from this dominion forever. And it is further enacted, that if any English woman being free shall have a bastard child by a Negro she shall pay fifteen pounds to the church wardens, and in default of such payment, she shall be taken into possession by the church wardens and disposed of for five years and the amount she brings shall be paid one-third to Their Majesties for the support of the government, one-third to that of the parish where the offense is committed and the other third to the informer. The child shall be bound out by the church wardens until he is *thirty years of age* [emphasis added]. In case the English woman that shall have a bastard is a servant she shall be sold by the church wardens (after her time is expired) for five years, and the child serve as aforesaid.[19]

In reality, because of the scarcity of white women, there was far more sexual contact between Englishmen and black slave women than vice versa. A child thus derived its status from its mother because of the economic benefit that accrued to her owner. If the legislature had followed the English legal doctrine that the status of the child was determined by the status of the father, thousands of blacks or mulattoes whose fathers were white would have been free (Higginbotham, 1978). In the same year another prohibition was enacted (and reenacted in 1792): "Whatsoever white man or woman being free shall intermarry with a Negro shall be committed to prison for six months without bail, and pay 10 pounds to the use of the parish. Ministers marrying such persons shall pay 10,000 pounds of tobacco."[20]

Apparently punishment of white women was necessary because indentured women, many of them Irish, resisted efforts to inoculate them with the virus of white racial prejudice (Bennett, 1969, p. 254). In 1848, the period of imprisonment for whites marrying blacks was increased to twelve months. It was not until 1932 that the statute was amended to impose imprisonment on *both* blacks and whites who intermarried (and increased the period of imprisonment to one to five years). These attempts to prevent black and white sociosexual relationships also applied to people of other races: Malayans, Filipinos, Chinese, Koreans, and Japanese.[21] As will be discussed in the next chapter, these attitudes toward interracial marriage were exported to the American overseas territories.

The taboo on interracial marriages went directly to the heart of the rigid American racial tradition with its creation of "genes-prisoners." As noted by Sickles (1972, p. 10): "the taboo . . . lends support to a caste system of superior and inferior social and economic roles for whites and blacks, who characteristically take their places in this system as nameless members of skin-color groups in which they are fixed for life."

On June 12, 1967, the Supreme Court handed down a landmark decision. The Virginia Act to Preserve Racial Integrity of 1924 prohibited the intermarriage of whites with any other race or any person of any traceable mixtures of races "with the sole exception of persons with one-sixteenth or less of Native American ancestry who were considered 'white' under the law." (This exception was an appeasement to old Virginia families who had long boasted of their "noble Indian" ancestry.) In *Loving v. Virginia*, the Court unanimously held Virginia's antimiscegenation law void under the due process clause of the Fourteenth Amendment. (By then the Lovings had been married for nine years and were the parents of three children.) A simple announcement by Chief Justice Earl Warren: "Judgment Reversed," decriminalized interracial marriage throughout America.

Interestingly, Judge Leon M. Brazile, the presiding Caroline County, Virginia justice, whose ruling was overturned in *Loving*, revisited a key point of the eighteenth-century debates between monogenists and polygenists. In announcing his sentence of the Lovings, whose marriage he perceived as a crime, he announced: "Almighty God created the races white, black, yellow, malay, and red, and he placed them on separate continents. And but for the interference with his arrangement there would be no cause for such marriages. The fact that he separated the races shows that he did not intend for the races to mix" (quoted in Sickles, 1972, p. 80).

By implication, persons from other races also should be prohibited from marrying whites.[22] For example, a provision of California's civil code, which was struck down by the State Supreme Court in 1948 in *Perez v. Lippold*, mandated that "all marriages of white persons with Negroes, Mongolians, members of the Malay race or mulattoes are illegal and void" (quoted in Sickles, 1972, p. 98). (This marriage was between a white woman and a Filipino man.) Another case, *Naim v. Naim* (1955), involved Ham Say Naim, a Chinese seaman, and Ruby Elaine, a white woman, who were married in North Carolina. The marriage was eventually dissolved after the couple returned to Virginia to live as man and wife. Following a series of legal challenges based on the protections afforded by the Fourteenth Amendment, the marriage was annulled, after Ham Say Naim appealed to the Supreme Court of Appeals of Virginia (Sickles, 1972, p. 102). The court upheld the appeal in 1955, but not without making references to Naim's Asian ancestry as that of "a mongrel breed."[23]

RACE, THE LAW, AND THE COURTS   71

The antimiscegenation taboo has been removed from the law, but not from the American racial tradition. As recently as 1994, Howland Humphrey, a white high school principal in Wedowee, Alabama, prohibited mixed-race couples from attending the senior high school prom. When asked by a female student of mixed white/black ancestry with whom she should attend, he disparaged the woman as the product of a "mistake." Humphrey was let go from his job; but he has retained a dominant position in local school politics.

RACE, IMMIGRATION, AND THE COURTS

This is not the place for an extended discussion of the racial and ethnic considerations in U.S. immigration legislation. But it is important to stress that as immigration reached record heights at the turn of this century, countless people found themselves arguing their racial identity in order to naturalize, and the American legal system responded in arbitrary ways. From 1907, when the federal government began collecting data on naturalization, until 1920, over 1 million people gained citizenship under racially restrictive naturalization laws. Many individuals from various nonwhite racial groups applied and were rejected, including applicants from Hawaii, China, Japan, Burma, and the Philippines, *as well as all mixed-race applicants from the overseas territories.* The protracted attempts of various groups to establish their "whiteness at law" constituted the essence of a number of court cases, which Ian F. Haney Lopez terms the "white-person prerequisite cases," which involved the highest state and federal judicial bodies in case-by-case studies to define who was white.[24]

Among the most important of the white-person prerequisite cases were those involving Armenians, Arabs, and Asian Indians seeking to be classified as whites. The courts were required to articulate rationales for classification, and by implication, to address the underlying purposes and intents for the divisions they were creating and sanctioning. Beyond simply issuing declarations in favor of or against a particular applicant, the courts, as exponents of the applicable law, had to explain the basis on which they drew the boundaries of "whiteness." In so doing, the courts established judicial precedents—guiding and determining other decisions yet to come, as is the essence of common law—whether race was to be measured by skin color, facial features, national origin, language, culture, ancestry, the speculations of scientists, popular opinion, or some combination of these factors. The courts became de facto responsible for deciding not only who was white, but why someone was white. A key criterion used by the courts for determining race was the "common knowledge rationale," that is, common beliefs about race in the community. While wholly unscientific, the rationale at least had the merit of permitting change as "community standards" evolved.

FORMAL AND INFORMAL ASPECTS OF THE AMERICAN RACIAL TRADITION

As we have seen, the American racial tradition has evolved from its fluid, uncertain beginnings in the seventeenth century to its different attitudes toward Native Americans, African Americans, and Asians, and to its mature form at the turn of the twentieth century. While generally of the rigid form, as described in chapter 1, the American racial tradition has had its flexible elements and has been changing in that direction recently. Currently, much is being made of an alleged shift from race to class as a criterion of social stratification in America over the last generation. Increased flexibility in racial attitudes—and consequently in social and economic outcomes—is evident. Among other evidence, statistical work by Andrew A. Beveridge and Steven Ruggles demonstrated the "greening of the black middle class."[25] Between 1970 and 1990 a remarkable increase took place in black participation in professional fields and an even more remarkable shrinkage in the white-black income gap in those fields. There is no question, however, that race, not class, remains the key social variable in America, and that the prevailing racial mores are still largely within the rigid mold set largely since independence. What explains such inertia, such durability, of the American racial tradition in the face of the undeniably important legislative and social changes of the 1960s and 1970s?

To understand the living dynamics of racial traditions, it is helpful to borrow some of the ideas of the "new institutional economics," associated largely with the names of Ronald Coase, Oliver Williamson, and Douglass C. North.[26] In that perspective, "institutions" are not the organizations, but mainly the *rules* of behavior that the organizations follow. To use a sports analogy, the "institution" of volleyball consists of the rules of the game and remains essentially the same regardless of the competing teams and the players. The game may be played badly or well, but it is still volleyball as long as the rules are not changed (for example, by doubling the height of the net). Racial institutions, too, do not change merely because the players are different—*it takes a change in the racial rules to change the racial game.*

In turn, institutions include both formal and informal rules. Formal, overt rules can be changed quickly but the informal rules cannot—and it is those informal rules/customs/attitudes that constitute the bulk of the institution—the much larger part of the iceberg that is below the water surface. In Douglass C. North's formulation, the "social stock" of rules of behavior (economic, social, political) is so large in any society that real change (as opposed to formal change) can only occur slowly and gradually—a phenomenon that North calls "path dependence." This is clear in the evolution of the American racial tradition as well: We are still dependent on the path on which eight generations of American policymakers and image-shapers have placed us.

When the institution of slavery was abolished, all formal rules pertaining to slavery disappeared overnight, and in theory African Americans were relieved of all restrictions that did not apply to other Americans. But the core of the racial tradition—the informal rules, customs, prejudices, and mental images—had not changed. At bottom, this was the reason for the failure of the Reconstruction efforts. And so it was that, a generation after the end of the Civil War, the underlying racial tradition reasserted itself and—through *Plessy v. Ferguson*—brought back the older formal rules of racial classification and behavior under a modernized formulation. Similarly, when the judicial successes of the civil rights movement in the early 1950s brought an end to federally sanctioned segregation, the quick change in formal rules was not complemented by a corresponding change in attitude and informal behavior. It took the subsequent two decades of social protest, federal intervention, awareness-raising by millions of white Americans, changing images through art, literature and—most of all—the immediacy of TV news, to produce a lasting change.

It is true that the end of de jure segregation meant that enforcement of racial rules could no longer be formal. In earlier times, enforcement was virtually automatic and assured by the legal infrastructure of slavery and, later, by Jim Crow laws in the South and strict residential segregation in the North. When the formal enforcement mechanisms became unavailable, the informal racial traditions came to be protected and preserved by informal "race enforcers." These individuals, normally from lower socioeconomic classes, have the function to penalize race trespassers or blow the whistle on nonpermitted activities. Their action is ostensibly on their own initiative, but is in fact part of an implicit compact (with their employer or their community) that awards them higher social status in correspondence with their racial enforcement role. Thus, a race enforcer is a bigot who has the power to act on his prejudices and obtains specific benefits or higher community status from doing so.

Examples are legion, and every black person in America has encountered some. In the tradition of the New Orleans conductor who interferred with Homer Plessy in the 1890s (acting for the state of Louisiana), let us only recall from the 1950s the Stork Club headwaiter who kept Josephine Baker at the peak of her fame waiting for service for hours (acting for club owner Sherman Billingsley); from the 1960s, Georgia restauranteur Lester Maddox and his ax handles (acting for his customers); from the 1970s, the South Boston thugs who threw under a train a black man who had gotten off at the wrong stop (acting for their neighborhood); and, as recently as 1993, the waitress at Denny's Restaurant in Annapolis, Maryland, who kept a group of black FBI agents waiting while serving their white colleagues at the next table (acting, allegedly, as an agent of the informal policy of her employer to discourage black patrons).

A historic opportunity was tragically missed after the Civil War. With vigorous and consistent political and intellectual leadership, the legal revolution could have been accompanied by sufficient change in racial attitudes to turn it into a social revolution. However, those who would lead the change could not, and those who could—including the new barons of the American industrial revolution—would not. Consequently, as immigrants arrived in larger and larger numbers from the late 1880s, they found in place rigid schemes of racial domination and exclusion. As all immigrants do, they conformed to the social consensus and became the engine for reproducing those racial schemes for future generations. Had they found a more liberal, more rational, racial tradition, they would undoubtedly have conformed with *it*, compounding the initial change in a positive direction. How different would America be today?

As argued above, the American racial tradition remains in the main a rigid one. However, the increased flexibility introduced since the 1960s is real and more sustainable than that introduced after the Civil War or in the early 1950s—because a genuine change in informal attitudes of tens of millions of people has accompanied the legislative and executive changes in the formal rules. As of mid-1995, nevertheless, one can find evidence either of further evolution or of a return to earlier rigid exclusionary schemes. Because the situation is historically fluid, much will depend—as it did in the early days of the new United States of America and during Reconstruction—on the actions of a few key individuals in a position to shape policy and mass images. Let us hope that, this time, the Patrick Henrys and John Marshall Harlans of America will prevail over the John Marshalls and Woodrow Wilsons. If the opportunity is again missed, the future of American racial and social relations may well be as bleak as its past. Either way, the impact will also be felt on the remaining U.S. overseas territories, to which we now turn.

NOTES

1. John Higham, *Strangers in the Land: Patterns of American Nativism 1860–1925* (1963; reprint, New York: Atheneum, 1974), p. 20.

2. Missionaries Samuel Austin Worcester and Elihu Butler were sentenced to four years in jail in 1831 for residing in the Cherokee Nation without a license. Until 1828, the land of the Cherokee Nation was off-limits to settlers. In 1829, when gold was discovered in Dahlonega, the state of Georgia seized much of the land and abolished Cherokee sovereignty based on Marshall's decision. Worcester and Butler sought to attract attention to the Indians' plight. The state enacted a law requiring all white men living on Cherokee land to obtain a state license. The two missionaries refused, were convicted of "high misdemeanor," and spent sixteen months at hard labor. Upon their release from prison the two missionaries joined the Trail of Tears, when Georgia forced up to 17,000 Cherokees to move west. Thousands died of exposure to cold weather and starvation. Another example of the dehumanizing attitude toward Native Americans was the fate of four Inuit, who were lured from their

native home by the explorer Robert Peary on the 1897 northern Arctic expedition and brought to the American Museum of Natural History in New York. They were kept in the basement, put on periodic public display and died in a few months. Their bodies were dissected and defleshed, and their skeletal remains put away in numbered boxes at the museum, where they remained until July 1993, when at last they were buried in a graveyard in Greenland. A similar treatment was meted out to Twa "pygmies" from Central Africa.

3. Congress passed the Dawes Severalty Act in 1887, which provided for the assignment to each Indian of an allotment of 160 acres of reservation land, to be held in trust by the federal government for twenty-five years. It applied to virtually all reservation lands with promise for agricultural development. Reservations in the desert and mountain regions were not covered. In Indian Territory all the reservations were liquidated under the terms of the Dawes Severalty Act as amended or under similar statutes. Each member of each tribe was assigned an allotment. The surplus lands in the West after allotment, amounting to over 60 million acres, were opened to homesteaders. Of the acreage assigned to Indians between 1887 and 1934, 27 million acres, or two-thirds of the land allotted, had passed from Indian to non-Indian ownership.

4. Ward Churchill and Glenn T. Morris, "Key Indian Laws and Cases," in *Genocide, Colonization, and Resistance*, ed. Jaimes Annette (Boston: South End Press, 1992).

5. Robert E. Bieder, "Scientific Attitudes Toward Indian Mixed-Bloods in Early 19th Century America," *Journal of Ethnic Studies* 8, no. 2 (1980), p. 19.

6. Lawrence Baca, "The Legal Status of American Indians," in *Handbook of North American Indians*, ed. Wilcomb E. Washburn (1978; reprint, Washington, D.C.: Smithsonian Institution, 1990), p. 230.

7. Among the white Americans claiming part–Native American ancestry are the following—all of whom cite only the Five Civilized Tribes—as whites refer to the Cherokees, Choctaws, Creeks, Chickasaws, and Seminoles—as ancestors: The 1973 Most Valuable Player in the American League, baseball player Dick Allen (part-Cherokee); baseball's first catcher to be named Rookie of the Year, Johnny Bench (one-eighth Choctaw); antigay crusader, former Minute Maid spokeswoman and singer Anita Bryant (part-Cherokee); country music superstar Johnny Cash (one-quarter Cherokee); pop superstar Cher (part-Cherokee); news anchor Dan Rather (his grandmother's father "took an Indian woman"); and humorist Will Rogers (one-eighth, who once told an audience of "blue bloods" at Boston's Symphony Hall, "My own forefathers . . . didn't come over like yours on the Mayflower—they met the boat."). Others include Kevin Costner, a "part-Indian," who was made an honorary member of the Lakota Sioux in 1990 and whose epic, *Dances with Wolves*, is about the group; Wayne Newton, who is the son of two "half-Indians," and Dolly Parton, part-Cherokee. Among the millions of African Americans claiming Indian ancestry are the late Red Foxx, whose maternal grandmother was a full-blooded Indian married to an African, and the late comedienne "Moms" Mabley, of mixed black and Cherokee ancestry. Cf. Stephanie Bernardo Johns, *The Ethnic Almanac* (New York: Doubleday, 1981), pp. 14–17, and Candy Mills, "More than Meets the Eye," *Interrace*, May/June 1992, p. 4.

8. Don Sharon, chairman of the Florida Eastern Creek Indians states that the desire to share in the services, fishing rights, and other benefits awarded to American

Indians in recent decades has also stimulated the increase in whites identifying with the group. He observed that when his tribe and others won payments in the 1960s, following a legal settlement with the federal government over land rights, many people came forward and tried to prove their Indian heritage: "When there was money involved, then people started identifying themselves this way. Everybody has the streak of greed in them." Barbara Vobejda, "More Americans Declaring Indian Identity," *Washington Post*, February 11, 1991, p. 1.

9. Hugh Johnston, writing in 1937, noted: "there developed, in the colonial period, much intermixture of the Indian and Negro slave. . . . The class commonly called the mulatto is the result, in many instances, of the union of the three racial elements. . . . To the visitor in the south the physical characteristics of many Negro slaves bore witness to their Indian origin" (quoted in Forbes, 1993, p. 191). Johnston also noted that many Indians were enslaved along the eastern seaboard: "The end of Indian slavery came with the final absorption of the blood of the Indian by the more numerous Negro slave. But the blood of the Indian did not become extinct in the slave states, for it continued to flow in the veins of the Negro" (Forbes, 1993, p. 191). In an article published in the *Journal of Negro History* Johnston wrote: "Where the Negro was brought into contact with the American Indian the blood of the two races intermingled, the Indian has not disappeared from the land, but is now part of the Negro population of the United States" (1929, p. 43).

10. Jack D. Forbes, *Africans and Native Americans* (Urbana: The University of Illinois Press, 1993).

11. In several Virginia counties, Indians were classified as "F.N." (free Negro). Forbes notes that is very rare to see a person classified as "Indian" in pre–Civil War Virginia records and *never* in the counties of King William, Queen and Queen, Caroline and Essex (p. 199). The 1800, 1810, 1820, and 1830 censuses used the "free person of color" category for most nonwhites, including Indians.

12. Henry Steele Commager, *Documents of American History* (New York: F. S. Crofts & Co., 1940).

13. Citizenship was not defined in the original Constitution.

14. Charles A. Lofgren, *The Plessy Case: A Legal-Historical Interpretation* (New York: Oxford University Press, 1987), p. 92. For a discussion of Ferguson's ignorance of Plessy's race, see pp. 53–58.

15. Loren Miller, *The Petitioners: The Story of the Supreme Court of the United States and the Negro* (New York: Pantheon Books, 1966), p. 165.

16. Jose A. Cabranes, "Citizenship and the American Empire: Notes on the Legislative History of the United States Citizenship of Puerto Ricans," *University of Pennsylvania Law Review* 127:316 (1979), p. 395.

17. Myrdal (1944) documented three stages of Negro-white sexual contact in the United States, which occurred in spite of the "antiamalgamation" doctrine. These periods were: (1) relations between Negro and white indentured servants during the seventeenth century, (2) miscegenation in the early eighteenth century as slavery and the plantation system became more firmly established, and (3) the Civil War period and its aftermath.

18. Robert J. Sickels, *Race, Marriage and the Law* (Albuquerque: University of New Mexico Press, 1972), p. 64.

19. A. Leon Higginbotham Jr., *In the Matter of Color. Race and the American Legal Process: The Colonial Period* (New York: Oxford University Press, 1978), pp. 43–44.

20. Ibid., p. 46.

21. The penalty was equally harsh for white women marrying Asians, who could lose their American citizenship (Takaki, 1989). Unlike Chinese and Japanese men, however, many Filipino men dated and married white women for several reasons. Among them was the reality that they came from a society where mestizos, or persons of mixed ancestry were present in large numbers and widely accepted (Takaki, 1989, p. 341). However, Filipino men and white women were subject to punishment under antimiscegenation laws in states such as Oregon and California. White women marrying Filipinos became targets of discrimination too. In 1930, in a case involving a German immigrant (Mrs. Anne Podien-Jesena who married Basalico Jesena), Monterey Superior Court Judge H. C. Jorgenson ruled that immigrant-white wives of Filipinos were not entitled to naturalized citizenship. The Federal District Director of Naturalization went even further, stating that white American women marrying Filipinos would lose their U.S. citizenship (Takaki, 1989, p. 342). Thus in addition to blacks and Filipinos, other nonwhites were also targets of antimiscegenation laws. These included Malayans, Native Americans, Chinese, Japanese, and the black and mixed-race inhabitants of the overseas territories.

22. Caroline County, Virginia, is home to a number of people, such as Mrs. Loving, who are of mixed African and Native American ancestries.

23. The noted African American writer James Weldon Johnson, writing in 1941, attributed white fears of interracial marriage to the white man's underlying sexual fears, particularly of Negroes:

> . . . in the core of the heart of the American racial problem the sex factor is rooted; rooted so deeply that it is not always recognized when it shows at the surface. Other factors are obvious and are the ones we dare to deal with; but regardless of how we deal with these, the race situation will continue to be acute as long as the sex factor persists. Taken alone, it furnishes a sufficient mainspring for the rationalization of all the complexes of white superiority. (*Along the Way* [New York: Penguin, 1990], p. 80)

24. Ian F. Haney Lopez, *White by Law: The Legal Construction of Race* (New York: New York University Press, 1996).

25. The title of an article by Sam Roberts in the *New York Times*, June 18, 1995, in which this statistical evidence was reported.

26. See, for example, Oliver E. Williamson, 1985, and Douglass C. North, 1989. The new economic theory of institutions is traced back to the work of Ronald Coase from the 1930s, work for which he received the 1991 Nobel Prize for Economics. (North's 1993 Nobel Prize was for his pathbreaking work in economic history.)

4 Race and American Territorial Expansion

THE PHASES OF AMERICAN TERRITORIAL EXPANSION

The United States emerged as a major colonial power as the result of the Spanish-American War in 1898, the later purchase of some territories, and the defeat of Japan in 1945—when it acquired the Pacific Trust Territories. The precedents of American colonialism and mode of territorial incorporation were established in relation to the thirteen colonies and the Northwest and Southwest territories from 1783 to the mid-1860s. This chapter examines American territorial expansion from the early nineteenth century onward, focusing on the role that race played in the process.

The acquisition of American territories follows three well-defined periods (Willoughby, 1905). The first period began with the confirmation by the Treaty of Paris with Great Britain of the claims of the thirteen original states to the territory stretching as far as the Mississippi River. This period can be said to have ended in 1853, with the addition of territory growing out of the admission of the Republic of Texas and the war with Mexico. The second period of territorial expansion in the Northwest and Southwest covered the next forty-five years to 1898. This was the period of industrial transformation of the American economy, of conquest of vast areas of low population density and, of course, of war and suppression of the Native Americans who lived in these areas. The third period began with the annexation of the Hawaiian Islands in 1898 and continued with the acquisitions of the former Spanish colonies after the Spanish-American War, and later the acquisition of a ten-mile wide strip across the istmus of Panama (1904), the purchase of the Danish Antilles (1917), and the receipt of the Pacific Trust Territories (1947).

Each period of territorial expansion was guided by different political objectives and constitutional principles. I am not concerned here with the first period of territorial expansion, but with the second and third periods. The key difference between the second and third period is that, after removal of the Native Americans, white settlers moved into the continental territories acquired before 1898. By contrast, the overseas territories acquired after 1898 were densely populated by nonwhite people of unique and "dissimilar" national characteristics. This single factor entailed a vastly different policy and treatment of residents of the territories—quite inconsistent with the precepts of the Northwest Ordinance of 1787, which was to have set the mode of continental consolidation. The continental territories were incorporated into full statehood in a comparatively short time. The overseas territories, the "flag territories," were not, nor were they encouraged toward early independence.

At its founding the United States federal system embodied "a body of countries . . . so closely connected by locality, . . . history . . . race, or the like, as to be capable of bearing, in the eyes of their inhabitants, an impress of common nationality" (Leibowitz, 1989, p. 102). As the United States expanded across the continent, constitutional interpretations reinforced the prevailing view of federalism as based on ethnic unity. Ethnic unity was encouraged by doctrines requiring equal treatment of all citizens through public education in the English language and through freedom of movement throughout the states.

CONTINENTAL EXPANSION

The Northwest Ordinance of 1787

As previewed in the previous chapter, the ordinance outlined the process for governing the areas north of the Ohio River and west of the Mississippi. Thomas Jefferson wrote the first ordinance in 1784, which called for the division of the regions into states, each with the same political powers as the original thirteen states. It was not until 1787 that an ordinance was approved establishing federal authority over the continental territories and laying out the path by which statehood would be granted. The ordinance, reaffirmed by Congress in 1789 following ratification of the U.S. Constitution, established the framework for developing future territories and admitting new states (General Accounting Office, 1985).

The Northwest Ordinance represented the most authoritative statement of the federal government's official policy toward territorial incorporation. It established the firm principle that the long-range objectives of territorial expansion was to admit new states. To prepare the territory for the most rapid possible transition to statehood, residents were subject to the same federal laws and taxation as the existing states. Whatever limits were placed on democratic government were expressly understood to be temporary, and the emphasis was on increasing measures of self-government as rapidly as the territories "matured." Knowledge of English and a law-abiding and orderly climate were among the criteria. White territorial residents were to receive the full protection of the American Constitution and, as noted, the territories would be admitted as soon as possible into the Union on an equal basis with the original states. The statements in the ordinance concerning coexistence and mutual respect vis-à-vis Native Americans were jettisoned whenever Native Americans found themselves in the way of land grabs (see chapter 2). But vis-à-vis the territories populated by white settlers the principles of the ordinance were followed closely.

The Role of the U.S. Congress in Statehood

Although the Northwest Ordinance established the basis for a cohesive territorial system, it did not prescribe detailed admission procedures. The power to do so is given to Congress by the U.S. Constitution. Article IV, Section 3 of the Constitution states: "The Congress shall have power to dispose of and make all needful rules and regulations respecting the Territory or other property belonging to the United States." In the view that evolved in Congress, a territory was considered "mature" enough for incorporation as a state upon fulfilling only three deceptively simple basic requirements:

1. The inhabitants of the proposed new state were imbued with and sympathetic toward the principles of democracy as exemplified in the American form of government
2. A majority of the electorate desired statehood
3. The proposed new state had sufficient population and resources to support state government and to provide its share of the cost of the federal government

Race and Conquest: "Manifest Destiny"

The experience of westward expansion is too extensive, and well-covered elsewhere, to be summarized further here,[1] except for bringing out the key links to the American racial tradition and to the later experience of overseas colonialism. Continental territorial expansion was motivated both by economic forces and by racial ideology, which interacted to reinforce one another. The two factors were combined in the notion of "Manifest Destiny," an expression first used by John L. O'Sullivan in an article on the annexation of Texas published in the July-August 1845 edition of the *United States Magazine and Democratic Review*, which he edited (Foner and Garraty,

1991, p. 697). O'Sullivan wrote that it was "our manifest destiny to overspread the continent allotted by Providence for the free development of our yearly multiplying millions." By the end of the century, expansionists were arguing that because of its "Anglo-Saxon heritage" America was supremely fit, and it was its "manifest destiny" to extend its influence beyond its continental boundaries into the Pacific and Caribbean basins.

On the economic and geographic side, the hallmark of this period was that the territories in question were contiguous, vast, sparsely populated and almost wholly undeveloped—thus affording easy opportunities for European settlement and thus the motive for removing Native Americans from their lands. The justification for doing so was provided by the racial ideology vis-à-vis Native Americans that was being developed concurrently with the westward expansion. And the approach was to extend to the territories American political, social, and economic institutions as far as practicable. However, those institutions would not cover, nor protect, the Native American inhabitants—and certainly not as nations or political entities. In the Northwest Territories, Native Americans were expressly excluded from full citizenship, as were African Americans and Asian immigrants. Race was always on the surface of the events of the day.

The ideology of cultural and racial "inferiority" of nomadic Indians (and Mexicans, as discussed later in this chapter) justified their active exclusion from incorporation in the territories. The bogus claim emerged that the lands inhabited by various Indian groups were "empty lands." The logical next step was the arrival of white settlers in larger numbers, who forced the Indians off the lands and proved that, in fact, they were empty. The federal government created and condoned "white man's territories."

The Creation of Indian Territories

The Constitution confers upon Congress the power of regulating the relations of Native Americans with one another and with non-Indians, as necessary for their "development and control." This was to be realized through Congress setting aside large areas of public lands, "Indian reservations," for occupation by the different tribes. These areas were created to maintain tribal forms of organization and to permit complete freedom to manage internal affairs. This policy presented no problem until mineral resources were found or scarce lands became coveted by white settlers, who pressured the government to open up reservations to settlement and move the Indians elsewhere. The parallel with the late-twentieth-century policy of establishing "homelands" in apartheid South Africa is strong. Under the guise of fostering the "independence" of various black nations, South African blacks were herded into "states" consisting of the least desirable land in the country. When it was discovered after the initial drawing of boundaries of the black "homelands" that some economically valuable land had been included, the boundaries were quickly redrawn at the urging of white interests.

White settlers turned quickly against the notion of special Indian territories. There were increasingly hostile clashes between settlers and Native Americans in the Northwest Territories. Settlers wanted to force Native Americans to abandon their tribal forms of government and consent to breakup their lands into individual holdings. Education was perceived as a useful means to that end, leading to the policy of "forced assimilation." As discussed in chapter 3, this policy was to "fit" Native Americans to move into white society and adjust to their new situation, thereby making it easier to alienate Indian lands.

The very term "Indian Territory" portended that (as would be the case of the overseas territories in the third period of expansion) Indian-dominated areas were unlikely to ever be admitted into the Union as states. The clearest case is that of the Shawnees. Aware of the congressional requirements for statehood, Shawnee Chief Tecumseh and his brother, "The Prophet," attempted to unite the Indians living west of the Mississippi into a confederation of tribes. This would have served two purposes: (1) fulfilled the population requirement for admission into the Union as a state, and (2) halted white expansion into Indian lands.[2] The attempt was unsuccessful. In a number of "treaties" between 1803 and 1809, General William Henry Harrison managed to purloin 30 *million* acres of land north of the Ohio River and rendered the question of Indian confederation moot.

The generally hostile policy toward Native Americans contrasted with official policy toward the five so-called "civilized" tribes: the Cherokees, Creeks, Chickasaws, Choctaws, and Seminoles. Indian Territory consisted of lands occupied by these groups, who were permitted to organize an autonomous government modeled after that of the United States. The structure consisted of a governor, a legislature of two houses elected by the people, a national court, a system of taxes, public schools, a territorial court, and other amenities. But even this was threatened by the steady increase in the numbers of whites moving into the territory, who would not tolerate Indian political autonomy, let alone submit to Indian authority. Willoughby (1905) notes that: "Though the whites became six times more numerous than the Indians, they had no voice in the administration of affairs, and it was hardly to be expected that such a situation would be allowed to continue indefinitely" (p. 73).

Congress thus began to enact a series of laws limiting the power of self-government of the five tribes, culminating in the Dawes Severalty Act of 1887, which terminated the status of Indian Territory. The act, signed by President Cleveland, permitted the president to supersede Indian governments and to convert traditional, communally owned tribal lands to private ownership. Specifically, each Indian family head was to receive 160 acres, with lesser amounts going to bachelors, women, and children. In addition, each Native American accepting a land grant was given full American citizenship. In 1890, Congress created the Federal Territory of Oklahoma, formerly known as the Indian Territory.[3] With the transformation of the Indian Territory into the white-dominated Oklahoma Territory, statehood went from impossible to inevitable.

The rest of the continent followed a similar pattern of initial white settlement: forcible expulsion of the native inhabitants to the least desirable areas, accelerated white immigration, complete marginalization of the native inhabitants—and statehood. Alaska and Hawaii appear to be exceptions. Annexed in 1867 and 1898, respectively, they acquired statehood only in 1959, much later than the other territories occupied at around the same time. Alaska is indeed an exception. Aside from the fact that territory is noncontiguous and remote from the rest of the country, it was believed to be wholly unfit for permanent settlement by whites and, aside from the Klondike Gold Rush, it was not known to contain important mineral resources or land resources in easily exploitable form. It was thus considered more of an administrative area than an occupied territory. By the "rules" of territorial incorporation, it did not present the characteristics needed to receive statehood. The exception of Hawaii, instead, is only apparent.

The "Unique" Case of Hawaii

Despite its unique characteristics, the case of Hawaii was consistent with the pattern of the continental territories, from "protectorate" in 1851 to statehood more than a century later. First, the same itinerary was followed of settlement/native exclusion/large-scale immigration/native marginalization/statehood. The key difference is that the large-scale immigration in Hawaii was of Asians and not of Europeans.

Second, the Hawaiian exception to the rule that only white-majority territories were considered candidates for eventual statehood is only apparent. It is true that the islands' racial makeup was atypical of the remainder of the United States. Hawaii had a richer ethnic mix than any other territory under U.S. occupation at the time.

The racial composition of Hawaii was reflected in the first census taken in 1832, which recorded a population of 130,313. The population counted in 1872 was considerably lower, with a total of 56,897, consisting of 51,531 Hawaiians and part-Hawaiians, for 90.5 percent of the total. The census of 1878, taken three years after the reciprocity treaty with the United States, which stimulated the need for plantation laborers, counted a total population of 57,985, comprising 47,508 Hawaiians and part-Hawaiians (81.9% of the total) and 10,477 of other races.

In 1900, of its 145,000 inhabitants only about 38,000, or one-fourth, were Hawaiian or part-Hawaiian—Hawaiians having been decimated in earlier times by disease and declining birth rates. With 61,000 residents, or 42 percent of the population, the Chinese constituted a plurality, and together with the 26,000 Japanese, Asians actually formed an absolute majority of the population of the Hawaiian Islands. Aside from a small number of other Pacific Islanders and a handful of Negroes, the 28,500 white Americans made up the remainder of the residents (including a number of foreign whites who were designated as American for this purpose!). Thus, over 80 percent of the population was nonwhite, a far cry from the demographics of the American West.

Nevertheless, from the beginning of the American presence there were powerful forces in favor of annexation and eventual statehood. As we know, they prevailed. The explanation lies in the fact that the white minority, although less than one-fifth of the population, was economically and politically dominant; it was this group that shepherded the territory to eventual statehood. This dominance played a key role in the decision of the U.S. Congress to annex the islands, treat them as a fully organized territory of the United States shortly after annexation, and eventually bring them into the Union, on a slower but similar track as for the continental territories. The chronology included the following key events.

The first American missionaries arrived in Hawaii in 1820. From that point on they and their descendants were mostly involved in attempts to establish dominance over the Hawaiian monarchy and to eventually destroy it. A major event in this direction resulted from the formation of a representative government by the monarchy in 1840. With the adoption of a constitution, establishing a representative body of elected legislators, the composition of the monarchy changed. Under this representative form of government, a number of Americans were appointed by King Kamehameha III to administrative and judicial office, thus putting them in a position to manipulate the monarchy.

Following a series of incursions by other European nations, the United States proclaimed in 1851, that foreign annexation would not be permitted. The increasing development of "manifest destiny" sentiment in the United States led to the opening of negotiations in 1854, for annexation to the United States, but this was terminated upon the death of King Kamehameha III in December. By this time, the country had established a constitutional bicameral government within a Christian context.

The events that would culminate in Hawaii's annexation to the United States occurred during the reign of Queen "Lydia" Liliuokalani. Among the defining events were her marriage to a white New Englander, the increasing decimation of native Hawaiians, the increased dominance of the descendants of white missionaries, and the ultimate annexation of the islands in 1897 and formal transfer of the islands to the United States in August 1898. The white annexationists organized themselves into several bodies, which manifested as the "Committee of Safety," then began to advocate for Hawaii's statehood. Also during the reign of Liliuokalani there was the considerable immigration of Asian laborers to work on white-owned sugar plantations, in addition to Spanish, Portuguese, and Filipino laborers. The increase of foreigners coincided with the decrease in the native Hawaiian population. White-dominated efforts for statehood followed the consolidation of annexation. In 1903 the territorial legislature had petitioned Congress for admission as a state, but it was not until 1959 that a long campaign culminated in Hawaii's admission as the fiftieth state.

In 1893, American troops landed at the request of the white "Committee of Safety," to "protect American lives and property" and commissioners sent to Washington by the committee negotiated a treaty of annexation, which President Harrison sent to the Senate.

In an unusual fit of common sense, the Senate refused to ratify the treaty for almost five years. However, continued white agitation for annexation finally produced a Joint Resolution approving annexation on July 7, 1898. It is significant that this action was taken in the midst of the Spanish-American War—just ten days before the surrender of the Spanish Army in Santiago, Cuba. American friends of the Hawaiians, and their strange bedfellows—senators concerned with the "race-mixing" problem—had succeeded in stalling ratification of the annexation treaty for almost five years. It is conceivable that opposition to annexation would have grown, had it not been for the emotionalism and new expansionist sentiment fostered by the war with Spain. Without that war, Hawaii might today be independent. But then, without that war, the course of history would have differed for all the former Spanish colonies, and American foreign policy would not have been the same.

On August 12, 1898, the sovereignty of the Republic of Hawaii was transferred to the United States, and in 1959, Hawaii finally became the fiftieth American state. Hawaii had been ready for statehood for nearly a decade, having adopted a state constitution in 1950. The delay resulted from a long series of congressional hearings on the threat of communism in the islands, led by Senator Butler, a staunch opponent of incorporation, on "race-mixing" grounds.

The political itinerary following the annexation resolution was the same as Congress had adopted in the annexation of Louisiana and Florida. In the first stage, "until Congress shall provide for the government of such islands, all of the civil, judicial and military powers exercised by the officers of the existing government in said islands shall be vested in such person or persons and shall be exercised in such manner as the President of the United States shall direct; and the President shall have power to remove said officers and fill the vacancies so occasioned." The second stage began with passage of an "organic act" in April 1900, which made of Hawaii a fully organized territory of the United States, extended to the territory all the provisions of the Constitution and laws of the United States, conferred citizenship upon qualified residents and created a bicameral legislature. In order to vote, a person had to satisfy the following requirements:

1. be a male citizen of the United States;
2. have resided in the Territory not less than one year preceding and in the representative district in which he offers to register not less than three months preceding the time at which he offers to register;
3. attained the age of twenty-one years;
4. have duly registered during the prescribed time for registration; and
5. be able to speak, read and write either the English or Hawaiian language.

The purpose of the last provision was to prevent political domination by the large numbers of Chinese and Japanese in the islands, and—because of the declining numbers and political vigor of the Hawaiians—in effect keep political power in white hands. In granting political autonomy leading to eventual statehood, it mattered to the Congress that the dominant political actors were whites. This was not the case of the territories gained from the Spanish-American War, and for which, therefore, the prospect of statehood was never in the cards.

OVERSEAS EXPANSION

There were at the end of the nineteenth century attempts at expanding the doctrine of manifest destiny beyond continental North America. On the surface, the American version of imperial doctrine largely parroted the "white man's burden" rationalizations made by other colonial powers,[4] and simply substituted the "American race" for the "British," or the "French," or the other self-appointed flag-bearers of the mission of oppressing other peoples in the name of superior civilization. But the emotional subtext was very different, very American, and heavily influenced by the racial tradition. We cannot do better than to reproduce a few of the more telling statements.

Josiah Strong, a religious and social reformer, considered the Anglo-Saxon to be "divinely commissioned to be, in a peculiar sense, his brother's keeper," and pictured "the American branch of the family moving down upon Mexico, down upon Central and South America, out upon the islands of the sea, over upon Africa and beyond." Professor John W. Burgess of Columbia University assigned to the Teutonic nations "the mission of conducting the political civilization of the modern world." A Darwinian lecturer and writer, John Fiske, shared with many historians and philosophers of his time the conviction that it was the mission of the English-speaking people "to establish sovereignty of the seas and bestow the blessings of benevolent rule and superior institutions on other races around the world."[5] Theodore Roosevelt was heavily influenced in his racial views by Nordic and Teutonic myths (Dyer, 1980). And finally, in the words of Senator Alfred J. Beveridge (talking about American aims in the Philippines):

> ... this question of [aims] is deeper than any question of party politics; deeper than any question of the isolated policy of our country even; deeper even than any question

of constitutional power. It is elemental. It is racial. God has not been preparing the English-speaking and Teutonic peoples for a thousand years for nothing but vain and idle self-contemplation and self-admiration. No! He has made us the master organizers of the world to establish [a] system where chaos reigns. He has given us the spirit of progress to overwhelm the forces of reaction throughout the earth. He has made us adept in government that we may administer government among savage and senile peoples. Were it not for such a force as this the world would relapse into barbarism and night. And of all our race He has marked the American people as his chosen nation to finally lead in the regeneration of the world. This is the divine mission of America. . . . We are trustees of the world's progress, guardians of its righteous peace.[6]

Nevertheless, all evidence indicates that, with the completion of territorial expansion throughout the continent, the manifest destiny sentiment was largely spent by the end of the nineteenth century. Few influential policymakers pushed, argued, or even welcomed any further territorial expansion beyond the continental limits. The challenge of consolidating American institutions from the Atlantic to the Pacific was monumental, and did not brook overseas distractions. As chapter 5 will explore in some detail, the United States was an "accidental imperialist," which backed into its overseas possessions as a result of an emotional war with Spain, the consequences of which had not been thought through.

The U.S. colonial possessions included the territories gained from the Spanish-American War of 1898: Cuba, Puerto Rico, the Philippines, and Guam. (Hawaii was annexed in July 1898, after the war with Spain opened the floodgates of expansionism. Cf. Blum et al., [1963] 1968). Later, the Danish Antilles were purchased in 1917 and became the U.S. Virgin Islands. The Pacific Territories consist of: American Samoa (1900), Microniesia (1947) (Yap, Truk, Ponape, and Kosrae), the Mariana Islands (1947), the Marshall Islands (1947), and Palau (1947).

Cuba became an independent republic shortly after the 1898 war, although it was under American military occupation from 1899–1902 and 1906–1909. The Philippines became a self-governing Commonwealth in 1935 and an independent republic in 1946. Guam, the largest of the Mariana Islands, was occupied in 1899 and was placed under the Navy Department. In World War II, it was seized by the Japanese and returned to the United States in 1944. Guam is an unincorporated, organized territory of the United States. It is "organized," because the Congress provided the territory with an Organic Act in 1950. Seeking to improve its current political status, the Guam Commission on Self-Determination has drafted a proposed Guam Commonwealth Act, which was approved in two 1987 plebiscites. In February 1988, the document was submitted to the Congress for its consideration and was introduced in four consecutive Congresses—the 100th through the 104th. A determination has not been rendered. American Samoa is an unincorporated and unorganized territory of the United States, which is administered by the U.S. Department of the Interior. It is "unincorporated" because not all pro-

RACE AND AMERICAN TERRITORIAL EXPANSION

Table 4.1
Trends in Self-Government

	Guam	Puerto Rico	American Samoa	The Virgin Islands	Northern Mariana Islands
Acquired by United States	1898	1898	1900	1917	Upon termination of trusteeship
First Organic Act passed[a]	1950	1900	none	1936	none
Received nonvoting delegate in U.S. House of Representatives	1972	1900	1980	1972	none
Elected first local legislature with full or substantial legislative authority	1950	1900	1960	1936	1977
Granted U.S. citizenship	1950	1917	Residents are mostly U.S. nationals[b]	1927	Upon termination of trusteeship
Elected first governor	1970	1948	1977	1970	1977
Granted constitution	Rejected by voters in 1979	1952	1960	Rejected by voters in 1979	1977

[a] Organic acts were passed by Congress to establish the local legal framework for governing each territory. Guam and the Virgin Islands continue to be governed under their respective organic acts, while Puerto Rico is now a constitutional government.

[b] A national is defined as a person who is either a citizen or noncitizen of the United States, owing permanent allegiance to the United States. In general, U.S. nationals enjoy the same protection and many of the same rights as U.S. citizens.

Source: Washington, D.C.: U.S. General Accounting Office, April 1985.

visions of the U.S. Constitution apply to the territory. It is "unorganized" because the U.S. Congress has not provided the territory with an Organic Act, which organizes the government much as a constitution would. The Marianas have become a Commonwealth, Micronesia is the Federated States of Micronesia, the Marshall Islands are a Republic, and Palau is a Republic. Puerto Rico is a Commonwealth; the U.S. Virgin Islands are an unincorporated territory. Table 4.1 lists the major events in the political history of the five remaining American territories.

In addition to the occupied territories, the American colonial sway can be said to have extended de facto throughout Central and South America. In 1823 the Monroe Doctrine, proclaimed by President Monroe in his annual message to Congress, stated that: "The American continents . . . are henceforth not to be considered as subjects for future colonization by any European powers. Thus, any attempt by European powers to interfere with their old colonies in the western hemisphere would not be tolerated by the United States."

The Platt Amendment of 1901 and the Roosevelt Corollary of 1904 expanded the Monroe Doctrine considerably; indeed, they turned the original policy against European interference in the Western Hemisphere into a prescription for American interference. The Platt Amendment to the Cuban constitution barred Cuba from entering into treaties giving other nations power over its affairs, going into debt, or stopping the United States from imposing a sanitation program on the island. The United States could also intervene in Cuban affairs to keep order or maintain independence. Cuba became virtually an American protectorate until abrogation of the amendment in 1934. And the Roosevelt Corollary (1904) stated that the United States would not interfere with Latin American nations that conducted their affairs with decency, but that "brutal wrongdoing" might require intervention by some civilized power, and that the United States could not "ignore this duty."

The overseas territories were treated in a manner entirely different from those gained during the previous period of continental expansion. As noted earlier, until the end of the nineteenth century, Congress generally pursued a policy of encouraging and preparing the white-dominated contiguous territories for statehood. This policy changed when the "flag territories" were acquired in 1898. Although they came under the jurisdiction of the American flag, these territories did not automatically enjoy the constitutional guarantees of the U.S. Constitution, which needed to be specifically and severally granted by Congress. As Table 4.2 shows, none of the "flag territories" had a white majority.

For the first time in American history, the United States acquired territory without promising eventual citizenship or independence. The Treaty of Paris, which ceded Spain's territories, did not hold the promise of statehood. Congress debated the policy implications of the treaty during the ratification process in early 1899. During the debate, Congress examined the propriety of acquiring territories without defining their legal status. Supporters of the treaty maintained that the United States had a sovereign right to acquire and govern territories. In the view of some, the United States was responsible for establishing suitable forms of interim government for the territories and preparing them for eventual self-government.

In February 1899, a joint resolution was introduced in the Senate. Although the resolution was not passed, its sentiment was to form a major

Table 4.2
Racial and Ethnic Composition of the U.S. Territories, 1994

Commonwealth of Puerto Rico: 99 percent "hispanic"; the Puerto Rican Census no longer asks for racial identity. Official language: Spanish; English is widely but not universally spoken.

Territory of Guam: 47 percent "chamorro" (native inhabitants); 25 percent Filipino; 10 percent Caucasian; 18 percent Asians (mainly Japanese, Chinese, Koreans). Official languages: English and Chamorro; Japanese is widely used as well.

Territory of the U.S. Virgin Islands: 80 percent black (45 percent Virgin Island native); 15 percent Caucasian; 5 percent Puerto Rican. Official language: English; Spanish and Creole also used in some areas.

American Samoa: 90 percent Samoan; 8 percent Tongan and other Pacific Islanders; 2 percent Caucasian. Official languages: Samoan, English.

Commonwealth of the Northern Marianas: The people of the Northern Marianas are predominantly of Chamorro extraction, although a number of Carolinians (Chuukese, Kosraens, Pohnpeians, and Yapese) and immigrants from other areas of East Asia and Micronesia have settled in the islands. Percentages are not available for the ethnic composition of the Northern Marianas.

Republic of Palau: Percentages are not available for the ethnic composition of the Republic of Palau. Official language: Palauan; English widely spoken.

Republic of the Marshall Islands: 99 percent Micronesian. Official languages: Marshallese, English.

Federated States of Micronesia: The population is approximately as follows: Pohnpei 31,000, Chuuk 52,000, Yap 12,000, and Kosrae 6,500.

Source: Fact Sheets, United States Insular Areas (Washington, D.C.: Department of the Interior, 1995), pp. 8, 31.

element of American colonial policy in the flag territories:

1. ... the acquisition by the United States through conquest, treaty, or otherwise, of territory not adjacent to and geographically part of the Continent of North America carries with it no constitutional or moral obligation to admit said territory, or any portion thereof, into the Federal Union as a State or States;
2. ... it is against the policy, traditions and interests of the American people to admit states erected out of such non-American territories, or portions thereof into our Union ... at any time or under any conditions.

Thus, in the prevailing racial views of the times (as described in the previous chapter), the nonwhite race of the population made the territories unsuitable for assimilation into the Union, but incapable of self-government at the same time. In that status limbo most territories were placed, neither fish nor fowl, and there many territories remain today.[7]

MIXED-RACE AND THE QUESTION OF ANNEXATION

The most disturbing single feature of the overseas territories to white Americans was their large mixed-race population. As explained in chapter 2, the central features of the American racial tradition are: (1) the bipolarity between whites and nonwhites (the latter defined as anyone with *any* degree of nonwhite ancestry); and (2) the miscegenation taboo. These views exerted a determinant influence on the question of the political status of the overseas territories.

The question had been foreshadowed fifty years earlier by the debate in the mid-1840s on the possible annexation of Mexico. The existence of a strong antimiscegenation sentiment, and antipathy toward the resulting mixed-race people, was evident in the public dialogue on the possibility of taking over Mexico after victory in the Mexican-American War. Texas was easily annexed because of the dominance of white American settlers in local politics. Concerning the possible annexation of Mexico itself, as reported in the *New York Evening Post*, the *Congressional Globe*, the *Cincinnati Gazette*, and other leading periodicals of the day, the racial ancestry of Mexicans featured prominently in the debate. More than half of the 8 million inhabitants of Mexico were of Aztec or Maya ancestry. Almost one-third were of mixed-race ancestry—black-white ("mulattoes"), white-Indian ("mestizos"), or black-Indian ("samboes")—evoking in American minds the very same negative stereotypes that held sway toward Negroes, Native Americans, and mixed-race people in the continental territories. Only a sixth of the Mexican population, descended from the conquering Spanish, was white.[8] Such a mixture, in the American racial ideology, would result in national degeneration if Mexico were to be annexed.

Similar sentiments were expressed toward the territories acquired in 1898. Thus, in Cuba, because of the flexible Spanish racial tradition, interracial concubinage and marriage were a long-established reality. Columnist Dorothy Stanhope spoke for the racial ideology of the time in a *New York Times* article in 1900. She lamented that Cuban society drew no discriminating line against the large proportion of the population that belonged to the "colored race." Havana was chided as a city reminiscent of any southern city in the United States, but with a disturbing difference: In the United States a Negro knew his place and kept it, making no attempt at establishing familiarity with white people and, in her peculiar view, even "looked down with contempt on any white person willing to associate with him as a social equal." Stanhope could barely contain her "surprise" at the ease of race relations in Cuba, which offended her as one used to segregation in the American South. She was astonished that "in their own estimation," Cuban Negroes considered themselves "every whit the equal of persons of fair skin," and it was not unusual to find that they consider themselves superior to whites, although, she wondered, "why is not exactly clear." Finally, she fixed on the ultimate taboo of white Americans. She lamented the frequency of black-white intermarriages in Cuba and the lack of laws against such marriages, and noted with dismay that they joined—not only the lowest classes ("as might be expected"), but often occurred among the middle classes, and occasionally among the "cultured," as well. Similar commentaries were made about Puerto Rico—see chapter 5—and the Philippines. For example, Senator MacLaurin, during the debate on the Treaty of Paris, expressed his fears that annexation of the Philippines would mean the "incorporation of a mongrel and semi-barbarous population into our body politic." In his view, Filipinos were "inferior to, but akin to the Negro in moral and intellectual qualities and in [a lack of] capacity for self-government."[9]

Thus, the final victory of Jim Crow and of racial segregation in the American South at the turn of the century portended a similar hardening of attitudes toward the nonwhite people of the overseas territories where racial mixing was widespread. It is not surprising, therefore, that annexation of the flag territories was opposed—although for diametrically opposite reasons—not only by eminent racists but also by black anti-imperialists who closely identified with the nonwhite populations and expressed fears about the extension of American racism to the territories. Evidence of this was evident in the black press that opposed President McKinley's Philippine policies and in the unusual rate of desertion of black troops serving in the Philippines, some of whom defected to Filipino resisters. On July 17, 1899, in anticipation of the upcoming presidential election, a meeting of Boston blacks was held to organize anti-imperialist sentiment among black Americans. The meeting adopted a resolution to "enter their solemn protest against the . . . unjustified invasion by American soldiers in the Philippine Islands." The resolution noted that:

While the rights of colored citizens in the South, sacredly guaranteed them by the amendment of the Constitution, are shamefully disregarded; and, while the frequent lynchings of negroes who are denied a civilized trial are a reproach to republican government, the duty of the President and country is to reform these crying domestic wrongs and not to attempt the civilization of alien peoples by powder and shot.[10]

The view of William Franklin Willoughby (1905), former Treasurer of Puerto Rico, remains basic to understanding official attitudes toward the territories to this date:

The character of at least a portion of the territory [acquired after 1898] is such that the United States is compelled to confront the fact that the prospect of such territory ever becoming of such a nature that it can safely be admitted into the Union as a State or States without detriment to the nation as a whole *is so remote that for all practical purposes it can be dismissed from consideration.* Willingly or unwillingly, the people of the United States are forced to recognize that by the accession of this territory the nation has come into possession of a territory that for an indefinite time at least will have to be held purely as a dependency. (P. 19, emphasis added)

However, the United States would not abandon the objective of political education and development:

The same and even greater efforts have been made to extend to these territories a system of government and laws conforming to those existing in the United States, and to educate their inhabitants in the principles underlying them and to imbue them with the spirit in which they should be administered. If success is achieved in these efforts, it will then be time to determine whether the territory shall be erected into a State of the Union or into a commonwealth enjoying autonomy in some other form. (Willoughby, 1905, p. 20)

THE LEGAL BASIS FOR THE STATUS OF THE TERRITORIES

As will be discussed in detail in the next chapter, American colonial policy and administration evolved in an ad hoc manner. The legal basis of the status of the new territories, however, was set early on, through the so-called "Insular Cases." Because the Constitution did not specify the policies for incorporating the new territories, the Supreme Court set the relevant precedents through a series of rulings between 1901–1922, known collectively as *The Insular Cases*. The Court interpreted the territorial clause of the Constitution (Article IV, Section 3) to permit broad congressional discretion in deciding questions of status for the overseas territories. The Insular Cases affirmed the *complete authority* of Congress over the territories, thus giving Congress much greater power than it had concerning the incorporated territories—although the latter power is explicit in Article IV of the Constitution itself.

Incorporated versus Unincorporated Territories

The Insular Cases explicitly established the all-important distinction of territorial "incorporation" and "unincorporation." In the incorporated territories the Constitution in its entirety automatically followed the American flag. In an unincorporated territory, only the fundamental provisions of the Constitution applied, "the general prohibitions in favor of the liberty and property of the citizen . . . which are an absolute denial of authority . . . to do particular acts" (*Report of the United States*, 1966). All other provisions and protections of the Constitution had to be extended individually by congressional decision. For example, when the nineteenth Amendment granting women the vote was passed in 1927, the right to vote was not automatically extended to women in the unincorporated territories, even when—as in

Puerto Rico—they were American citizens. In addition, incorporated territories were presumed to have an inherent right to be considered for statehood, but unincorporated territories did not (GAO, 1985, p. 10). The distinction between incorporation and unincorporation should not be confused with the distinction between "organized" and "unorganized" territories—that is, those with an explicit system of participatory governance and those ruled as administrative entities. Unincorporated territories normally progressed to organized status through congressional passage of an "Organic Act" specifying the system of governance.

Thus, the United States was confronted with the situation that, for an indefinite time to come, the territory under its sovereignty would be divided into two classes having a different political status. One, constituting the United States proper, would enjoy full political rights and privileges, and the other, dependent, territory would be subordinate to the former and would have its status determined for it by the U.S. Congress.

Status Uncertainty in the Unincorporated Territories

As we shall see in detail in chapter 5, Puerto Rico played an important role in the evolution of colonial status through Insular Case law. The key questions were: (1) whether the Constitution followed the flag; (2) whether the inhabitants of the newly acquired territories, including Puerto Rico, were automatically citizens of the United States; (3) whether the inhabitants of the newly acquired territories, including Puerto Rico, had the protection of the Bill of Rights vis-à-vis the federal government; and (4) whether the Constitution prevented the imposition of tariffs on imports from these territories.

In 1900 Congress responded negatively to each question. The Supreme Court ruled in the Insular Cases that the former Spanish possessions were neither foreign countries nor integral parts of the United States. As unincorporated territories, these possessions were not assumed to be on a statehood track. In addition, their inhabitants were declared to be American nationals but not American citizens. Tariffs could be imposed on goods exported to the United States, but their form of government would be whatever Congress decided. In short, with Puerto Rico setting the precedent (see chapter 5), the new territories were placed in status limbo, "an indeterminate state of ambiguous existence for an indefinite period," as a dissenting judge noted.

Similar status uncertainty applies to the other overseas territories. The case of the U.S. Virgin Islands is examined in detail in chapter 7. As noted, that the Virgin Islands are "unincorporated" does not mean that they are "unorganized." With the 1936 Organic Act, revised in 1954, the Islands obtained a detailed framework of government, albeit with explicit reminders that this was not to be taken as an indication of eventual statehood.

The U.S. Virgin Islands remain today—without any realistic prospect for change—subject to the power of Congress which is still empowered by the Constitution to make suitable rules and regulations to govern the territory.

Since the end of World War II, Congress and the executive branch have adhered to a policy of self-determined political, economic, and social development for the territories and insular areas under U.S. administration. The federal government has adopted a flexible approach in dealing with the political aspirations of territorial inhabitants. The degree of autonomy and participatory rights vary among the unincorporated territories. Currently, they typically have an elected governor and legislature, substantial autonomy in local affairs, and send a nonvoting delegate to Congress. The inhabitants of all of the territories are U.S. citizens, except inhabitants of American Samoa, who are "nationals" of the United States.[11]

The territories with the greatest degree of autonomy have come to be called "Commonwealths." Today, the term "Commonwealth" is applied to Puerto Rico and the Northern Marianas. (As of mid-1997, a "Guam Commonwealth Act" was pending.) The meaning is of course vastly different both from that in colonial America (e.g., "Commonwealth of Massachusetts") and from its application to the former British colonies—where it denotes a loose commonality of cultural and political interests.

D. K. Fieldhouse (1965) summarizes:

The American empire never acquired a formal constitution; but its legal structure, as defined by the U.S. courts, fell into three parts. Caribbean states held by treaties were foreign. Alaska and Hawaii were incorporated into the Union by Congress and came within the constitution. In 1959 they became full states. All others were unincorporated territories—colonies in all but name. Citizenship followed the same distinctions. Inhabitants of incorporated states were citizens of the United States as well as of their own states; others were either "foreign" . . . or "nationals of the United States" and citizens of their own territories. Congress extended full citizenship to all Puerto Ricans in 1917, Virgin Islanders in 1927 and Guamanians in 1950.

The next chapter describes how this legal uncertainty played out in actual colonial policy and administration.

NOTES

1. Compare Dee Brown, *Bury My Heart at Wounded Knee* (1970; reprint, New York: Holt, Rinehart & Winston, 1971); Vine Deloria, *American Indian Policy in the Twentieth Century* (1983; reprint, Norman: University of Oklahoma Press, 1985); idem, *Custer Died for Your Sins* (1969; reprint, New York: Macmillan, 1970); Reginald Horsman, *Expansion and American Indian Policy 1783–1812* (1967; reprint, Norman: University of Oklahoma Press, 1992).

2. Tecumseh and The Prophet advocated racial separation and full Indian independence.

3. The region had been ruled by Native Americans since passage of the Indian Intercourse Act of 1834.

4. The cult of Anglo-Saxon superiority was immortalized by Rudyard Kipling, in a 1898 poem written especially for the Americans, celebrating *The White Man's Burden*.

5. Strong (*Our Country*), 1885, quoted in Blum et al., 1968, p. 521; Burgess and Fiske quoted in ibid.

6. Quoted in Schirmer and Shalom, 1987, p. 26.

7. In 1976, Congress approved a mutually negotiated Covenant to Establish a Commonwealth of the Northern Mariana Islands (CNMI) in Political Union with the United States. The CNMI government adopted its own constitution in 1977, and the constitutional government took office in January 1978. The Covenant was fully implemented on November 3, 1986, pursuant to Presidential Proclamation no. 5564, which conferred U.S. citizenship on legally qualified CNMI residents. The Commonwealth of the Northern Mariana Islands has a nonvoting elected Resident Representative in Washington, D.C., who represents the Commonwealth before the Congress and the federal government. The Compact of Free Association between the United States and the Republic of Palau entered into force on October 1, 1994. The Compact places full responsibility for Palau's defense with the United States and provides grant funds and federal program assistance, principally through the Department of the Interior. The people are citizens of Palau. The Republic of the Marshall Islands signed a Compact with the United States in 1986, which gives the State Department responsibility for government-to-government relations. The U.S. Department of the Interior is responsible for the oversight and coordination of U.S. programs and funding assistance. The Marshallese are citizens of the Marshall Islands. The Federated States of Micronesia signed a Compact with the United States in 1982. Although a sovereign state, the Federation's defense is the full responsibility of the United States. The Federation also receives grant funds and federal program assistance. Micronesians are citizens of the Federated States.

8. Merk, 1963, p. 157.

9. Quoted in Constantino, 1966, p. 1.

10. As reported in the *Boston Post*, July 18, 1899 and quoted in Schirmer and Shalom, 1987.

11. On April 17, 1900, the chiefs of Tutuila and Aunu'u ceded to the United States the sovereignty of their islands in Samoa. On July 14, 1904, the King of Manua'a did likewise for his islands in the archipelago. The Cession of Tutuila and Aunu'u guarantees "preservation of the rights and property of the inhabitants of the said islands . . . their lands and other property . . . , and respects the authority of the chiefs." The Cession of Manua'a pledges that "the rights of the chiefs in each village and of all people concerning their property according to their customs shall be recognized." (U.S. House Committee on Interior and Insular Affairs, 1986, *Hearings*, p. 32)

5 "For a Mess of Pottage": Pragmatic Materialism and American Colonial Policy

The evolution of the American racial tradition and its influence on territorial expansion within the continent and overseas have been examined in previous chapters. It is time to focus on the characteristics of American colonial policy and administration. The main theme is that, just as in the biblical story, Esau sold his birthright to his brother Jacob "for a mess of pottage," so the territories exchanged their long-term political development for an assortment of short-term material benefits. This tradeoff, which was in turn related to considerations of race, was the hallmark of American colonial policy. But let us begin with an analysis of the major differences between European and American colonialism.

THE RELUCTANT IMPERIALIST

The legacy of the American Revolution, although tainted from the very start by its exclusion of nonwhite persons, entailed the notion that holding people of other lands in a state of permanent subjection is incompatible with the principles of the Declaration of Independence and the American Constitution. The self-image of the United States was that of an unwilling participant in assuming a colonial burden. "Manifest Destiny" had been expressly limited to continental expansion (despite half-hearted attempts at stretching the concept to encompass overseas territories); there was little expansionist jingoism in the 1890s; earlier opportunities to take part in the international partition of Africa were rejected (although the United States attended the Conference of Berlin as an observer). Even the semantics differed: Americans have never referred to the territories in terms such as "colony," "dependency," or "protectorate." Euphemisms have been used, such as "insular" areas and outlying or overseas "territories."

The U.S. government never employed sociologists or anthropologists in formulating policy as did the British and other Europeans, so that even among social scientists today little is known about America's colonial policies. Americans have shown little interest in the overseas territories, and few have undertaken comparative analyses of European and American colonial policies and practices. What studies were carried out are bifurcated, focusing *either* on denial of American colonies (Bough and Macridis, 1970), or solely on economic factors (Emerson, 1949), or on diplomatic issues (DeConde, 1992). Among the exceptions are the works of Rubin Weston (1972) and Reginald Horsman (1981). In the view of Ruth Van Cleve (a former Interior Department official concerned with administration of the territories):

The relative absence of literature and the consequent absence of widespread knowledge of the subject may derive in part from a sort of national paranoia, a sense of embarrassment that a country born in revolt against colonialism should today have appended to it areas (territories) that are in some manner subordinate to the nation at large, areas not full-fledged parts of the Republic, areas that, to varying extents, are accorded second-class treatment. (1974, p. 4)

The disinterest or *denial* (in the psychological sense of the term) of the reality of colonial expansion after 1898 precluded the very attempt to formulate colonial policies on a coherent ideological basis. One could not very well set independence of the territories as the long-term goal and work toward it, if one did not even admit that the territories were colonial dependencies. On the other hand, the influence of the domestic racial tradition, and in particular the concern with "racial purity," ruled out assimilation of colored peoples as a long-term objective. A "policy" of sorts was spliced together after the fact—"pragmatic materialism"—and is discussed later in this chapter. But in general, American policy toward the overseas territories was characterized by ad hockery, an opaque administration entrusted to the military or to minor functionaries, and spasmodic attempts at either "doing good" or bringing the natives in line—depending on the administrative mood of the moment.

It is indeed true that the United States backed into its colonial possessions. Listen to President McKinley: "Hold it just a moment! Not quite yet, gentlemen! Before you go I would like to say just a word about the Philippine business. I have been criticized a good deal about the Philippines, but don't deserve it. The truth is I didn't want the Philippines, and when they came to us, as a gift from the gods, I did not know what to do with them."[1]

Still, willing colonialist or not, the United States did manage to acquire a colonial empire which, although not vast by comparison to European colonies, was far-flung across two oceans. It became very convenient for external security, too, providing an excellent network of strategically placed bases. In addition, the U.S. experience of direct territorial possession strengthened the older imperial strain originating with the Monroe Doctrine and removed any residual restraint to interventionism in the Western Hemisphere. American occupation of Nicaragua in 1911 and 1916, and Haiti in 1915, were only the more visible manifestations of the daily reality of Central America, which was to all intents and purposes a *colonial* reality. American colonialism did matter, greatly, to those affected.

THE DIFFERENCES BETWEEN AMERICAN AND EUROPEAN COLONIALISM

Aside from the obvious disparity of size of empire and length of colonial experience, the key differences between European and American colonialism concern ideology and the influence of race.

The Role of Ideology

Among the domestic influences that shaped European colonial policies—primarily French and English—were the French Revolution and the movement to abolish slavery, respectively. There were, of course, large differences between the colonial policies of European countries (and glaring discrepancies between the rhetoric and the practice as well), but the common element was the influence of ideology. This was sharply at variance from the American colonial experiment, so heavily influenced by its domestic racial tradition and bereft of an ideological basis for a long-term vision about its territories.

British policy in the heyday of colonialism was influenced by the Lockean notions of basic human rights and specifically by the antislavery ideology. Its main characteristic was "differentiation" through the maintenance of separate institutions. Nonwhites would be allowed—even helped—to progress to the full extent of their capacity in their own social and economic sectors. However, they were to remain separate and apart from the dominant whites (except for their system-maintenance service functions) and would not participate in the formulation of colonial policy and exercise of colonial power. The alleged long-term goal of British colonialism was the *political and economic maturity* of the colonial peoples (the "White Man's Burden," in Rudyard Kipling's wonderfully hypocritical poem) and their *separate development*.

French colonial policy was inspired, in theory, by the liberty, equality, and brotherhood triad of the French Revolution. There resulted a conception of basic cultural unity between metropolitan France and her dependencies.

Colonial people of a certain socioeconomic and cultural level were intended to be assimilated through adoption of French language, culture, and outlook. Consequently, French citizenship was extended widely to certain classes of nonwhites in the colonies, and a considerable measure of direct representation was provided in the metropolitan parliament. The alleged long-term goal of French colonialism was the *cultural maturity* of the colonial peoples and their *eventual assimilation* into the "Union Francaise."

Portugal, too, purported to follow a policy of assimilation, and a great deal of ink was expended (particularly in the mid–twentieth century under Salazar) on the rhetoric of a "lusophone" community—along the French model. It is true that colonial administration permitted mixed-race colonial people of high cultural level (*asimilados*) relatively easy access into the colonial elite. But the underlying rationale of Portuguese colonial expansion was an outlet for surplus population. (Among colonial powers, Portugal was economically the most underdeveloped, with a high rate of unemployment among unskilled people.)

Less noble, but less hypocritical as well, was the motive-force of German colonialism—founded on an ideology of power dominance, with the long-term goal of projecting national power. Even the Italian colonial late-comers had an implicit motive-force: helping to bring the young unified Italian state up to par with the major European powers—through acquisition of the colonial territories, which a respectable European power was expected to have.

By contrast, the United States backed into its colonial possessions. Aside from the systematic influence of the American racial tradition (and particularly the miscegenation taboo—see chapter 2), there was never *any* coherent ideological basis, "good" or "bad," to American colonialism. (The only other such case is Belgium, where the government was finally forced to take over administration of the Congo following the personal rule of King Leopold II. As in the case of Portugal, Belgium's adoption of the rhetoric of cultural assimilation was thoroughly cosmetic—as shown by the virtual absence of any educated Africans at the time of independence in 1960.) A major explanation of the lack of an ideological basis for colonial policy is the anticolonial genesis and belief system of the United States itself, discussed earlier.

Race in European Colonial Policies

The influence of the racial tradition on American territorial expansion has been discussed in the preceding chapters. Racial attitudes played a much smaller role in European colonialism than they did in U.S. territorial expansion. The main, and sufficient, explanation of this difference is that most of the European countries did not acquire a significant nonwhite population until very late in the nineteenth century. Further, European racial attitudes first evolved in relation to the first generations of the colonial population, who were relatively unconfrontational about race and racism in the metropolitan country.

Although race was never the same all-consuming preoccupation in European colonial policy that it was in the United States, it did play an important part. For example, all rhetoric notwithstanding, the French objective of assimilation was largely an illusion, as Frantz Fanon correctly assessed (Fanon, 1967). But the illusion was and remains very useful. As early as the days of the merchant houses of Bordeaux in the mid–eighteenth century, the French government realized that the active cooperation of mixed-race people in the colonies would be essential for the administration and maintenance of the expanding empire. As Robert July points out (1970, p. 350), the mulattoes were able to safeguard French political interests through their control of fraudulent local elections and offices and their role of economic intermediacy. Thus, the flexible nature of the French racial tradition had its roots in deliberate (and far-sighted) policy, and its openings to individual mobility of mixed-race persons served well to weaken group action and resistence.

In British perceptions of race, blacks were judged inferior on the basis of both culture and physical appearance. From Elizabethan times (the sympathetic depiction of Shakespeare's Othello notwithstanding), blackness was associated with evil, savagery, and depravity. The development of the negative black image had a historic precedent, as we saw in chapter 2, in thirteenth-century British relations with the Irish, who were depicted as savage heathens who were "more incivill, more uncleanly, more barbarous and more brutish in their customs and demeanures, than in any other part of the world that is known" (quoted in Cashmore, [1984] 1988, p. 153). This view justified, through military conquest and legislation such as the Penal Laws of 1697, depriving the Irish of their religious, civil, and land rights. (By the beginning of the eighteenth century almost 90 percent of the land was in the hands of non-Catholics of foreign origin.) Cartoons in magazines such as *Punch* depicted the Irish as evolutionarily less developed and compared them to Africans. The racism was virulent. Charles Kingsley wrote that "to see white chimpanzees [the Irish] is dreadful; if they were black, one would not feel it so much, but their skins, except where tanned by exposure, are as white as ours." And the American historian Edward A. Freeman said that "This would be a grand land if only every Irishman would kill a negro, and be hanged for it" (Kingsley and Freeman quoted in Cashmore, [1984] 1988, p. 154). (We saw in chapter 2 how these attitudes of English settlers had a significant influence on the development of the American racial tradition.) The negative stereotypes of blacks came to be widely used as a justification of slavery and the slave trade.

From the mid–nineteenth century, however, the British imperial theme stressed more and more the political backwardness of colonial peoples rather than any inherent racial inferiority and the corresponding responsibility to bring them up to civilized governance—albeit, unlike the French, on the basis of systematic separation. (It is no accident that apartheid emerged in a former British colony. It can be seen as the exasperated, but logical, extreme of the British traditional policy of separation.) But not all of the British colonies or their inhabitants were viewed as equally "fit" for higher political evolution. Thus, the white settler "daughter" colonies—in North America, New Zealand, Australia, and South Africa—were expected to gradually undergo a transition to self-government and ultimately rise to the status of self-governing dominions. Progression to dominion status by the territories populated by nonwhites was another matter. (With its ancient history and rich political institutions, India was an exception.) Each colony was to develop according to its own traditions, cultures, circumstances, and potential, but political independence was so off into the future as not to be worth considering. In practice, therefore, British policy allowed nonwhite colonial peoples to follow their cultures and religions, but kept them resolutely out of politics and of central governance.[2]

Of the other European powers, as mentioned, the stated colonial ideology of Portugal, France, and Belgium was "assimilation," by which a small select group of the colonized (usually mixed-race people) could aspire to join the social and legal ranks of the colony's European elite. The degree to which assimilation actually occurred was very small (it was *zero* in the Belgian colonies), but it was important for psychological reasons that indigenous individuals believed it to be *possible*. In practice, racial barriers were unyielding and few locals were encouraged to get an education or to develop leadership capabilities (Kanza, 1972). The vast majority of colonial people falling outside the *accultured* or *asimilado* categories experienced civil, social, and political discrimination every bit as strong as in colonies of other European powers.

In contrast, the social policy of the United States pertaining to people of the territories was much more clear cut and reality based. As in the United States itself, no social or cultural distinctions were sufficient to warrant inclusion of other-race or mixed-race people into a separate and higher-status category. As chapter 2 explained, the American racial tradition recognized classes within each race; but the racial polarity was clear, and no illusion of "racial graduation" by economic or cultural achievement was possible. Segregation, social avoidance, and discrimination were applied equally to all nonwhites in the territories, *as they did in the United States*. One consequence of this policy is that the socioracial status of lower-class whites was raised upwards—closer to that of whites of higher socioeconomic status—thus guaranteeing their active cooperation in systems maintenance.

AMERICAN COLONIAL POLICY AND ADMINISTRATION

As Furnivall (1948) has noted, colonialism is defined by results more than by rhetoric. That American colonialism lacked an ideological basis does not mean, of course, that a policy was never developed.[3] A colonial policy did emerge, although haphazardly and after the fact, from the interaction of the American racial tradition and the impulse for material advancement. Its key feature can be termed "pragmatic materialism," by which term I mean the swap of claims to early political advancement in exchange for material short-term economic benefits. Because the short-term benefits are continuously renewed, they become permanent—in the administrative system as well as in the psychology of both metropolitan and local people. Because political advancement is continuously postponed, a permanent political solution of either incorporation or independence becomes unreal. The policy of pragmatic materialism was heavily influenced by Booker T. Washington and his white mentors, mainly General O. O. Howard and Samuel Chapman Armstrong, and strongly supported by President Theodore Roosevelt.

The Architects of American Colonial Ideology

The American approach to the colonies was an export from domestic racial politics, a straightforward application of the "Atlanta Compromise" to the territories. Of the leadership types that emerge in the rigid racial tradition discussed in chapter 1, the accommodationist is the most appropriate for understanding American colonial practices. The paramount accommodationist leader in American history was Booker T. Washington, who was greatly influenced by the political outlook of his white mentors, particularly General O. O. Howard and Samuel Armstrong, and influenced in his turn the views of President Theodore Roosevelt.

General O. O. Howard (1830–1909) was Commissioner of the Freedmen's Bureau (formally known as the Bureau of Refugees, Freedmen and Abandoned Lands) and a key architect of post-Reconstruction policies for newly emancipated African Americans. He had served as an officer in the American Civil War and was deeply interested in the welfare of the former slaves. The Freedmen's Bureau's lack of success (and of genuine interest) in furthering civil rights for blacks was offset by its significant achievements in providing financial aid for the establishment of industrial schools and colleges. The depth of General Howard's influence is best reflected in his founding of Howard University in Washington, D.C., which was meant as the lynchpin for implementing General Howard's education policy for Negroes. Howard University is regarded by many as the premier historically black university in America, and it has educated thousands of potential leaders from throughout the world, particularly from the American territories.

The circular relationship between colonial and African American leadership through the Howard University channel continues to this day. Consider the appointment in August 1995 as Education Commissioner in the U.S. Virgin Islands of James E. Cheek, former president of Howard University for two decades, by Virgin Islands' Governor Roy Lester Schneider, a Howard University–educated oncologist, who attended the medical school while Cheek was president.[4]

The second major influence on Booker T. Washington's political philosophy was Samuel Chapman Armstrong (1839–1893), the Hawaii-born son of American missionaries, who died five years before Hawaii was annexed. Armstrong graduated from Williams College in 1862 and then entered the Union Army, achieving the rank of brigadier general at the end of the Civil War. His command of Negro troops led to his postwar interest in black education. From 1866 to 1872 he served in the educational department of the Freedmen's Bureau. He believed strongly in "industrial education" (i.e., vocational training) as the means for former slaves to advance up the economic ladder. In 1868 he founded an industrial school for Negroes, Hampton Institute in Hampton, Virginia, and served as its head until his death on May 11, 1893. Hampton Institute (now a university), continues to play an important role in the education of black leaders in the United States and in the territories, particularly from the U.S. Virgin Islands before the founding of the College of the Virgin Islands (now university) in 1970. Armstrong was also interested in the "Indian question" and he linked the two sets of issues by developing an Indian Education Program at Hampton Institute. As he shrewdly noted in a letter to his wife: "The Indians . . . are a big card for the school. . . . There's money in them I tell you."[5]

Whatever one thinks of the views of Booker T. Washington (1856–1915), his influence on domestic and international racial policies of the time is unparalleled in American history. Washington, a former slave of black-white ancestry, was Armstrong's most noted student at Hampton Institute, and from 1880–1881 supervised the Indian boys' dormitory—the Wigwam—at the institute (see chapter 2). Armstrong helped arrange Washington's appointment as Principal of Tuskegee Institute in Macon County, Alabama, where he remained for the next thirty-four years. From this position he attained national and international acclaim. Washington was particularly indebted to Armstrong and often noted his gratitude to the man he described as the "noblest, rarest human being" he had ever known and whose influence was "the greatest and most lasting."

Booker T. Washington strongly supported the pragmatic views of his mentors and developed their seminal notions into a sophisticated political and socioeconomic philosophy that was well received by prominent whites, including President Theodore Roosevelt. Washington believed that with time, patience, and careful tutoring, blacks could change their economic circumstances and eventually approach the *economic* status of whites. Toward the end of this fluid period in American race relations (see chapter 2), he outlined his pragmatic philosophy in the widely acclaimed "Atlanta Compromise" speech, delivered at the 1895 Atlanta Cotton States and International Exposition. The speech was important not only in establishing domestic policy for African Americans, but would later find a receptive audience among American colonial policymakers as well.

Washington urged the former slaves to forego political activity and any attempt at social equality with whites. He counseled Negroes to accommodate the New Order in the postemancipation South, accept Jim Crow, and concentrate on industrial, mechanical and agricultural education, and spiritual uplift, rather than classical learning or striving for social equality. The Atlanta speech, which set the tone for forty years of race relations in America also sketched the outline of the pragmatic materialism that would become the cornerstone of American colonial policy:

Cast down your bucket wherever you are. . . . Cast it down in agriculture, mechanics, in commerce, in domestic service, and in the professions. . . . The wisest among my race understand that the agitation of questions of social equality is the extremest [*sic*] folly, and that progress in the enjoyment of all the privileges that will come to us must be the result of severe and constant struggle rather than of artificial forcing. (Washington, 1895, p. 3)

He also urged blacks to behave as good citizens, but forego political participation until a nebulous time far, far off into the future. As would later be argued for the nonwhite inhabitants of territories acquired in 1898, the right to vote and full political rights would have to wait until African Americans were ready and able to exercise those rights—in the judgment of the white majority, naturally: "It is important and right that all privileges of the law be ours, but it is vastly more important that we be prepared for the exercises of these privileges."[6]

Booker T. Washington died in 1915, two years before the Virgin Islands were purchased from Denmark, and seventeen years after the "flag territories" were acquired. But the impact of his ideas on colonial policy lasted long after his death, particularly through their earlier influence on Theodore Roosevelt and his policies.[7]

No examination of the influences shaping American colonial policy can overlook the views of Theodore Roosevelt. Roosevelt had been assistant secretary of the Navy just prior to the Spanish-American War; he fought in the war; became vice-president on the McKinley ticket in 1900; succeeded McKinley as president on the latter's assassination in 1901; and was reelected in 1904 serving through 1908—at the formative time in American policy toward the new colonies. He was an admirer and close friend of Booker T. Washington, with whom he often consulted on race relations, and his invitation to Washington to visit the White House in 1901 created a storm of controversy.[8] He was also a close friend of Rudyard Kipling, from whom he absorbed the "White Man's Burden" myth.

(The reader interested in a highly readable and penetrating analysis of Roosevelt's racial views is referred to Thomas Dyer (1980)—from which much of the following summary is derived.)

Theodore Roosevelt was an unapologetic imperialist in the heyday of the "age of imperialism," who perceived the world in Manichean and romantic terms of good and evil, strong and simple, savage and civilized.[9] Heavily influenced by Nordic and (particularly) Teutonic myths, he placed Anglo-Saxons at the apex of the racial hierarchy, entrusted with a special destiny which, among other things, justified colonialism. Destiny pointed to a world ruled by white people. His notion of altruism was the firm belief that the best thing a white country could do for a colored country was to take it over and let the superior whites administer the affairs of the inferior inhabitants. In his own words:

The rude, fierce settler who drove the savage from the land lays all civilized mankind under a debt to him. American and Indian, Boer and Zulu, Cossack and Tartar, New Zealander and Maori—in each case the victor, horrible though many of his deeds are, has laid deep the foundation for the future greatness of a mighty people. . . . It is of incalculable importance that America, Australia and Siberia should pass out of the hands of their red, black and yellow aboriginal owners, and become the heritage of the dominant world races.[10]

In general, Roosevelt's fascination with natural science, combined with the American racial tradition of his times, gave him a "firm belief that nature's creatures could be classified" (Dyer, 1980, p. 4), leading him to assume a natural hierarchy of races. The hierarchy was not seen, however, as immutable: influenced by the prevailing Lamarckian theories of the time, Roosevelt believed that racial characteristics could be influenced by the environment and—over *very, very long* periods—evolve into higher forms. This permitted him, in Dyer's words, to "develop an explanatory scheme for the contradiction between American democratic ideology and the reality of a caste society based on race. . . . If democratic beliefs compelled him to argue that blacks should be received into American political society, he insisted on the need for a very gradual entry without 'social equality' " (Dyer, 1980, p. 92).

Thus, the emotional racism absorbed from his southern mother was reinforced by the "intellectual" influence of his mentors at Harvard and Columbia, and combined with Lamarckianism and (misunderstood) Darwinism to produce a pseudointellectual justification of Roosevelt's imperialism (which also provided a natural outlet to the man's unbounded energy and zest for acquisition).

By contrast, the crude genetic racists of much of the antebellum South were utterly uninterested in colonial adventures as, in their view, there was no possibility that inferior races could be made to evolve into something higher through the tutelage of their betters. In this sense, from the point of view of its targets, its "scientific" racism, which Theodore Roosevelt exemplified, was worse than its crude variety which was, at least, predictable. (Roosevelt could also be very "unscientific," however, as exemplified by his childish cruelty in frightening and humiliating the family's black housemaids [Dyer, 1980].)

Roosevelt was not, however, a rigid racist. For example, he placed the Japanese on a par with Anglo-Saxons, their civilization being "equally high." Nor was he a hypocrite. He detested, for example, the unspoken code of behavior that allowed southern whites to exploit sexually black women while "shrieking in public about miscegenation" (quoted by Dyer, 1980, p. 107).

Concerning the people of the American territories, his views were generally benign, but typically condescending toward "our little brown brothers." He wrote of the Filipinos: "[They] were quite incapable of standing by themselves when we took possession of the islands" (Roosevelt, 1937, p. 112). This also characterized his view of Puerto Ricans, who also had to "be made fit for self-government," and he fully shared the view expressed by General George W. Davis in 1899 that: "Great care must . . . be taken lest [the] extension of [political power] be made too rapidly, resulting in the introduction of institutions for which the people are unprepared."[11]

Counterbalancing his refusal to accept political advancement of the people of the territories (except, theoretically, at a glacial "evolutionary" pace quite irrelevant from a practical policy point of view), Roosevelt was committed to improving their material situation—which brings out the essential kinship with Booker T. Washington's ideas. Thus, *the Atlanta Compromise, intended for domestic purposes, was transformed into the basic bargain of American policy toward the overseas territories.*

Colonial Policy: The Components of Pragmatic Materialism

The Basic Bargain. As mentioned, the implicit compact of American colonialism was a trade-off between claims to rapid political advancement and a package of material benefits. The first component of pragmatic materialism was therefore the provision of basic social, educational, and infrastructural services: streets and highways; public parks and promenades; lighting, sewage, and water supply; public baths, lavatories and slaughter-houses; commercial fairs and markets; public education and libraries; sanitation and hospitals; public charities and cemeteries; construction of public buildings; and regulations for the police, public order, and health.

Naturally, only some among this impressive list of basic public services were actually provided and then in uneven fashion to different groups. Nevertheless, the policy had results. For example, in the case of the Virgin Islands, infant mortality declined sharply. And in Puerto Rico, school enrollment jumped from about 25,000 at the time of the American occupation to over 152,000 by 1917, and external trade expanded eightfold. In response, pragmatic materialism was well received by territorial leaders, and the basic bargain was kept: Early movements of protest and agitation for status change and political development in the territories fizzled out when sprinkled with the tangible benefits provided by the colonial authorities— the schools, the roads, the hospitals, the parks and, above all, the jobs.

The Benefit Theory. A second element of American colonial policy was the benefit theory; that is, the rejection of exploitation of the colonies in favor of their "uplift." In the words of a well-meaning early colonial official:

The one essential justification that has ever been offered for the acquisition of new territory and the holding of it even temporarily in dependence has been that such action has been for the benefit of the territory itself. As the most important consequence of this principle, the United States has in no case sought to make of dependent territory a source of revenue to the federal government. (Willoughby, 1905, p. 12)

The federal government assumed the costs incurred in the annexation of the territories following the Treaty of Paris, and the receipts from subsequent customs duties and excise taxes accrued to the territories themselves. In addition, several of the territories (e.g., Puerto Rico and the Virgin Islands) were allowed to develop their own systems of excise taxation. What evidence does exist of the net flow of resources to or from the United States and the territories is ambiguous. It is easily demonstrated that, from a fiscal point of view, the federal government contributed more resources to the territories than it derived in taxes or other revenues. Thus, in the case of Puerto Rico, after passage of the Organic Act of 1900 and the establishment of civilian administration (see chapter 5), all revenues collected in the island accrued to its own treasury. Furthermore, all taxes collected in the United States on goods imported from Puerto Rico were placed at the disposal of the president of the United States to be used by him for the benefit of the government of the island. However, the benefit-cost balance shifts considerably toward the United States if a reasonable monetary value is imputed to the network of military bases (not to mention their benefit in terms of national security). Furthermore, in the larger territories of Puerto Rico and the Philippines American private firms gained substantially from the fact of American suzerainty. On balance, it is plausible that the American economy as a whole received some net benefit from the colonial possessions. But this was never the main motive-force of American colonialism, whose benevolent strain was very real. Listen again to President McKinley agonizing over the Philippines:

I walked the floor of the White House night after night until midnight; and I am not ashamed to tell you, gentlemen, that I went down on my knees and prayed [to] Almighty God for light and guidance more than one night. And one night late it came to me this way—I don't know how it was, but it came: (1) that we could not give them back to Spain—that would be cowardly and dishonorable; (2) that we could not turn them over to France and Germany—our commercial rivals in the Orient—that would be bad business and discreditable; (3) that we would not leave them to themselves—they were unfit for self-government—and they would have anarchy and misrule over there worse than Spain's was; and (4) *that there was nothing left for us to do but to take them all, and to educate the Filipinos, and uplift and civilize and Christianize them, and by God's grace do the very best we could for them, as our fellow-men for whom Christ also died.* And then I went to bed, and went to sleep, and slept soundly, and the next morning I sent for the chief engineer of the War Department, our map-maker, and I told him to *put the Philippines on the map of the United States* (pointing to a large map on the wall of his office), and there they are, and there they will stay while I am President!" (Emphasis added)[12]

Education for citizenship. The third element of colonial policy was educational training. Despite the indefinite postponement of a permanent political solution inherent in the American colonial bargain, participation in local administration was encouraged. Training in public administration was provided to locals, particularly to the Filipinos and the Puerto Ricans, who under Spanish colonialism "had little experience in the management of public affairs, and to whom the fundamental principle that government should be administered for the benefit of the whole people instead of for those who happen to be in authority was unknown" (Willoughby, 1905, p. 85).

Colonial Administration. The fourth element of American colonial policy was the intention to create an efficient administration. Whereas it can be argued that the first three elements of colonial policy discussed above were all to some extent put into reality, American colonial administration remained haphazard and fragmented. The official intent was to extend to the territories a system of government and laws conforming to those existing in the United States and educating territorial inhabitants in the principles underlying them.

With the formation of civilian government after the initial period of military administration, the political and administrative system was revamped. Typically, a governor was appointed by the president of the United States and confirmed by the Senate, and executive departments were created—usually including at least a secretary of state, attorney-general, treasurer, auditor, commissioner of the interior, and commissioner of education. A legislative assembly was composed of an Executive Council (appointed by the president of the United States and a House of Delegates elected by qualified voters. The Spanish codes of administrative, civil, and criminal law were replaced by the laws and procedures found in the United States, and the judiciary included a U.S. District Court, with the jurisdiction of both district and circuit courts. The financial system was reformed along American lines, and the U.S. dollar became the local currency. This apparently orderly model of local administration, however, did not always correspond to administrative realities, nor were the territories subject to uniform treatment and guidance by the federal government.

The "denial" of empire, resulting lack of vision, and the influence of the race factor implied ad hoc, haphazard and fragmented guidance from the Washington colonial center and a central colonial administration largely staffed by second-rate, junior, or reluctant functionaries. In European countries colonial service provided an acceptable public career route for the higher echelons, and a well-organized colonial office was an important part of the machinery of government. The United States never evolved a single U.S. governmental agency with exclusive responsibility for administering the territories, and involvement in territorial administration was, if not a dead end, certainly not a stepping stone to bureaucratic success.

The territories were administered through a series of ad hoc arrangements. In the nineteenth-century phase of territorial expansion—continental expansion west of the Mississippi (see chapter 3)—the practice became established of giving the Interior Department administrative authority over the new territories, which were slated for eventual statehood.[13] In 1873, the department was given an official general mandate through an Act of Congress, which provided that the Secretary of the Interior would exercise all the powers and perform all the duties in relation to the territory of the United States.

As explained in chapter 4, the legal and political status of American territorial holdings changed with the Spanish-American War. The cessions of the disparate islands, with "exotic cultures unfamiliar to most Americans" gave rise to disparate administrative arrangements in Washington. Guam (and, later, the U.S. Virgin Islands) were administered by the Navy Department for a prolonged period. After a short two years of military administration, Puerto Rico was put under the Department of State until 1907, when it was placed under the authority of the War Department's Bureau of Insular Affairs. The Department of the Interior had previously assumed responsibility for Hawaii and Alaska and, in 1931, assumed from the navy authority over the Virgin Islands.

It was only in 1933 that a Division of Territories and Island Possessions was created in the Department of the Interior, with theoretical responsibility for Alaska, Hawaii, the Virgin Islands, the Philippines, and Puerto Rico. (After World War II, Guam and American Samoa were added to its mandate.) The division, however, had neither a political head nor executive authority. It advised the president, Congress, and local governments of the colonies, and linked them with other departments, but it did not provide administrative or political guidance to the territories.[14] The Division of Territories and Island Possessions was transformed into the Office of Territories in 1950, which was replaced in 1971 by a new entity. The new entity did not have a name: It was simply directed by a newly created deputy assistant secretary for territorial affairs, who reported to the assistant secretary for land management! In 1973, the Office of Territorial Affairs was created. These ad hoc changes and fragmented authorities are symptomatic of the underlying ambiguity of the political status of the territories.

The absence of a coherent administrative architecture continues to this day. Administration policy toward the remaining territories is largely left to interested committees of the U.S. Congress. The state of affairs is summarized in a recent congressional hearing:

Today, the United States, through Article IV, Clause 3, Paragraph 2 of the Constitution, asserts that Guam, the Virgin Islands and American Samoa have no sovereign powers of their own, but are ruled solely by Congress and have only such powers as Congress decides to delegate to these territories. Congress determines the tax policy of these territories; Congress amends these tax policies, quite often unaware that the interest of all or some of the territories may be very adversely affected. Other times, Congress may not care because their constituents' interests are opposed to those of the nonvoting territories. (U.S. House Committee on Interior and Insular Affairs, 1986, *Hearings*, p. 15)

THE LINK TO THE AMERICAN RACIAL TRADITION

The American racial tradition was quickly exported to the new territories by the U.S. military. Because the territories were acquired as the result of war, the first colonial administrators were military men. Military administration was in place for varying periods of time—from a short two years in the case of Puerto Rico and Cuba, to a long seventeen years in the case of the Virgin Islands. And the military was among the most rigidly racist of American institutions of the time. Until 1948, when President Truman desegregated the U.S. Armed Forces, the American military was characterized by strict racial segregation and dominated by white southerners at all levels of the chain of command.

Military personnel exhibited strong antimiscegenation attitudes. With reference to Cuba, DeConde (1992) writes:

When American soldiers and their officers first met some of their Cuban allies, they were surprised to find that many were black and "only partially civilized." The Anglo liberators characterized these people, as they had other non-whites, as "born of a mongrel spawn of Europe, crossed upon the fetishes of darkest Africa and aboriginal America." Obviously, in this perspective, the Cubans were incompetent to govern themselves. (P. 62)

These perceptions affected all territories, from the Philippines through the Virgin Islands and even Puerto Rico, where the immediate first consequence of American administration was the downward-leveling of the socioracial status of the mixed-race "near whites," who were just Negroes in American eyes (see chapter 7). Paramount carriers of the American racial tradition, the military administrators did not recognize the distinctions of mixed-race ancestry, the differences in culture, the role of class. To them, all mixed-race people and all unmixed colored people of the Philippines, Cuba, Guam, Puerto Rico, the Virgin Islands, and so forth, were, simply, niggers. There was a determination that the "special race" of Anglo-Saxons, now embarked upon a mission of expansionism, not be contaminated and weakened by inferior people.[15] The crystalline simplicity of the American racial dichotomy could not possibly comprehend the nuances and subtle distinctions, verbal language, body language, clothing, occupation, money, and, of course, skin color and somatic variations, of the flexible racial traditions of the Spanish or Danish types.

A sympathetic observer of military administration noted of the navy's stewardship in the Virgin Islands between 1917–1931 that "the building of streets and roads, of water systems and school houses; the protection of public health, the administration of police—these tasks were performed easily and well by the naval administrators." Yet, even he admitted that "Negroes expect a separate status, but they do not expect that status to be accompanied by galling discriminations. When discriminations cannot be avoided, wisdom dictates that colonial administrators keep them as few and inoffensive as possible. If possible, questions of race prestige must be kept from arising."[16]

Seen in this light, even the provision of material benefits had its social costs. When coupled with the rigid racial attitudes of the American administrators, the policy intensified social conflict among the different racial groups in the territories, and created new conflicts where none had existed. Because the distribution of the economic benefits was unequal, and visibly race-based, economic cleavages emerged or were reinforced—coinciding more and more with socioracial distinctions and heightening conflict and tension throughout the system.

It can now be seen that, for all its surface benevolence, the colonial policy of pragmatic materialism was in essence a corollary of the American racial tradition, by which nonwhites were viewed as neither capable nor interested in political self-determination, but might prove responsive to material gain.[17] Let us sum up: (1) the guiding colonial policy of pragmatic materialism emerged from American unwillingness to incorporate the overseas territories through statehood, or to grant them independence; (2) such unwillingness stemmed in turn from the predominance of colored people in the territories and the American racial tradition that could accept neither the incorporation of colored people on a basis of equality nor the idea they they could govern themselves; and (3) the emergence of accommodationist local leadership in the territories was a natural response to their predicament, and acted to consolidate the colonial policy of trading off material benefits for political and social equality. The next two chapters describe this circular dynamic in detail and trace its effects on today's society and politics in the two best-known remaining territories: Puerto Rico and the U.S. Virgin Islands.

NOTES

1. In his remarks to a visiting delegation of Methodist church leaders, quoted in Daniel B. Schirmer and Stephen R. Shalom, *The Philippines Reader: A History of Colonialism, Neocolonialism, Dictatorship and Resistance* (Boston: South End Press, 1987), pp. 22–23.

2. See von Albertini, 1971, p. 88. The British colonial empire included very different geographical, cultural, and political entities. Besides the Muslim protectorates and mandated territories in the Middle East, there were the Asian colonies Ceylon, Malaya, and Borneo; in West Africa, Nigeria, the Gold Coast, Sierra Leone, and Gambia; the South East African territories of Northern Rhodesia; and in the East, Nyasaland, Uganda, and Kenya, and the mandated territory of Tanganyika and the Sudan. Other important colonies were Gibraltar, Malta, Cyprus, Aden, Hong Kong, and Jamaica, and in the South Pacific, the Fiji Islands.

3. For various discussions of American colonial policy in the territories, good sources are: Ruth G. Van Cleve, *The Office of Territorial Affairs* (New York: Praeger, 1974); Arnold Leibowitz, *Defining Status: A Territorial Analysis of U.S. Territorial Relations* (Leiden, Netherlands: Nijhoff, 1989); Alan Weisman, "An Island in Limbo: State, Nation or Commonwealth? Puerto Ricans Hotly Debate Their Future," *New York Times*, February 18, 1990.

4. General Howard served as the third president of the university; he resigned to return to military service, and, ironically, participated in anti-Indian campaigns in the West.

5. Quoted in Hultgren and Molin, 1989, p. 18.

6. Washington shrewdly recognized that the economic well-being of African Americans was threatened by European immigrants, particularly southern Italians, and he urged American whites not to cast their economic lot with European immigrants:

To those of the white race who look to the incoming of those of foreign birth and strange tongue and habits for the prosperity of the South, were I permitted I would repeat what I say to my own race, "Cast down your bucket where you are." Cast it down among the eight millions of Negroes whose habits you know, whose fidelity and love you have tested in days when to have proved treacherous meant the ruin of your firesides. Cast down your bucket among these people who have, without strikes and labor wars, tilled your fields, cleared your forests, built your railroads and cities, and brought forth treasures from the bowels of the earth.... Casting down your bucket among my people, helping and encouraging them as you are doing on these grounds, and to education of head, hand, and heart. (Washington, 1895, p. 6)

For a brief reference to Washington's visit to Sicily, see Jerre Mangione and Ben Morreale, *La Storia: Five Centuries of the Italian American Experience* (New York: Harper Perennial, 1992). Washington is quoted thusly:

The Negro is not the man farthest down. The condition of the coloured farmer in the most backward parts of the Southern states in America, even where he has the least education and the least encouragement, is incomparably better than the condition and opportunities of the agricultural population in Sicily. (P. xv)

7. Washington also attracted the admiring attention of some European colonial administrators, such as Governor Alan Burns. Cf. Burns, 1949. For a discussion of Washington's views on colonial policies in Africa and the role of Tuskegee Institute in training Africans in developing a cotton industry, see Louis R. Harlan, "Booker T. Washington and the White Man's Burden," in *American Historical Review* (January 1966), pp. 441–66. For interesting discussions of the political views of Booker T. Washington, see: Logan, [1954] 1965. Logan notes: "The preeminent significance of the speech stems from the acceptance of the doctrine of compromise by a Negro with close personal contacts with powerful men who had made compromise the national policy" (p. 276). See also White, [1985] 1990, and Harlan, 1972.

8. Bartle Bull (1988) recounts the following story about Roosevelt's attitude toward African Americans:

Big game hunter Quentin O. Grogan wrote that the President became very candid when they hunted alone, particularly when they rested under a tree during the heat of the day in Africa. One afternoon they discussed the painful difficulties of race relations in the United States. It was a time when lynchings were not uncommon and the progressive President, a close friend of the American black leader Booker T. Washington, was concerned about racial oppression and the protection of individual rights. Grogan asked him, "if by pressing a button, you could eliminate all the negroes in the United States, would you press it?" Roosevelt replied, "I would jump on it with both feet." "Without a button," asked Grogan, "What is the solution?" "As far as I can see, integration is the only answer." (P. 114)

9. His son, Theodore Roosevelt Jr., who served as governor of Puerto Rico and governor of the Philippines, had very different views: "Those who are raising altars to the so-called different races seem to be either woefully lacking in historical knowledge or in humor. The great countries of Europe, and therefore their offspring in other parts of the world, are composites in varying degrees of many peoples. *Racial purity for a nation practically does not exist today.*" (Roosevelt, [1937] 1970, p. 5; emphasis added.)

10. Quoted in Morris, 1979, p. 464.
11. *Civil Affairs of Porto Rico*, 1899.
12. On the same occasion cited earlier; see note 1.
13. Except as noted, this discussion is based on Van Cleve, 1974.
14. Fieldhouse, 1965, p. 344.
15. Horsman, 1981, p. 272.
16. Evans, 1945, p. 279.
17. To be sure, the American policy of material uplift was also in part rooted in the progressive reform movement in the United States, which incorporated the belief that progress would result from increased technical efficiency and education for citizenship. The "impossibilists" argued that it was better that a nation be allowed to work out results for itself, even at the expense of waste, muddling, and violence. The "pragmatists" insisted that intelligent guidance from without could sometimes accelerate the process of natural growth and save much waste (Weatherly, quoted in Schmidt, 1971, p. 157).

6 *The Case of Puerto Rico*

This chapter examines the social and political consequences of American colonialism in Puerto Rico. After a brief look at the racial attitudes and practices of the Spanish, we describe the implications of the change in the dominant racial tradition that followed the replacement of Spanish with American colonial rule; political developments through the evolution of "commonwealth" status; the current ambiguity in status; the nature of political leadership; and the prospects for political status evolution in light of Puerto Rico's racial mix. In Puerto Rico as in the other territories, racial considerations did and do matter, although mitigated by the issues of cultural nationalism, identity, and language.

THE COUNTRY

The Commonwealth of Puerto Rico, about 50 miles east of Hispaniola (Haiti and the Dominican Republic) in the Caribbean Sea, comprises the main island of Puerto Rico, together with the small offshore islands of Vieques and Culebra and numerous small islets. The land area is 3,515 square miles (Connecticut is 5,018 square miles, Delaware is 2,045, and Rhode Island is 1,212), and the population, as of July 1, 1995, was 3,812,569 (not counting the large number of Puerto Ricans living in the United States—primarily in New York).[1]

The economy benefits substantially from a variety of preferential fiscal and other provisions under U.S. legislation, and 1997 per capita income is $7,300, well below the poorest American states of Mississippi ($9,648) and

West Virginia ($10,520). Puerto Ricans have been described by Clara E. Rodriguez as "the Rainbow People," based on the variety of racial types in a single family (1989, p. 49). This is the result of the history of racial mixing. The people represent a great variety of ethnic and racial backgrounds, primarily lineal descendants of pre-Colombian Indians, Spaniards, and African slaves.

Executive power is vested in the governor, who is elected for a four-year term by universal adult suffrage. Legislative power is held by the bicameral Legislative Assembly (Camara de Representantes), comprising the Senate (Senado) with twenty-nine members, and the House of Representatives with fifty-four members. The members of both chambers are elected by direct vote for four-year terms. The resident commissioner, also elected for a four-year term, represents Puerto Rico in the U.S. House of Representatives, but—as with the delegates from the U.S. Virgin Islands and Guam—can vote only in committees. (The right to vote on the floor, given to the delegates by the Democratic majority 103rd Congress, in 1993, was rescinded by the new Republican majority 104th Congress in 1995.) In the nineteenth century the distinction of resident commissioner had implications for statehood. With the acquisition of the flag territories, the distinction no longer exits. The term "resident commissioner" originally had status implications for the continental territories that later became states. But with acquisition of the flag territories, no such presumption of statehood existed. For example, both Puerto Rico and the Philippines were granted resident commissioners (the latter had two). But the Philippines became independent and Puerto Rico is a Commonwealth that does not carry a presumption of statehood. In contrast, Alaska and Hawaii were granted delegates, and both became states. In the 1970s, Congress gave Guam and the U.S. Virgin Islands a delegate, but this did not imply statehood. Finally, Puerto Ricans are citizens of the United States, but those resident in Puerto Rico may not vote in presidential elections, although they participate in national party primaries and in conventions. The official language is Spanish, but English is widely spoken.

POLITICS AND RACE UNDER SPANISH RULE

Despite its name—"Rich Harbor"—Puerto Rico never completely matched the economic role of other Spanish colonies in the Western Hemisphere. Politics, race, and society, however, were run along very similar lines.

Colonial Politics

The system of government established for Puerto Rico was derived from the Code of Laws of the Indies (1691) and the revised Code of Spanish Laws (1795) both of which followed the doctrine of royal absolutism. The governor was omnipotent as chief executive, head of the army and navy,

THE CASE OF PUERTO RICO

chief fiscal official, supreme judge, and as royal vice-patron. The inhabitants—largely a mixture of the Negro-Indian population and the Spaniards—were politically more aware than in many other colonies, giving rise to constant political agitation for increased participation.

Islanders could become members of the Spanish Parliament, the *Cortes*, but their influence was limited and laws were either enacted in Spain or decreed by the Spanish-appointed executive officials. Some municipal self-government was provided, but its real autonomy was often negated by administrative handpicking of the candidates for local office. The number of persons permitted to vote in public office was limited sharply by rigid educational and property qualifications.

Resistance to Spanish rule and the push for political self-determination were gathering steam toward the end of the nineteenth century. The best-known event is the September 23, 1868 *Grito de Lares* (the "Outcry from Lares"), when some 400 men and women were involved in a short-lived insurrection and proclaimed independence from Spain in the town of Lares. During the 1880s, the movement for political self-government under Spain was led by Roman Baldorioty de Castro, one of the island's leading political and literary figures, and a prominent abolitionist. The year before annexation by the United States, the Spanish National Constitution improved the situation somewhat and a Charter of Autonomy was decreed. The charter provided for the election of delegates with full voting rights to both houses of the *Cortes*. In addition, there was to be an elected Chamber of Representatives on the island and a fifteen-member Council of Administration, with seven members appointed and eight selected through direct elections. The powers of the governor were correspondingly reduced, although he retained the right to suspend civil rights and to refer insular legislation to the Council of Ministers of Spain. The Puerto Rican Legislature was given general power to pass on all matters of insular importance, including the key authority to establish the budget and determine tariffs and taxes.

The Charter of Autonomy was decreed in November 1897. In July 1898, American troops occupied Puerto Rico. It could be argued that the 1897 charter was in effect a blueprint for transition to independence. If this is true, the transition was suddenly aborted. It is undeniable, in any event, that hopes of political emancipation were kindled by the Spanish-American War only to be dashed by the replacement of one colonial regime with another. American rule entailed a sharp reduction in local political participation for twenty years—until the Organic Act of 1917 (discussed later in this chapter).

Race and Society

In sharp contrast with the American taboo, not only interracial concubinage but intermarriage were common in the West Indian territories colonized by Spain. The Spaniards found the Islands of Puerto Rico, Cuba, and

Santo Domingo inhabited by Native Americans, whom they conquered, enslaved, converted, and whose women they took as concubines. African slaves were also introduced into the colonies, and the Spaniards intermixed freely with them as well (Reuter, [1918,] 1970). Slavery played a relatively minor role in the colonial economy of Puerto Rico and did not have continuous economic value during the early centuries. The first slaves were introduced from Spain in 1510.[2] In 1518, Charles V authorized the importation of 4,000 slaves to the islands of Puerto Rico, Cuba, Jamaica (and to Spain itself). These slaves were imported primarily to fill the growing needs of the infant sugar industry of the sixteenth century.

By and large, the Spanish racial tradition was flexible, particularly until the nineteenth century. (The reader is reminded that use of the word racial "flexibility" is not necessarily coterminous with softness or gentleness.) Thus, Negroes appear never to have formed a separate sociocultural segment within the structure of Puerto Rican society under Spain; mixed-race individuals had an intermediate socioracial status; and slaves were freed more routinely. The practice of manumission, long established in Spain, served to increase the numbers of free Negroes in Puerto Rico during periods of economic contraction. In 1776, the number of free men of color, both those of mixed-race (*pardos*) as well as Negro (*negros*), exceeded by many thousands the number of slaves. Furthermore, escaped slaves from other colonies were allowed to enter Puerto Rico as freemen. For example, a group of eighty fugitive slaves from the Danish island of St. Croix were granted their liberty upon entering Puerto Rico in 1714, organized into militia, and given two *cuerdas* of land each.

During the nineteenth century legal changes were made, in the direction of a more rigid racial tradition and systematic discrimination. Julian Steward ([1956] 1972) writes that the heavy importation of slaves in the early 1800s, the imposition of repressive labor legislation, and the renewed identification of the political interests of the insular upper class with the interests of Spain, combined to shift the emphasis from the unity of all Puerto Ricans to encouraging the growth of a large slave population with few rights and a small chance of political integration.

This involution in the status of blacks was foreshadowed in the *Instrucciones* given to one Don Ramon Power to ask for the duty free–introduction of slaves as established by the *Cedula de Gracias* of 1815 (Steward, [1956], 1972). Discrimination also began with respect to free people of color: A clause of the 1815 legislation granted white immigrants the right to occupy twice the amount of land for cultivation as granted to Negro or "mixed" immigrants. In 1833, further limitations were imposed, and Negroes were entirely barred from military service. In 1848, following a series of abortive slave revolts, the governor-general of the island invoked the Black Code *(Codigo Negro)*. Among its draconian provisions were the following: Persons of color, whether free or slave, were all subject to judgment by courts-martial; slave owners were empowered to punish their slaves for minor offenses without recourse to military or civil authorities; and restraints were placed on the growing group of free Negroes, mostly small farmers and artisans in towns and on *haciendas*, who served as leaders of the movement for the equality of Negroes within the island.

The informal racial customs and an agricultural boom, however, prevailed over the formal legislation. (See chapter 2 for a discussion of the crucial distinction between formal and informal "institutions.") Steward concludes that the Black Code did not accomplish its aims: Both black and white free laborers worked at the same manual tasks in the fields with Negro slaves, as dictated by the expanding demand. Thus, economics and the informal racial tradition combined to frustrate official intentions and reduce the importance of race in Puerto Rican society.

The passing of slavery narrowed the gap between whites and blacks and created some political common ground. The struggle for abolition, which increased in intensity during the middle of the nineteenth century, became a part of the general Puerto Rican fight for political autonomy from Spain. The struggles for abolition and autonomy became joined. Steward ([1956], 1972) writes:

The integration of Negro subgroups into Puerto Rican nationality thus came to be closely tied to the fight for greater self-determination on the part of the island.... Negro patriots, such as Dr. Jose C. Barbosa played an important role in the crystallization of common Puerto Rican identity. The Negroes could best realize their objectives in the struggle for equality at that time by identifying themselves with the ideal of self-government in Puerto Rico, through which the separate identities of white and Negro Spanish subjects might be subordinated to the dominant concept of Puerto Rican nationality. (p. 497)

RACE AND SOCIETY UNDER AMERICAN RULE

Superimposing the American Racial Tradition

Although at the time of the Spanish-American War there still remained a large economic and social gulf between whites, blacks, and mixed-race people in Puerto Rico, the differences had been narrowing and the influence of race on social and economic status was diminishing. Racial identification was becoming subordinate to cultural identification, largely because the system of racial identification in the flexible tradition was based more on phenotype and "social color" than on genotype. As noted by a contemporary observer of race at the turn of the century: "There is little or no race prejudice, and the white or whiter mixtures of the two races pass muster as whites, and not as in the United States, as blacks" (quoted in Mathews, 1974, p. 316).

A sharp reversal of these trends took place with the superimposition of the rigid American racial tradition onto the relatively flexible Spanish variant. The first immediate consequence was the lowering of the socioracial status of the intermediate racial groups. Ironically (but predictably, based on the theory of a rigid racial tradition) the first in Puerto Rico to suffer loss of status were the prominent "near white families"—who had been largely pro-American based on their resentment of "pure Spanish" *hidalgo-ism*.

The earliest illustration of the leveling downwards of the socioracial status of Puerto Ricans is provided, once again, by the ubiquitous Booker T. Washington (who was himself of mixed black/white ancestry). From the identification of the people in the new territories as colored, came the "logical" step of sending Puerto Ricans and Cubans to Tuskegee Institute to be educated in industrial methods and, upon returning to their countries, starting the same type of institutions there. In letters to the editors of the *Christian Register*, on August 18, 1898, and the *Boston Transcript*, on September 3, 1898, Washington wrote: We are ready to begin the work as soon as funds are secured or guaranteed. In what better or more permanent way can we help Cuba than by educating a number of these people? What I have said of Cuba applies as well to Porto Rico, where over half the population are negroes."[3]

Nevertheless, when convenient, Puerto Ricans could also be considered white by American politicians and judges. It will be recalled from chapter 3 that the legal construction and definitions of race often served a concrete purpose (as in facilitating the expropriation of Native American lands). This was the case, for example, when it became necessary to assure that Filipinos would not be considered eligible for naturalization—nor the Philippines for possible statehood: The Jones Act of 1916 promised eventual independence to the Philippines; the Jones Act of 1917 conferred American citizenship on Puerto Ricans.

As explained earlier, the naturalization legislation prohibited nonwhites from acquiring citizenship (see chapter 3). In order to grant Puerto Ricans citizenship, it became necessary to define Puerto Ricans as white. Thus, American interests at the turn of the century converged with the myths of the earlier Spanish colonizers to invent a predominantly white society in Puerto Rico, contrary to the realities described in the previous section.

Puerto Ricans are a mixed-race people whose ancestry includes Boriquenos or Indians who were exterminated, Africans, and a small, but dominant Spanish group. The former groups were in the most oppressed stratum of the social pyramid during the early period of Spanish colonization and had more contact with one another than either had with the dominant Spanish group, resulting in their mixing.[4] The Spanish population was small and unstable throughout the first two centuries of colonial life. For example, in 1534, the governor of the colony gave an account of his efforts to stop the Spanish population's mass exodus to the mainland in search of riches. The island, he wrote, was "so depopulated that one sees hardly any people of Spanish descent, but only Negroes." As noted by Gonzalez:

> The Spanish ingredient, then, in the formation of a popular Puerto Rican culture must have taken the form of agricultural laborers, mostly from the Canary Islands, imported to the island when the descendants of the first African slaves *had already become black Puerto Ricans*. It is because of this that I believe . . . that the first Puerto Ricans were in fact *black* Puerto Ricans. . . . As for the white campesinos or countrymen of those early times, in other words the first *jibaros*, the truth is that this was a poor peasantry that found itself obliged to adopt many of the life habits of those other poor people already living in the country, namely the slaves.[5]

Yet, indicative of the contortions to which the most committed of racist ideologues was willing to undergo, Representative Thomas Spight of Mississippi said in 1900 about Puerto Ricans:

> Its people are, in the main, of Caucasian blood, knowing and appreciating the benefits of civilization, and are desirous of casting their lot with us. . . . How different the case of the Philippine Islands, 10,000 miles away. . . . The inhabitants are of wholly different races of people from ours—Asiatics, Malays, negroes and mixed blood. They have nothing in common with us and centuries can not assimilate them. . . . They can never be clothed with the rights of American citizenship nor their territory admitted as a State of the American Union. . . . But the case is essentially different with Puerto Rico. Its proximity to our mainland, the character of its inhabitants, and the willingness with which they have accepted our sovereignty, together with the advantages—commercial, sanitary and strategic—all unite to enable us to make her an integral part of our domain, without any violence to principle or any danger of foreign entanglements. (Quoted in Cabranes, 1979, p. 425)

Cabranes attributes the relatively tender treatment accorded to Puerto Rico (in contrast to the harsh views of the Philippines) partly to the representations made to Congress concerning the racial composition of the island. For example, Representative Payne (1900) readily accepted highly questionable War Department reports showing that white people, descendants of the Spaniards, possibly mixed with some Indian blood, but none of them of Negro extraction—outnumbered by nearly two to one the combined total of Negroes and mulattoes.

Partly because of this utter ignorance of the racial makeup of the island, the rigid American racial tradition never entirely overcame the local history of racial flexibility. But it did shift boundaries and introduce new ones and created an admixture of racial rules every bit as complicated as the admixture of the races themselves. One consequence has been a "disconnect" between the mythology and the reality of race relations in the island.

A Pathology of Normality

Because of the mixing of the very different Spanish and American racial traditions, Puerto Ricans have acquired an ambivalence toward race that Florestan Fernandes (with reference to Brazil) has termed a "pathology of normality." This is a psychological mechanism based on the denial of race-based social and economic cleavages. It is more profound in Puerto Rico than in other U.S. overseas territories because of the mixed racial composition of most Puerto Rican families. The color spectrum in a single family can run from very dark to practically white. Puerto Ricans often use the probing question: "Donde esta sua abuela?" ("Where is your grandmother?"). There are two possible implications: (1) as a test of racial heritage: if grandmother is "white" then the individual can also lay claim to this racial identity, and (2) as a light hearted put down of someone who assumes airs of racial superiority and brags about Spanish ancestors. The latter meaning is more common.

In the main, the denial of African ancestry and the assertion that race "does not matter" serve an important social purpose by lowering the potential for interracial conflict. As explained in chapter 1, a lower level of racial conflict is associated with a greater number of socioracial status groups, the resulting ambivalence about racial identity on the part of individuals, and thus an absence of group polarization. The racial identity of subordinate groups, particularly those of African descent and phenotype, is often sublimated in the denial that race matters at all. This is exhibited in a powerful "white-bias," manifested in "bleaching" through intermarriage and otherwise attempting to eradicate Negro features, and identifying with a higher status socioracial group.

All of the above theoretical expectations are abundantly met in the case of Puerto Rico. There is a preoccupation with "raising the color" of individuals and otherwise moving up in the color/status continuum. In reality, such attempts to attain higher socioracial status rarely succeed, even in highly flexible racial traditions. This matters little, however. What is important in cases such as Puerto Rico is the *belief* that *individual* mobility is possible and desirable—through intermarriage, concubinage, cultural and economic achievement, or simple denial of racial ancestry. It is often those at the lowest socioracial stratum—who most resemble Africans—who are the great believers in the myth of racial democracy and most protective of the socioracial status structure. For them, the myth serves as a psychological mechanism to preserve hope in circumstances that do not justify any.

This syndrome explains why the racial self-identification of Puerto Ricans has become increasingly "white," with little or no real shift in the real somatic or genetic distribution of the population. In a relatively short span of time, Puerto Ricans have gone from predominantly "black" to predominantly "white."[6] An 1846 survey registered an absolute majority as "Negro"; the first racial survey undertaken by the War Department in 1898 recorded a 60 percent "white" majority (589,390 out of a total of 953,243); and in 1950 only 23 percent were classified as Negro. The census asked the race of inhabitants until the year 1950, at which time racial classifications were dropped (1950 U.S. Census of Population, Vol. 2, "Characteristics of the Population," Parts 51–54 cited in Willoughby, 1905, p. 82). The 1950 census classified the population into Whites, Negroes, Other. As the result of an agreement between the government of Puerto Rico and the U.S. Census Bureau in 1958, it was decided not to continue to ask for racial classifications. The rationale illustrates the statistical analogue of "no entiendo" discussed on pages 127–28: It is not part of the culture to ask about race, therefore the government of Puerto Rico requested that it be dropped. Thus, since 1960, the "Hispanic" classification has been introduced, and specific information on "white" or "Negro" Puerto Ricans is no longer easily available.

Today, the operative racial tradition in Puerto Rico is undeniably more flexible than in the United States, and the intensity of racial hostility and conflict is far lower.[7] Anyone who has had extended contact with Puerto Ricans is struck by the great variety of shades of complexion from purest white to darkest black. Puerto Ricans also insist that racial discrimination does not exist in their country (Hollister, 1967). At the same time, some who deny that discrimination exists admit that there are social, economic, and other advantages often enjoyed by whites and mulattoes that are not shared by Negroes. In the main, however, the notion of a color-blind society is a myth—as even a casual observer of the physical features of Puerto Rico's political, economic, and social leaders can so easily see.

The overwhelming majority of the prominent Puerto Rican politicians *of all political tendencies* have been in recent times phenotypically "white"— including every single elected governor, from Luis Muñoz Marin to Roberto Sanchez Villella, Luis A. Ferré, Rafael Hernández Colón, Carlos Romero Barceló, and Pedro Rosselló; and independence leaders Antonió Gonzales, Juan Mari Brás, Ruben A. Martinez Berrios, among a host of others. Of course, even while they hold fast to the color-blind myth, Puerto Ricans know quite well the social reality; namely, the story about a dark Puerto Rican politician who, told by his assistant after a minor traffic accident that he looked "pale," replied: "Quick, get the camera!"[8]

It was not so in the earlier years after the American takeover. Among the leading political personalities of Puerto Rico, several were clearly identifiable as Negroes. Among these was José Celso Barbosa (1857–1921), a Negro physician and educator, and founder of the Puerto Rican Republican Party in 1900. Barbosa was an ardent admirer of the United States, who aspired to lead Puerto Rico to statehood, regardless of whatever "transformations the Congress deem necessary in accordance with the civic and cultural state of the country" (quoted in Carrión Morales, 1983, p. 141).

Interestingly, the individual supporting independence was Pedro Albizu Campos, an ardent nationalist, of mixed-black/white ancestry. Unlike José Celso Barbosa, Albizu's education at Harvard University, and his experiences in the segregated American army, as well as serving a prison term for nationalist activities (which he served in Atlanta, Georgia), did not leave him with an undying faith in American political institutions. His reaction was the very opposite and the United States and its institutions—as well as its rigid racial tradition—were the object of a "fiery, uncompromising attack" (Hanson, 1960, p. 221), which culminated in his help in planning a shooting attack in the Gallery of the U.S. Congress, on March 1, 1954.

Earl Parker Hanson wrote: "Pedro Albizu Campos was and is a bitter man who hates the United States venomously. That he was an illegitimate child and dark in skin are said to have added to his bitterness. Certainly in all his political speeches he ceaselessly and relentlessly attacked the United States on the one point in which we are weakest in human relations—the race issue" (p. 71). Albizu was drafted into the U.S. Army during World War I and allowed to transfer for duty in Puerto Rico, where he was sure that no color line would be drawn (p. 70). He was wrong on this account. The U.S. Army had introduced the color line, which it maintained until 1948, and Albizu was assigned to the 375th Regiment, a Negro regiment whose activities were confined to doing degrading manual labor and garrison duty in Puerto Rico and Panama. Hanson concluded: "Acutely sensitive to the many snubs he had received as a Negro, he now began to devote his life to the cause of Puerto Rico's independence" (p. 71). For much of the period during which Albizu lived in the United States and served in the military, *Plessy v. Ferguson* was the law of the land. He died in 1965.

Another prominent black, an exception to the contemporary rule of mostly white political activists, was Ernesto Ramos Antonini, speaker of the Puerto Rican House during the 1950s, who was a supporter of Commonwealth status. Although hard to demonstrate, it is not coincidental that, as the American racial tradition influenced the island more and more, the skin tone of its political leadership lightened to the point where virtually all leading politicians of today are white.

The white bias is also apparent in the type of women who have represented the islands in international beauty pageants (and won the Miss Universe title in the 1970s and 1980s). It's very rare, too, to find dark-skinned Puerto Ricans in the upscale tourist industry, in the financial world, and in business. The situation described by Francesco Cordasco and Eugene Bucchioni in the 1970s still stands:

The upper class is concerned with "limpieza de sangre" ["cleanliness of the blood," from African traits], and the perpetuation of special privileges within its own select group. Because of this, members tend to exclude any outgroup, and Negroes are easily defined because of their obvious physical differences. . . . Even though there are some Negroes who reach high business, professional and political positions, they are still considered to be unacceptable as members of the intimate circles . . . treated as complete equals in business or political encounters among men, but never accepted in the home or in intimate social gatherings. An upper class man may marry a mulatto woman without too much censure, but his wife will never be completely accepted and will know that she will be "excused" from many of the functions of the other women of her husband's group.[9]

Thus, as Cordasco and Bucchioni put it, "the white Puerto Rican has a weighty burden: he must be 'white' not only to white continentals, but also to other 'white' Puerto Ricans."[10]

The burden of *dark* Puerto Ricans, of course, is much heavier. While there is no official segregation, darker Puerto Ricans are heavily concentrated in lower socioeconomic positions and in the poorer residential areas. Research confirms what a simple car drive through San Juan and other towns makes so evident. The few blacks encountered in the higher-income residential areas of San Juan are often maids, particularly from neighboring islands. Again from Mathews (1974):

The black Puerto Ricans are quick to point to the examples of the lack of racial barriers or discrimination. With pride they recite the social event they have been invited to, the intimate parties of upper-class whites in which they have been admitted and made to feel at home, the absence of any personal experience of denial because of race, and so on. Such acceptance, such admittance, would disappear if they began to be aggressive or were identified as [disturbing] the social serenity by questioning the order of things. Furthermore, their own chances of advancement, which obviously depend on the whiter elements of the society would be jeopardized if they contributed to a polarization of the racial issue. (P. 318)

In America, most Puerto Ricans enter a no-man's land of racial marginality. They are not accepted as whites by white Americans, and they are reluctant to identify as African—though they are often forced by the strict de facto residential segregation in America to live in black neighborhoods. One defense is to engage in patterns of behavior clearly distinguishing them as not Negro, such as speaking only Spanish. Listen to the exchange between Langston Hughes' fictional character Jess B. Simple and a dark Puerto Rican in a Harlem bar:

[Jess] said: "Puerto Rican? Are you one?"

He said, "Si, are you one too?"

I said, "You look just like me, don't you? Who's the darkest, me or you?"

He said, "You, darkest."

I said, "I admit I have an edge on almost anybody. But you are colored too, daddy-o, don't forget, Puerto Rican or not."

He said, "In my country, no."

I said, "In my country, yes. Here in the U.S.A., you, me, all colored folks are colored."

He said, "*No entiendo.*"[11]

POLITICAL DEVELOPMENTS UNDER AMERICAN RULE

The Milestones

In the Treaty of Paris following the end of the Spanish-American War, Puerto Rico was formally annexed by the United States. The annexation added a territory geographically separated from the United States with large numbers of people culturally distinct from the dominant Anglo-Saxon culture of North America. The political and constitutional issues that arose from the acquisition of the overseas territories after 1898, discussed in chapter 3, initially affected Puerto Rico in the same manner as all other territories. Thereafter, Puerto Rico followed a distinct political evolution. In contrast with the reflexive exportation of the American racial tradition and lack of recognition of the different social relations, in the political arena there was a realistic attempt to take into consideration the preexisting conditions of Puerto Rico.

Thus, the Foraker Act of 1900 established a temporary civil government for Puerto Rico in place of the military administration to which the island had been subjected (as in the other territories) for the first fifteen months after the war. (As described in the next chapter, the U.S. Virgin Islands experienced very different treatment, and navy administration there lasted fifteen *years.*) The Senate report that accompanied the Foraker Act stated the intention to permit Puerto Rican participation in government and to avoid, as far as possible, radical changes in the Spanish Charter of Autonomy (discussed earlier).

In 1904, the Supreme Court ruled in *Gonzalez v. Williams* that Puerto Ricans were not "aliens" and, therefore, could not be refused entry into the United States, and in 1917, an Organic Act, known as the Jones Act, replaced the provisions of the Foraker Act. The 1917 Organic Act provided for a territorial constitution, increasing Puerto Rican political autonomy and self-government, and conferred U.S. citizenship on all Puerto Ricans. Congress, however, reserved to itself the power to nullify all insular legislation and the president of the United States continued to have the final authority to promulgate insular laws. Also, the other political disadvantages of being an unincorporated territory were not removed by the 1917 Organic Act. As explained in chapter 3, these disadvantages included the denial of many constitutional protections unless specifically mandated by Congress and, of course, lack of representation in Congress. Thus, when the nineteenth Amendment granting women the vote was passed in 1927, the right to vote was not extended to Puerto Rican women, although they were American citizens.

Under the leadership and push of Luis Muñoz Marin, this state of affairs was changed in 1950, with congressional passage of Public Law 600, "in the nature of a compact" by which "fully recognizing the principle of government by consent . . . the people of Puerto Rico may organize a government pursuant to a constitution of their own adoption." PL 600 was to be approved or disapproved by a referendum held in accordance with the laws of Puerto Rico. Approval would result in a convention to draft a constitution. The law was approved, and the first Puerto Rican constitution, PL 447, was eventually drafted and submitted to Congress following popular endorsement through another referendum. The draft constitution included the provision that any amendments must be consistent with the U.S. Constitution, the Puerto Rican Federal Relations Act, and PL 600 itself.

In 1952 the Congress of the United States formally approved the Constitution of Puerto Rico, and entered into a compact that established a "Commonwealth relationship" between Puerto Rico and the United States. Under the compact, Puerto Ricans formed an autonomous political community in permanent union with the United States based on the irreversible bond of American citizenship. In 1953, the General Assembly of the United Nations recognized the creation of the Commonwealth and removed Puerto Rico from the list of non–self-governing territories. The political status of Puerto Rico today remains essentially the same as that established in 1952.

The Ambiguity of Current Political Status

As noted in chapter 3, the Insular Case rulings placed the territories gained after the Spanish-American War "in an indeterminate state of ambiguous existence for an indefinite period." As a dissenting judge noted, the rulings postponed indefinitely a decision on status and placed Puerto Rico in political limbo. The granting of "Commonwealth status" in 1952, while a major clarification and a huge step forward in political evolution, did not put to rest the issue of political status.

The debate on further political evolution continued, with the three main political parties identified with the three status options of Commonwealth, statehood, or independence. Periodically, referenda have been held on changing political status, without success. In 1967, a referendum was held in Puerto Rico on three political status alternatives: statehood, independence, or continued Commonwealth status. Commonwealth status was supported by 60.4 percent of the voters, 39.0 percent favored statehood, and 0.6 percent supported independence (GAO, 1985). In 1991 a referendum was organized by the Partido Popular Democratico (PPD) to adopt a charter of "democratic rights," which included guarantees of U.S. citizenship, regardless of future changes in Puerto Rico's constitutional status, and the maintenance of Spanish as the official language. The proposed charter was rejected by a margin of 53 percent to 45 percent. The result was widely interpreted as an indication that the majority of voters wished to retain Puerto Rico's Commonwealth status. In 1993 a referendum was held on a petition to clarify the nonterritorial nature of the bilateral compact between Puerto Rico and the United States and to guarantee future economic, political, and social resources. The referendum also had significance for the status issue. Enhanced Commonwealth status received 48 percent, statehood 46 percent, and independence less than 4 percent. The question of status remains a permanent feature of political dialogue and daily conversation. Forty years after the approval of the Puerto Rican Constitution, it is a rare occurrence in Puerto Rico to have a social gathering without somebody bringing up at some point the question of status.

The debate is kindled in part by genuine uncertainties about the permanence of Commonwealth status in the face of periodic doubts raised on the American side. As recently as 1991, questions were raised about the permanence of: (1) American citizenship for persons born in Puerto Rico; and (2) the Commonwealth relationship itself. In a bill proposed by the Bush administration (S. 244), the continuation of citizenship was linked to statehood. However, as Lawrence H. Tribe argued: "American citizenship of the people of Puerto Rico is not rendered vulnerable by . . . any . . . Supreme Court decision or legal doctrine. Puerto Ricans cannot be stripped of their citizenship by Congress, and it would be completely fallacious to suppose that only statehood for Puerto Rico would assure permanent citizenship." He concluded that the contest between statehood and commonwealth must be resolved on its own merits and termed the citizenship issue "an irrelevant distraction."[12]

The second issue raised in S. 244 pertained to Puerto Rico's "unique juridical status . . . under which Puerto Rico enjoys sovereignty, like a State . . . [and] an autonomy consistent with its character, culture and location." The Bush administration termed this status as "totally inconsistent with the Constitution." Again, legal precedents do not support this view. The U.S. Supreme Court has on several occasions recognized and accepted the "unique" status of Puerto Rico and deemed it sovereign over matters not ruled by the Constitution of the United States.[13]

As noted, the question was (temporarily) put to rest by the rejection of the statehood option in the 1993 referendum. It is nevertheless true that Commonwealth status remains ambiguous and inherently uncertain. Indeed, even the semantics differ, with the term "Commonwealth" translated into Spanish as *Estado Libre Asociado*—Free Associated State. On the American side, the situation illustrates the problem of a generic policy of self-determination with no ultimate status signal (GAO, 1985). On the Puerto

Rican side, the "neither fish nor fowl" nature of Commonwealth status keeps alive the options of statehood and (much more remote) independence.

STATUS OPTIONS AND POLITICAL ACTIVITY

Political Leadership and Parties

Chapter 1 explained how a flexible racial tradition, such as that inherited by Puerto Rico, leaves more space for political ideology as opposed to race-based political action. In Puerto Rico, however, ideology has been entirely dominated and defined by the status issue, which remains the subtext of Puerto Rican politics just as the cold war used to dominate American foreign policy. Other important political issues or ideological differences have been accordingly sidestepped, neutralized, or neglected.

From the very beginning of the American period in Puerto Rico to this date there has been continuous tension between proponents of closer ties with the United States and independence advocates. Thus, Eugenio Maria de Hostos called for self-determination and a plebiscite for independence soon after the Treaty of Paris ceded Puerto Rico to the Americans.

Later, Pedro Albizu Campos, a Harvard-educated lawyer, founded the Nationalist Party and is considered the father of the Puerto Rican independence movement. Albizu Campos was of mixed-race, with definite Negro somatic features, a man of integrity, strong convictions, and even stronger principles. After his initial political successes on the island (indeed, *because* of his successes), he became the subject of systematic federal persecution and spent much of his later life in prison—partly from violating the 1930s "gag law" which, in a manner incomprehensibly antithetical to all American laws and values, prohibited the expression of nationalist opinions. Albizu Campos remains to this day a figure much admired by Puerto Ricans of all political convictions.

At the opposite end of the political spectrum, José Celso Barbosa, a black physician, was a fervent advocate of statehood, and founder of the Republican Party in 1900. An intermediate position was occupied by Luis Muñoz Rivera and, later, by his son Luis Muñoz Marin. Although Muñoz Marin was originally an associate of Albizu Campos, he founded the Popular Democratic Party in 1938; devised the compromise "Commonwealth" status between independence and statehood (echoes of Booker T. Washington); and set the background for the economic transformation of Puerto Rico through "Operation Bootstrap."

Frustrated by the restrictions on overt political activity, and by the weakening of proindependence sentiment arising from the material benefits given by the federal government, an extreme manifestation of independence sentiment took place in 1950. A group of Puerto Rican members of the Nationalist Party attacked Blair House in Washington (where President

Truman was residing while the White House was being renovated); in a separate episode, others unleashed a shooting within the U.S. House of Representatives. Albizu Campos was held responsible, arrested, and again imprisoned until shortly before his death in 1965. While the attack was a clear failure in its own terms, it may have been a political success in ways its authors never intended. It may have helped persuade Congress to grant the substantial expansion of political autonomy launched with PL 600 and, eventually, incorporated in the new Constitution of Puerto Rico.

Except for a nostalgic remnant of cultural nationalists, who urge the creation of a system centered on Spanish language and culture, political leadership and parties in Puerto Rico are still organized around the three status options. Thus, the political spectrum encompasses: (1) statehood advocates, clustered around the National Progressive Party (*Partido Nuevo Progresista*—PNP—the successor of Celso Barbosa's Republican Party); (2) proponents of continued Commonwealth status, organized around Luiz Muñoz Marin's Popular Democratic Party (*Partido Democratico Popular*—PDP); and (3) independence supporters, organized in several small parties, of which the largest is the Puerto Rican Independence Party (*Partido Independentista Puertorriqueno*—PIP), founded in 1950 by "independentista" dissidents from within Muñoz Marin's Partido Popular Democratico (PPD), led by lawyer Gilberto Concepcion de Gracia.

Although Puerto Ricans don't vote in federal elections, they do participate in party politics and are represented at the Republican and Democratic conventions (as are Guam and the Virgin Islands). The PNP is affiliated with the national Republican Party and generally takes conventional Republican positions.[14] The PDP is affiliated with the Democrats and similarly adopts middle-of-the-road positions. The PIP has a left-wing ideology whose vagueness is compensated for by vigorous rhetoric, but whose credibility among its natural potential constituency of working people is weakened by its decidedly upperclass political leadership.[15]

The Status Options

Since the mid-1970s, a number of status initiatives have been put forward. In 1975, a modified Commonwealth proposal, the "Compact of Permanent Union Between Puerto Rico and the United States" was introduced to Congress but was never reported out of committee. In 1976, President Ford proposed statehood for Puerto Rico, but no action was taken. In 1978 and 1981, Presidents Carter and Reagan, respectively, also supported statehood as an option, if the Puerto Rican people expressed such a desire in a plebiscite. In 1991, as mentioned earlier, a bill was put forward to force the issue, by linking continued American citizenship to the acquisition of statehood, but the 1993 referendum turned down the option. What do the status options actually entail?

Statehood. Prominent statehood advocate (currently Puerto Rico's non-voting congressman in the House of Representatives) Carlos Romero Barceló calls Puerto Rico "a nation of disenfranchised U.S. citizens." In his February 9, 1989, address to Congress, President Bush apparently agreed: "I've long believed that the people of Puerto Rico should have the right to determine their own political future. Personally, I strongly favor statehood. But I urge the Congress to take the necessary steps to allow the people to decide in a referendum."

It was the grant of U.S. citizenship to the people of Puerto Rico in 1917 that made statehood a possible alternative.[16] For Puerto Rico, statehood would mean that:

—the Commonwealth of Puerto Rico would be admitted into the Union permanently as a State on an equal footing with the other States. The current constitution and laws of Puerto Rico would be accepted as the constitution and laws of the new State, and the Constitution and laws of the United States would be extended in full to Puerto Rico;

—the U.S. citizenship of persons born in Puerto Rico would be constitutionally guaranteed and be equal in all respects to the citizenship of persons born in the other States. Citizens of the new State would be entitled to vote for the President and Vice President and would elect the apportioned number of Members of the House of Representatives and two Members of the Senate;

—residents of the new State would be treated equally with residents of the other States in all Federal programs and would assume all obligations of residents of the States of the Union;

—residents of Puerto Rico would lose any special benefits associated with commonwealth status, and other provisions therein would similarly be deleted. However, the Congress would act to provide a reasonable and fair transition for the economy of Puerto Rico.

The two most contentious issues are the loss of the special economic benefits from the current status and the question of language. Spanish is the official language of Puerto Rico under Commonwealth status. It is doubtful, with the increasing strength of the movement in favor of declaring English the official language of the United States, that the U.S. Congress would admit to statehood a Spanish-speaking territory.

Commonwealth. At the beginning, the PDP stood four-square for eventual independence, and most of the prominent members were independentistas. As mentioned earlier, Muñoz Marin turned gradually away from early independence and devised the intermediate Commonwealth status. The goal of eventual independence was not formally abandoned; indeed, the Puerto Rican term for "Commonwealth" is *Estado Libre Asociado*, or Free Associated State, clearly implying the possibility that the "free state" may well decide to sever its "association." But for the foreseeable future, the question of status was put on the back burner. The PDP was organized to improve the conditions of the lower classes, particularly the *jíbaro* (peasant) of the mountain interior. The party's platform was summarized in the slogan: "Bread, land and liberty." In concert with the populist New Deal Governor Rexford Guy Tugwell, the PDP initiated such economic reforms as land redistribution, enforcement of minimum wage and hour laws, a progressive income tax, and the establishment of an economic development program.

The kinship between the "Commonwealth" solution and the "pragmatic materialism" component of American colonialism is evident. Indeed, whether Muñoz Marin was motivated by U.S. support for his personal political ambitions, or because he had become persuaded that independence was impossible (or some combination of both), his program—to forego claims for early independence in exchange for a measure of autonomy and material benefits—was a linear descendant of Booker T. Washington's Atlanta Compromise. And, analogous to views about Booker T. Washington, he is viewed as either a national realist who made the best of an unfavorable situation, or a turncoat who gave up his ideals and friends for personal political gain.

Since 1989, the option of "enhanced Commonwealth" status has been discussed. The approach would be to enable Puerto Ricans to obtain the same economic and social benefits as other U.S. citizens while attaining maximum cultural and political autonomy but in a context of permanent union with the United States. The PDP proposal calls for "more equitable participation . . . in all federal programs that provide grants or services to citizens of the United States . . . [and] safeguards for the distinct cultural identity of the people of Puerto Rico." Enhanced Commonwealth could mean the following:

—Puerto Rico would be in a permanent union with the United States that could only be altered by mutual consent. The Commonwealth would be an autonomous body politic, not incorporated into the United States, and sovereign over matters governed by the Constitution of Puerto Rico, consistent with the U.S. Constitution;

—the American citizenship of persons born in Puerto Rico would be guaranteed and secured, and equal to that of citizens born in the United States. The individual rights, privileges, and immunities provided for by the U.S. Constitution would automatically apply to residents of Puerto Rico;

—residents of Puerto Rico would be entitled to benefits under federal social programs equally with residents of the several states contingent on equitable contributions from Puerto Rico as provided by law;

—to enable Puerto Rico to govern on matters necessary to its economic, social, and cultural development under its constitution, the Commonwealth would be authorized to submit proposals to the United States for the entry of Puerto Rico into international agreements, or the exemption of Puerto Rico from specific federal laws. The U.S. government would consider such proposals on an expedited basis through special procedures.

The enhanced Commonwealth proposal has been criticized as wanting one's cake and eating it too. This is too harsh. While the proposal does call for additional material benefits and powers for Puerto Rico, it counterbalances the requests by offering permanent union with the United States (albeit as an unincorporated autonomous entity).

Independence. Since World War II, the highest measure of support for independence in contemporary times came in the 1952 elections, when the PIP obtained 19 percent of the vote. Since then, the independence movement has splintered into several small parties, some of which were identified with specific individuals and have now disappeared. The PIP has remained as the largest single party, although it, too, had suffered substantial loss of support, generally receiving less than 5 percent of the vote. Recognizing the fears and concerns of the average Puerto Rican, the current PIP independence platform is very moderate and has the following components:

—an independent Puerto Rico would have a republican form of government through a constitution guaranteeing the full protection of human rights;
—the United States would be requested to provide a reasonable and fair economic transition to independence for a minimum period of ten years. The relevant precedent is U.S. Senator Tyding's bill of 1945 calling for Puerto Rican independence after a twenty-one year transition period, in which the island was to receive special economic treatment. Transitional measures to be considered could include: (1) annual block grants corresponding to present federal spending in the Commonwealth; (2) continued preferential entry of Puerto Rican products into the U.S. market; and (3) incentives for American investors and lenders similar to those presently provided by law;
—eventual demilitarization of Puerto Rico;
—independence would not affect the continued use in Puerto Rico of U.S. dollars, nor the rights of individuals to benefits acquired by virtue of services rendered to the United States, nor impair the American citizenship of persons born before the date of independence.
—other questions would be negotiated after independence directly between the United States and an independent Puerto Rican government.

The evident reasonableness of the independentista platform also poses the political problem of lack of substantive differentiation from the option of enhanced Commonwealth status. Other than a passport of a different color, it is hard to see the real difference between the "moderated independence" option and the "enhanced Commonwealth" option. "Moderated independence" may well be a prescription for the final political oblivion of the PIP.

A Look into the Future

Independence leader Ruben A. Martinez Berrios explains the status problem in terms of the racism in American policy:

> It is not at all surprising that even today, one still finds support in the United States for the notion that colonialism by consent is not a bad thing, so long as the colonial power is the United States. It should not be difficult to perceive the undertones of racism in all of this. Isn't there, really, at the root of our problem an unstated premise that Puerto Ricans can't really administer a republic responsibility, that the American presence provides a "checks and balances" element to the otherwise "unsteady Latin temperament" that for Puerto Ricans to be wards of the United States is really for the Puerto Ricans' own good. (Quoted in Falk, 1986, p. 35)

The argument is articulate and could even be convincing, except for the inconvenient fact that Puerto Ricans insist on voting against independence by huge margins, in elections and referenda that all observers have found to be free and fair. Certainly, the prospect of losing the benefits provided by a century of "pragmatic materialism" (see chapter 5) may well explain the voters' attitude. One could therefore argue that Puerto Rican opposition to independence has been bought with American goodies. Be that as it may, the fact remains that self-determination and respect for human rights must give the people of Puerto Rico the power to decide, whatever one may think of their motives and lack of perspective. They have made it quite clear that independence is simply not in the cards.

Statehood commands much greater support, but has repeatedly failed to muster a majority. It is therefore impossible to be sure whether Congress would ever accept Puerto Rico as a new state if Puerto Ricans did vote to so request statehood. While it is clear that the influence of race has been waning, it would be naive to believe that the racial make-up of the Puerto Rican population is irrelevant to the question. Important, also, are the cultural differences. If Puerto Ricans were to insist on cultural differentiation *by law*, greater than that possessed by other states of the Union, the statehood option would be seriously compromised. Nor is there a credible prospect of Puerto Ricans willing to abandon legal protection for their language and cultural institutions. In any case, to repeat, the willingness of Congress to accept Puerto Rican statehood, and the conditions it might require, cannot be tested unless there is first a formal request for statehood, through a majority vote of Puerto Ricans in a free and fair referendum. In 1993 the option was turned down once more. Many years are likely to pass before it is presented again.

And so, continuation of the present Commonwealth status, enhanced or not, appears the most likely outcome for the foreseeable future. The heritage of pragmatic materialism will continue to be felt, in its positive and negative aspects, throughout the relationship between this Caribbean island and its former colonial power. It is even possible (though improbable) that, through its new element of "permanent union," enhanced Commonwealth might put to rest the status dispute for a long time to come (at least until a new generation rediscovers the old debates of their grandfathers.)

NOTES

1. As of 1995, Puerto Rico had a larger population than Delaware, 706,000; Rhode Island, 997,000; Arizona, 3,187,000; Colorado 3,231,000; and was slightly smaller than Connecticut, which had 3,275,000 people. *U.S. Census, July 1, 1995* (Suitland, Md.: Government Printing Office, 1995).

Information for 1997 was obtained from a phone conversation, March 1997, with the Puerto Rico Federal Affairs Administration, Washington, D.C.

2. This section is based on Julian H. Steward et al., *The People of Puerto Rico: A Study in Social Anthropology* (1956; reprint, Urbana: University of Illinois Press, 1972), pp. 496–97, which is based on Jose Colomban Rosario and Justina Carrión, *Problemas Sociales: El Negro:Haiti-Estados Unidos-Puerto Rico* (San Juan: N.P., 1940).

3. Quoted in Harlan et al., 1975, p. 455.

4. Jose Louis Gonzalez, "The Four-Storeyed House: Africans in the Forging of Puerto Rico's National Identity," in *Slavery and Beyond: The African Impact on Latin America and the Caribbean*, ed. Darien J. Davis (Wilmington, Del.: Jaguar Books on Latin America, 1995), p. 180.

5. Ibid., pp. 180–81 (italics in original).

6. Mathews, 1974, p. 301.

7. This is evident, among other things, from various colloquialisms—e.g., the use of "negrito" ("blackie") as a term of affection.

8. Quoted in Carr, 1984, p. 59. Frederick J. Hollister reported on a survey of college students, which he undertook at the University of Puerto Rico at Mayaguez during the spring semester of 1966–1967 to investigate the opinions of Puerto Rican college students regarding the relationships between skin color and respect and opportunities in Puerto Rico. Puerto Ricans in his sample: (1) denied the significance of skin color as affecting feelings of respect. Among those who disagreed, those who considered themselves to be white were more likely than mulattoes to express the opinion that white skin color carried advantages as far as respect was concerned. (2) Respondents agreed that persons of all skin colors had the same opportunity. Mulattoes expressed greater optimism regarding equality of opportunity than did whites. (3) Respondents agreed, in spite of their denial that skin color was important and that white skin color was the best to have as far as opportunity and respect were concerned. Mulattoes expressed the belief that their skin color was the best to have. (4) Mulattoes rated Negro skin color as worst to have with greater frequency than did whites. (Hollister, "Skin Color and Life Chances of Puerto Ricans," *Caribbean Studies* 9, no. 3 [1967].)

9. Cordasco and Bucchioni, 1973, p. 58.

10. Ibid.

11. Hughes, 1958, p. 21.

12. This information on the political developments of 1989–1991 is found in

Puerto Rico Proceso Plebiscitario, 1989–91, Vol. 1 (Washington, D.C.: Puerto Rico Federal Affairs Administration, 1992), p. 94.

13. In a 1974 ruling, the Court supported the view of lower federal courts that Commonwealth status implies sovereignty over matters not covered in the U.S. Constitution (*Calero-Toledo v. Pearson Yacht Leasing Co.*), and in 1976 it explicitly recognized the status of Puerto Rico as "unique" (*Examining Board of Engineers, Architects and Surveyors v. Flores de Otero*). Also relevant is the 1988 ruling in *Puerto Rico Department of Consumer Affairs v. Isla Petroleum*.

In December 1992, President Bush, who is prostatehood, issued a seven-paragraph memorandum rescinding a thirty-one-year-old directive by President John F. Kennedy that placed the federal government squarely behind the island's "unique position" as a self-governing American Commonwealth. Under the Bush memo, Puerto Rico is described as "a self-governing territory" that federal agencies should treat "as if it were a state." Bill McAllister, "Bush Gift to Puerto Rico Called Mainly Symbolic," *Washington Post*, December 3, 1992, p. A19.

14. The Republican Party is generally prostatehood.

15. The leader of the PIP for the last generation has been blond, blue-eyed Ruben A. Martinez Berrios, who holds degrees from Yale and Oxford.

16. Some congressional estimates put the cost to the U.S. Treasury for Puerto Rican statehood at as much as $3 billion a year. That would include the costs of bringing funding for all federal programs on the island up to the levels of the states. Cf. Bill McAllister, "Bush Gift to Puerto Rico Called Mainly Symbolic," *Washington Post*, December 3, 1992, p. A19.

7 The Case of the U.S. Virgin Islands

This chapter examines the American colonial experience in the U.S. Virgin Islands and its social and political consequences. Particular attention is given to the impact of substituting the rigid American racial tradition for the more flexible Danish model and the significance for social structure and political status. The chapter concludes with an assessment of prospects for significant change in political status.

THE COUNTRY

The U.S. Virgin Islands, purchased from Denmark in 1917, consist of about one hundred small islands and islets, located about forty miles east of Puerto Rico, in the Anegada Passage. As of 1995, the population can be estimated at about 97,229 and per capita income at about $11,000. The three main islands, accounting for only 132 square miles, are St. Croix (82 square miles and two towns: Christiansted and Frederiksted), St. Thomas (27 square miles, with the town of Charlotte Amalie as the seat of local government), and St. John (19 square miles, mostly the Virgin Islands National Park and the Rockresort at Caneel Bay). The islands have no mineral resources and are physically different from each other, which has shaped their politics. St. Croix has been and remains the most racially conservative of the three, as well as the most industrial. Its fertile plains suited its past as a plantation and slave society. St. Thomas is rugged and mountainous; its beautiful beaches, natural harbors, and duty-free commercial outlets make it a tourist and shopper's favorite. St. John's national underwater park, trails, and camping grounds operated by the Department of the Interior are popular with naturalists.

Congress granted U.S. citizenship to islanders living in the territory in 1927. From 1917–1931 the islands were administered by the U.S. Navy. In 1931, administration was transferred from the navy to the Department of the Interior. Universal suffrage was granted in 1936 to all who could read and write English. Until 1970, the governor was appointed by the president of the United States and since then has been elected by popular vote. There is a unicameral fifteen-person legislature elected for a two-year term and a nonvoting delegate serves in the U.S. Congress. The political status of the islands is that of an "unincorporated territory" (see chapter 3). The "constitution" of the islands is the Revised Organic Act enacted by the U.S. Congress in 1954. Islanders do not vote in presidential elections, although they send delegates to the national Democratic and Republican conventions. There are two political parties organized into three factions: the Democratic Party of the Virgin Islands, the Independent Citizens Movement, and the Republican Party of the Virgin Islands. English is the official language. A person born in the islands is a U.S. citizen at birth.

Tourism has replaced sugar as the major economic activity, accounting for about two-thirds of GDP and of employment. Tourist expenditures are estimated to fluctuate around $700 million annually. The small manufacturing sector consists of textiles, electronics, pharmaceutical and watch assembly; one of the world's largest petroleum refineries is in St. Croix. The agricultural sector is minuscule.

POLITICS, RACE, AND SOCIETY UNDER DENMARK

European rivalry for the islands was keen, and they were controlled by several European nations in rapid succession, including England, France, and Holland, and finally Denmark from 1764 to 1917, when they were purchased by the United States.

Colonial Politics

Under the Danes the islands were administered under the "superior" direction of an appointed governor acting in accordance with instructions from the king of Denmark. A system of dual administration was maintained for the districts of St. Croix and St. Thomas–St. John. Each district consisted of a separate municipality complete with its own Colonial Council, which was empowered to carry out legislative functions. Membership of the St. Croix Council consisted of thirteen elected members, plus five members nominated by the Crown. The Council of St. Thomas–St. John was comprised of eleven elected members; plus four royal nominees.

St. Croix was further divided into electoral districts consisting of town and country. St. Thomas–St. John was divided into three elective districts consisting of town and country. Each subdivision had a set number of elected representatives. Section 36 of the 1906 Colonial Law (No. 124–1906) granted the governor power to dissolve the Colonial Councils. Voting qualifications, reflecting the Danish class bias, were narrowly based on economic rather than racial grounds. In addition to royal nominees, the franchise was limited to a man of "unblemished character . . . who has the right of nativity or has resided in the Danish West Indies for five years, has attained the age of 25 and who either owns property in the municipality calculated to yield a yearly rent of at least 300 francs in St. Thomas and St. John and of at least 700 francs in St. Croix."

Plantation Society

Settlement of the islands was spurred by a series of incentives offered by the Danish crown to Danes willing to settle there. Newcomers were offered land at a nominal fee, they were exempted from taxes for a period of eight years, and all imports and shipments of produce were duty-free for the same period. In 1674 Christian IV decreed that the Danish West India Company could trade with African chiefs. Between 1700 and 1786, the Danes shipped out a yearly average of 2,000 Negro slaves. The growth of slavery depended on the development of the plantation system. The Danes annexed St. John in 1717 and purchased St. Croix from France in 1733. St. Thomas became a plantation colony in 1688.

The success of the settlement program is indicated by the numbers of slaves and plantations. The first census enumerated for St. Thomas in 1688 surveyed 90 plantations. By 1691, the number had increased to 101 and by 1715, there were 160 (Campbell, 1946). There was a corresponding increase in the number of African slaves: from 555 in 1688 to 3,042 by 1715. An ordinance issued on March 24, 1718, decreed that on St. John each planter was required to have one white man on each plantation, a requirement partly designed to increase the island's white population. On St. John in 1728, there were 123 whites and 677 blacks. By 1733 (the year of the slave insurrection on the island), there were 208 whites and 1,087 slaves (Johnston, 1910, p. 347). By 1764, the population numbered 2,500, of which whites accounted for 104. Of the three islands, St. Croix was best suited to plantation crops by virtue of climate and fertility of the soil. This island became the richest sugar island in the Caribbean for a time. Under the ownership of Denmark it reached its peak of wealth about 1796 (Lewisohn, 1964). As St. Croix grew and prospered, the number of slaves increased. From 1773 to 1791, the number increased to over 21,000; by 1802 there were 27,000 slaves (Dookhan, 1972).

The settlement program was successful in attracting Europeans of other than Danish nationality. Harry Johnston (1910) noted that not many Danes came to settle either at St. Croix or St. Thomas. The European planters were chiefly French Protestants—Huguenots—who were unable to live in any French possession, Jews of various nationalities, as well as English, Spaniards, and Swedes. On St. Thomas and St. John, the largest group in 1765 was the Dutch, of which about four-fifths were of "Zeeland and Holland origin" (Westergaard, 1917). The remaining nationalities included Danes, French, Germans, English, and Irish.

Of the three islands, St. Croix and St. John were most thoroughly identified with sugar. The social distinctions among the slaves included natives and newly arrived Africans, house, and field slaves. The first Danish laws defining the legal status of slaves resembled those of the English and French. Basic slave rights included private property, marriage, fixed holidays, family gardens, and lighter work for expectant mothers, the sick and the old (Johnston, 1910). The Danes forbade polygamy, and the Moravian missionaries attempted to establish regularity and order in slave marriages. A royal ordinance of 1755 permitted baptism, Christian instruction, and Christian burial for Christian slaves, protection against harsh treatment by planters, and safeguards to maintain intact families. A decree of 1792 promoted marriage between slaves and encouraged stability in slave relationships. The ordinance decreed: "every Negro pair that lived together continually should be considered a married couple and should have their names recorded in a protocol. Thereafter they were to be looked upon as married until there was some misunderstanding which had to be registered in the protocol before they could be considered separated" (Lewisohn, 1964, p. 195).

Official attitudes toward slave marriages were, however, weakened by the attitude of plantation owners, many of whom disregarded slave marital and social rights. Many plantation owners seduced slave women.

In 1792, a royal ordinance prohibited the importation and exportation of slaves, making Denmark the first slave-owning nation to prohibit the slave trade. While local auctions continued, the export of slaves from the Danish West Indies ceased in 1793. The antislavery movement grew in both Denmark and in the islands. A series of events led to an uprising on July 2–3, 1848, which resulted in the emancipation of slaves on St. Croix. The uprising followed more than a decade and a half of liberal changes introduced by Governor von Scholten.

The Danish Racial Tradition

The flexible racial tradition of the Danes contrasted strongly with that of the Americans and was more in line with existing patterns throughout the Caribbean. The socioracial status of free Negroes could be changed by royal decree, as in 1831 and 1834. For example, King Frederick VI issued a series of proclamations from Copenhagen, which were intended to equalize the socioracial status of a small segment of wealthy and free mixed-race individuals with the status of upper-class whites. The decrees, known as the "Plans for an improved and more distinct organization for the free colored inhabitants of the Danish West India Islands, St. Croix, St. Thomas and St. John," established the criteria for upward mobility and socioracial status reclassification.

The plan abolished the "free briefs," previously held by all free coloreds and in its place substituted classifications based on the establishment of new distinctions among free coloreds, most of whom were mulattoes.[1] The plan established two divisions: the free colored elites and the free colored masses. The first group was further subdivided into three classes. To the first class belonged the high-ranking officers of the colored militia; to the second class belonged the free colored officers. The third group included noncommissioned officers and privates of the free colored corps. A second division was composed of "all the rest of those whose names were registered in the protocols of the colored persons."

The section of the ordinance, which had the effect of regulating behavior and rewarding cultural affectations, authorized the governor to put into the various branches of the first division, individuals who, while not holding a position in the militia, deserved "distinction more or less, on account of superior education, mental capacity, good conduct, situations in life, or from other considerations." (Slave owners also published lists of those with "bad characters.") An interesting section of the plan allowed the governor to manipulate membership in racial groups and to raise socioracial status by transferring an individual from one racial group to another. The relevant section of the plan stated:

Where free persons of color of both sexes assimilate in color to the whites, and they otherwise, by a cultivated mind and good conduct render themselves deserving to stand, according to their rank and station in life, on an equal footing with the white inhabitants, *all the difference which color now causes ought to cease*. The right of deciding thereon, must be left with the Governor-General, who also will direct the names of such persons to be struck off the protocols for the registry of the free colored population, and to be entered as white inhabitants. (Campbell, 1946, p. 15, emphasis added)

The plan also facilitated the movement of a few coloreds into the merchant class, an important group in Danish colonial society: "To a few select members of the first class of the first division was granted the right to hold a Burgher's brief [merchant's license], whereby they will be placed on an equal footing, according to their rank and condition, with His Majesty's white subjects in the colonies who hold burgher's briefs" (Campbell, 1946). The plan also addressed civil rights for coloreds and again reflected the extent to which the racial tradition was flexible in relation to individuals. The police master on St. Thomas was informed that the "free coloreds of both sexes, that belong to the first division, shall be considered and treated in every manner as the white inhabitants." When traveling abroad and in the granting of passports to America, Europe, and other foreign lands, as well as in other public documents, they were not to be referred to as "free coloreds," but by the titles of Mister and Mrs., unless they requested otherwise.

Sociosexual Components of the Danish Racial Tradition

The Danish racial tradition varied in another significant way from the American tradition. While the latter has been fixated on the taboo of interracial sociosexual relations, under the Danes common law marriage between coloreds, blacks, and whites was not legally prohibited, although there does appear to have been informal sanctions against legalizing these relations for economic reasons for and inheritance requirements. The white population during this time was predominantly male, and this contributed to the development of concubinage relations between white men and black or colored women.

An observer of the period describes the accepted pattern in the Danish Antilles: "There are white men who live with Negro women in an ordinary married state, still without having been legally married and they consider their children as legitimate successors." (quoted in Campbell, 1946). Insight into the prevailing mores was offered by Charles Edwin Taylor, an observer of the period, who noted that: "Many years ago the good people of St. Thomas dispensed with marriage. . . . They were not a marrying people. As late as 1835, only 662 persons were married out of a population of 11,071. There were few married among the whites and still less among the coloreds" (Taylor, 1888, p. 34).

But interracial marriages did occur, not only between white men and nonwhite women, but also between white women and colored men. Marriages of the first type, one observer claims, were "more commonly found among lower-class men, with the couples occasionally returning to Europe to live" (Campbell, 1946, p. 20). It appears that patterns of concubinage or marriage differed, depending on whether one was a principal or a secondary white, in a reversal of the pattern noted by M. G. Smith in colonial Jamaica: "Generally the 'principal' whites, who were the wealthier and politically dominant class of white society, had white wives and white families. . . . 'Secondary' whites . . . lacked white wives and white families and the legal sanctions of marriage for their procreative relationships" (Smith, 1965, p. 94). Instead, the early history of the Danish Antilles reveals extensive concubinage among principal whites and occasional intermarriage among secondary whites. It was not unusual during this time for attractive mixed-race women to enter into connubial relationships with powerful white men. The women used their access to the political power of the white partner to wield influence. This informal system of influence and power was a particularly interesting aspect of the Danish racial tradition, and it contrasts strongly with the in-the-shadows relationship which existed, for example, between Thomas Jefferson and Sally Hemins. (The existence of the relationship remains controversial, and the mulatto children allegedly fathered by Jefferson have been consigned to historical obscurity.) The steady erosion of European marriage forms under the pressures of black/white sex and Danish Lutheran pietism gave way to interracial concubinage.

The story of Anna Heegaard illustrates how open concubinage with powerful white men could become, in the hands of clever and attractive women, avenues to wealth and respectability (Lewis, 1972, p. 31). Anna Heegaard was the colored (one-fourth black) mistress of Danish Governor von Scholten, with whom she lived in idyllic conditions in the enchanting hillside mansion of *Bulows Minde* in St. Croix. Heegaard, whose life with von Scholten has been celebrated in a contemporary Danish film, is credited with convincing the married governor, who was deeply in love with her, to emancipate the slaves on St. Croix.

Anna knew that the Governor was the only man in any position able to do much for the slaves. She knew how much the Governor wanted to help the slaves; he was in love with her and that, too, gave her great influence. Together they made a team and together they began a series of measures designed to educate and elevate the slaves . . . toward the day when freedom was granted by the King. (Lewisohn, 1973)

A number of principal whites, such as the governor, did not bring their wives to the Danish territory. It was also customary for the mistresses of these men to function as unofficial wives, with few formal legal rights, but a great deal of influence. Visitors to *Bulows Minde* observed that Heegaard presided over the twice-weekly "At Homes" at Government House. Upperclass whites and coloreds attended these affairs. Whites who did not have the requisite economic and social status were excluded. These patterns replicated themselves in much of the rest of colonial society under the Danes. By contrast, from the very beginning of American contacts with the islands, there was a strong preoccupation with lack of "racial purity" among the islanders. Mixed-race people were among the first to feel the sting of the antimiscegenation sentiment of the American racial tradition.

THE AMERICAN PURCHASE AND ECONOMIC TREATMENT OF THE ISLANDS

The Purchase of the Danish Antilles

American interest in the Danish West Indies predated the Spanish-American conflict. Negotiations in 1866 between Secretary Seward and the Danes led to the signing in October 1867 of a treaty to purchase St. Thomas and St. John for $7.5 million, and a referendum was held in the islands, whose populated voted overwhelmingly in favor of transfer to the United States. In 1870, however, the U.S. Senate refused to approve the purchase, and it was not until 1917 that the islands were purchased by the United States for $25 million.[2] The motive of the United States was frankly strategic, in view of the islands' central location, particularly in relation to Panama, and the canal, and the concern that they might fall into German hands. Once the positive results of the referenda in Denmark and the islands were completed, the Danish government ratified the treaty on December 22, 1916, and President Woodrow Wilson signed it on January 16 and proclaimed U.S. sovereignty on January 25, 1917. On March 3, the president approved the congressional authorization for the necessary appropriation for the temporary government of the islands under naval administration. On March 9 the king of Denmark issued a proclamation to the inhabitants of the islands announcing their transfer to the sovereignty of the United States. And on March 31, at transfer ceremonies in Charlotte Amalie, Secretary of State Lansing handed Danish Minister Brun a draft on the U.S. Treasury for $25 million in gold.

Economic Conditions at the Time of Purchase

Flexibility in racial attitudes notwithstanding, at the time of purchase the islands were in poor economic condition. Infant and adult mortality were high, sanitation and health facilities were lacking, and an inadequate water supply and sewage system presented health hazards. The dominant economic activity on St. Croix were the sugar estates, which provided barely subsistence wages. Conditions were little removed from the days of slavery. Shortly after the purchase, the American naval governor noted that: "There are practically no food crops except yams and sweet potatoes. . . . The islands are incapable of self-support and must continue to be aided by federal appropriations. . . . The natives should be given instruction above all else in the use of their hands."[3] A 1927 visiting Educational Survey Commission from the Hampton Institute noted that even after ten years of American administration, conditions were woeful. (See chapter 4 for the linkage between Booker T. Washington's philosophy and American colonial policy.) The commission commended the efforts of the administration to provide public services through increasing the length of paved roads and improving the water and sanitation systems. The commission noted a decline in population caused by emigration and a decrease in the use of natural and industrial resources of the islands. Infant mortality rates were still among the highest in the "civilized" world. During a visit in 1931, the last year of naval administration, President Hoover referred to the islands as the "poorhouse of the Caribbean."

The nascent outline of the American colonial policy of pragmatic materialism (see chapter 4) is found in a report of the Bureau of Efficiency, which visited the islands in 1929–1930. The bureau's primary recommendation was to: "increase appropriations sufficiently to do energetically at once the things that are necessary to bring about improved conditions and thus make it possible to help Virgin Islanders help themselves . . . with the ultimate result of making the islands entirely self-supporting" (*Report*, 1931 quoted in Evans, 1945, p. 235). Herbert D. Brown, bureau chief, specifically recommended the "priming of the pump of private industry" in partnership with the federal government. It was proposed that tourism be emphasized on St. Thomas; homesteading would be encouraged on St. Croix, where agricultural laborers would grow their own food. The Hampton Institute was encouraged to institute a program of vocational and agricultural education. The implicit quid pro quo was social order and quiet acceptance of American racial mores; this trade-off—pragmatic materialism—remains the economic cornerstone of American policy in the Virgin Islands to this day. The economic and political turning point came in 1931, when administration of the islands were transferred from the Navy Department to the Department of the Interior, which launched an economic improvement program.

Economic Treatment of the Islands

Congressional committees have, since the early days of the purchase, played a major role in administering the Virgin Islands, through providing personnel, capital, and directing economic policy. The outline of the policy that eventually developed was summarized in the Governor's *Annual Report* for 1934, which noted that in matters of health, the eighteen years of American administration had brought tremendous material advances. The water supply was greatly improved. Sewage and waste disposal systems were developed where none existed before. Preventative health measures were greatly increased and included free medical services for those who could not afford to pay. Out-patient clinics and district nursing were established. Health and sanitation expenditures were tremendously increased from those of Danish times. The result was a considerable decrease in the general death rate and in the infant mortality rate, as well as a general rise in the health standards of the people, a condition that separates the U.S. Virgin Islands from other islands in the region. The death rate dropped from 30 per thousand in the last few years of Danish rule to an average of 22.4 per thousand in the period 1919–1930. Public health programs also eradicated malaria and filariasis.

A major concern of American administrators has been the minimization of social unrest by alleviating underlying poor economic conditions.[4] The Virgin Islands Corporation (VICORP), established in 1949 by the U.S. Congress, was given the task of coordinating programs in homesteading, housing development, establishing sugar factories, rum distilleries, and encouraging bay rum production. Other activities included the encouragement of vegetable crops and handicrafts (with scant results), and of a tourist industry and related hotel construction—with remarkable success.

The 1954 Revised Organic Act provided for the return of internal taxes to the territorial government on a matching basis (Van Cleve, 1974, p. 113). The act also provided that products of the islands could enter the United States duty-free if their foreign components did not exceed 50 percent of their value. A third provision of the act permits island taxpayers to satisfy income tax obligations to both the United States and the Virgin Islands by paying tax upon income from *all* sources to the Government of the Virgin Islands. Manufacturing was encouraged by tax exemptions, established by a special provision of the U.S. Tariff Act, to benefit local manufacturers. Tax concessions are also given to American industries locating in the islands, and, in addition to a watch factory, two major industrial operations were established on St. Croix—the Martin-Marietta aluminum-processing plant and the Amerada Hess oil refinery, one of the world's largest. Unfortunately, the technology is highly capital-intensive in both industries, and few local jobs were created. Still, between 1963 and 1973, manufacturing employment rose from less than 700 to over 2,800 in St. Croix.[5] The oil refinery, in particular, has benefited from quotas to encourage shipping to the U.S. mainland, and the company also pays a royalty per barrel to the local government.

There are other economic benefits of pragmatic materialism as well. The Virgin Islands' government offers liberal concessions to private industry, largely modeled after neighboring Puerto Rico's endeavor. The Caribbean Basin Economic Recovery Act, also known as the Caribbean Basin Initiative (CBI) of 1983, however, reduced the competitive advantage of the Virgin Islands by encouraging U.S. private investment *throughout* the Caribbean— the political motive of which was to economically isolate Cuba and Nicaragua. The CBI also created a free trade area through which products manufactured in beneficiary countries could be exported to the United States duty-free. Nevertheless, in general, the economic position of the U.S. Virgin Islands has remained favored. As noted earlier, this is the other side of the American colonial coin, intended to soften the harsher aspects of the American racial tradition and preempt agitation for political status advancement. The rapid economic growth has resulted in, among other things, excess demand for labor—particularly for menial jobs. In turn, this has fostered immigration from other Caribbean islands, which has added to population pressures and contributed to raising the level of social tension and conflict.

The success of the policy is manifested in the islander's satisfaction with the political arrangement which, unlike neighboring Puerto Rico, minimizes political autonomy. As is discussed in the last section, the islanders have not demanded radical status change, mainly because of the benefits of pragmatic materialism and awareness that the American racial tradition would result in setting the predominantly black territory adrift if there was too much political agitation.

The success of pragmatic materialism is seen in Table 7.1, which shows the high per capita income of Virgin Islanders (and Puerto Ricans) relative to other Caribbean nations in 1970 and 1994. (The islands' per capita income, however, remains slightly lower than the lowest among American states—Mississippi and West Virginia.) Tourism has been by far the major contributor to the increase in wealth, both from its direct revenue and from the multiplier impact on construction and spinoff activities.

The high average per capita income, however, masks very unequal income distributions: The vast majority of the population enjoy far lower incomes than the average. Also, it does not offset other problems for the islands resulting from their status limbo and absence of true self-determination. For example, the Virgin Islands have been prevented in major cases before the Third Circuit and the D.C. Circuit Court from establishing a preference for local residents for government employment; the D.C. Circuit Court also prevented the transfer of petroleum excise taxes.[6]

THE RACIAL STRUCTURE

The Racial Structure of the U.S. Virgin Islands

The political status of the islands has been and will continue to be influenced by their racial mix. With the substitution of American racial attitudes for the largely class-based Danish tradition, there has emerged a segmented society in which race is the primary criterion of social stratification. At the time of purchase, reflecting the flexible classification system, "Negroes" of unmixed African ancestry accounted for 74.9 percent of the population, and the mixed-race group 17.7 percent, with whites accounting for just over 7 percent. Today, whites account for almost one-fourth, and mixed-race people are included in the "black" category. The black population decreased slightly from 1930 to 1960, primarily from outmigration. After 1960, black outmigration has been more than offset by the arrival of West Indians from neighboring islands, and by 1990 blacks accounted for the same three-fourths of the population as at the time of purchase. In relative terms, the black population would have increased much faster except for the large influx of white continentals from the late 1950s. (As discussed later, population growth from 1960 to 1980 has been remarkably high, with annual rates of growth in the neighborhood of 10 percent.)

Since 1917, the mixed-race group has been reclassified as black, along the lines of the American racial classification system. As discussed in chapter 2, the U.S. Census does not include Euro-Africans as a separate category, as is the customary practice in most of the Caribbean. (Until 1974, the cate-

Table 7.1
Per Capita Income in Selected Caribbean Countries, 1970 and 1994
(US$ per year)

Country	1970	1994	Percent Increase
Haiti	150	250[a]	67
Jamaica	798	1,340	70
Trinidad & Tobago	900	3,940	337
Puerto Rico	2,450	6,590	169
U.S. Virgin Islands	2,400[b]	11,000[b]	358

[a]The figure is a rough estimate; the World Bank does not list a specific figure for 1994.
[b]International statistical publications do not contain data for the U.S. Virgin Islands. The 1970 estimate is from Harold Mitchell, *Caribbean Patterns: A Political and Economic Study of the Contemporary Caribbean* (New York: John Wiley & Sons, 1972), and the 1994 estimate from the *World Factbook 1995* (Washington, D.C.: Central Intelligence Agency, 1995). The difference in sources make the comparison doubtful. In particular, the 1970 figure is likely to be an underestimate—as it would imply an extremely high annual growth rate of almost 9 percent over twenty years. However, there is corroborative evidence of a 1992 per capita income around $11,000.

Sources (except as noted): World Bank, *World Tables* (Baltimore: Johns Hopkins University Press), for 1970, and *World Development Report*, 1994.

gory "Mixed and other races" in the U.S. Census classification for the islands referred to "Japanese, Chinese, Filipinos and Native Americans.") This apparently trivial "technical" change is symptomatic of the more general ideological stance in matters of race. In practice, however, the small number of individuals of "other races" in the Virgin Islands suggests that the number of Euro-Africans is only slightly overestimated by the data in the "Mixed and other races" category. The proportion of the total population accounted for by that group has remained approximately constant at around 18 percent from the date of purchase to 1960, with a sharp relative decline thereafter attributable to the influx of migrants, both West Indian blacks and white continentals.

Unlike in Puerto Rico, where race is no longer asked on the census at the specific request of the Puerto Rican government (see chapter 5), the population of the Virgin Islands is censed along racial lines, and there is high racial consciousness on the part of all groups. Today, the population of the Virgin Islands is stratified in terms of both race and social status. The racial breakdown of the population from 1917–1990 is shown in Table 7.2.

The Blacks

Among nonwhites the determinants of status have changed since 1917. Prior to 1917, the black elite based their claim to upper-class status on

Table 7.2
Racial Structure of the U.S. Virgin Islands, 1917–1990

Year	Blacks		Whites		Mixed and Other Races		Total
	Number	%	Number	%	Number	%	Number
1917	19,523	74.9	1,922	7.4	4,606	17.7	26,051
1930	17,243	78.3	2,010	9.1	2,759	12.5	22,012
1940	17,176	69.0	2,236	9.0	5,477	22.0	24,889
1950	18,561	69.6	2,945	11.0	5,159	19.3	26,665
1960	20,643	64.3	5,373	16.7	6,092	19.1	32,108
1970	45,309	72.5	11,339	18.1	5,820	9.3	62,468
1980	70,655	73.2	17,305	17.8	8,700	9.0	96,660
1990	75,338	74.0	17,741	17.4	8,730	8.6	101,809

Source: U.S. Census, Washington, D.C.: Department of Commerce.

mixed-race ancestry and on the social divisions institutionalized by the class-conscious Danes. Some blacks and mixed-race individuals held relatively high social status on the basis of culture, former legal status (slave or free), phenotype, and occupation. From 1917, race took over as the primary determinant of status. However, since the boom in real estate began during the 1960s, ownership of land and professional training have become other important status criteria. Therefore, the educational and professional training opportunities provided under the American policy of pragmatic materialism did finally serve to attenuate the rigid elements of the American racial tradition. In this very limited sense, Booker T. Washington's approach has borne some fruit—albeit after fifty years and in a context of black majority rule.

The black middle class in the Virgin Islands includes clerks, secretaries, government employees, skilled artisans, health professionals, and teachers. As in the United States, the term "middle class" is loosely defined when applied to blacks; an income or job that would place a white worker in the "working class" qualifies blacks to be placed in the "middle" class. As Gordon Lewis (1972) noted, in the Virgin Islands the public image of a job counts more than its monetary rewards. Nevertheless, it is noteworthy that the growth of numbers of nonwhites in "upper-class" and "middle-class" occupations, almost five-fold from 1960 to 1970, far outstripped the growth in population and labor force, approximately 100 percent over the same period.

Until the economic boom of the 1960s, most black islanders were very poor, and the poorest were largely darker-skinned native Virgin Islanders—a heritage from the days of plantation society. From 1960, the economic condition of all Virgin Islanders improved markedly—even though income distribution became more unequal, as a result of the influx of wealthy white continentals and of very poor Caribbean islanders. As of the tapering down of the boom, in 1970, the census shows 38 percent of families with a yearly income of less than $5,000 and 15 percent higher than $15,000, compared to a mean family income of $9,062. Today, it is questionable whether a significant number of native islanders are still within the lower economic strata. The poor are mainly "aliens" from neighboring Caribbean islands. "Native" Virgin Island blacks, consequently, now find themselves in an intermediate group between whites and "alien" black immigrants; regrettably, they often express toward immigrant blacks attitudes and prejudices resembling those to which they themselves have been subjected.

The African American Connection

African Americans have long been attracted to the islands, and there is a significant black "continental" group in residence. Among all the overseas territories, the Virgin Islands have experienced American racism in its closest form to that in the United States. The American racial tradition has forged a similar outlook between African Americans and Virgin Islanders, as indiscriminate white racism has affected both groups. Islanders traveling to and living in the United States experienced identical discrimination to African Americans and were reminded of the second-class status they assumed along with American citizenship.

African Americans have held high-level appointments in the island's government. Prior to 1917, two black Americans, Louis van Harm and David Payne, served as American consular representatives to the Danes. After the bleak initial period of appointing only white (navy and civilian) governors, there have been three black "continentals" appointed as governor: William E. Hastie (1946–1949), as the "first Negro Governor"; Archie Alexander (1954–1955); and Walter A. Gordon (1955–1961).[7] African Americans have held other high positions in the insular government, including as commissioners of education and of police. The "connection" has also brought Virgin Islanders to leadership positions in stateside black communities. For example, the late J. Raymond Jones was legendary for his work as a black Tammany Hall leader in Harlem, and Roy Innis, Chairman of the Congress of Racial Equality (CORE), is a native of St. Croix.

The Puerto Ricans

Since the early days following American acquisition of the islands, St. Croix in particular has attracted Puerto Ricans from the neighboring islands of Culebra and Vieques. Puerto Ricans have increasingly been accepted in the islands, and they account for approximately 25 percent of the population, many of whom are Virgin Islands born. Puerto Ricans have also been accepted into the political system, and they have served in the legislature and held the position of lieutenant-governor of the Virgin Islands. Their acceptance has not been without rancor, however, and Virgin Islanders are particularly wary of occasional proposals to merge their island with Puerto Rico.[8]

The Whites

White Americans have long been involved with the islands, predating the purchase. After the purchase, the islands were administered by the U.S. Navy and the U.S. Marines, almost all of whom were white southerners. White "continentals" have been and remain dominant in the islands, both economically and politically, despite their numerical minority of less than 15 percent of the population. Whites differ widely by place of origin and by length of residence in the islands. Their numbers have increased in absolute and relative numbers since 1917 and most sharply since 1960. In addition to white continentals, there are small groups of Danes, Jews, and French.

The Danes have always constituted a tiny resident minority even in the days of Danish rule. Today, their numbers are minuscule—well under one hundred individuals—ranking highest in the social structure on account of culture, European heritage, and what is believed to be their relatively liberal racial attitudes.

A Jewish community—initially of Sephardic origins—has been in the islands since about 1685, when Jews arrived from Spain, Portugal, and neighboring Caribbean islands. The synagogue in St. Thomas was established in 1795 and as of 1995 there were 118 family membership units. The community, never very large, has decreased consistently until recent years—from 400 in 1837 to 257 in 1880, 100 in 1901, and just 50 in 1942. From the 1950s, Jewish Americans began to arrive in significant numbers. The social status of Jews is high on account of culture, economics, and civic-mindedness. Virgin Island Jews have intermarried with islanders, and three governors have been Jewish—Gabriel Milan, Morris de Castro, and Ralph M. Paiewonsky—as have several members of the legislature and an attorney-general.

The small French community of less than 3 percent descend from fisherman migrants from the Caribbean island of St. Barthelemy and has resided mostly in St. Thomas for about a century. Prior to the purchase, the French ranked low in the social structure because of their occupation, income, and general lifestyle. Speaking a French patois (which accounts for their derogatory name of "cha-cha," as blacks decided their chatter sounded), they were "clannish, unassimilated and wearing 18th century clothing . . . snubbed by St. Thomians, light and black" (Paquin, 1971). After 1917, the French saw an instant raise in status on account of race, and they were readily accepted by the new American residents despite the major differences in language, culture, and lifestyle. Naturally, they reciprocated by becoming increasingly race conscious themselves.

The "Aliens"

Significant numbers of people from other Caribbean islands have come into the U.S. Virgin Islands, either to stay or as a transit point for hoped-for entry into the continental United States. Because of illegal entries, it is impossible to estimate their number with precision. As of 1992, probably an estimated 55,000 "aliens" were believed to be in the Virgin Islands, virtually all of African ancestry, dark phenotype, and Caribbean culture. They occupy the lowest rungs of the social and economic ladder and are heavily discriminated against by other Virgin Islanders—white or black. One of the most disturbing consequences of the American racial tradition has been its internalization by many Virgin Islands' blacks, who behave toward the aliens in much the same way as white continentals have behaved toward them—from gross stereotyping to outright discrimination and hostility.

SOCIAL AND RACIAL CONFLICT

Racial Discrimination

Race relations have been characterized by resentment and hostility in this "American Paradise" virtually from the day of purchase, generated overnight by the racial tradition carried by the American administrators. In his 1990 autobiography, *Memoirs of a Governor: A Man for the People*, former Governor Ralph M. Paiewonsky called racial discrimination "more serious than any of the other problems I had to deal with, because of its implications for the Virgin Islands as a whole and its potential for destructive development."

While racism was very strong during the military administration, with the transfer of authority to the civilian administration and the limited local autonomy provided by the 1936 Organic Act (discussed below) a modus vivendi in the still-small community had been reached. As Paiewonsky noted, it was "with the entry of white Americans to live here after World War II [that] race relations began to change" for the worse.[9] This is confirmed by *U.S. News & World Report* that reported in May 1961 "racial trouble is being imported by U.S. citizens who are moving here in growing numbers—and bringing their segregationist customs with them."

An investigation by the Governor's Commission on Human Relations, during this time, found that discrimination based on race was widely practiced by real estate agencies and social clubs, particularly on St. Croix. An example of de facto segregation (supported in this case by the federal government) is the case of Water Island, located just off St. Thomas harbor.

THE CASE OF THE U.S. VIRGIN ISLANDS 155

The island, the fourth largest of the Virgin Islands group, has been developed as a primarily all-white community of affluent continentals. The island was owned by the Interior Department and leased to Water Islands, Inc., which, in turn, subleased it to the Sprat Bay Club. On December 12, 1996, the Department of the Interior returned Water Island to the territorial government. On St. Croix, whites have steadfastly resisted the construction of much needed low-income housing, while permitting the construction of high-income residential communities. Even routine tourism was systematically affected: until the mid-1970s, car rental agencies on the islands required black customers to fulfill lengthy prerental requirements not required of white customers.

During the 1970s, the small white community increasingly sent their children to private schools. The proportion increased as the level of schooling became higher. In 1970, for example, whites accounted for 13.8 percent of the total private and secondary school population, but only 6.5 percent of public school enrollment and 38.3 percent of private and parochial school enrollment (McFerson, 1979a). The ugliest overt expression of racial conflict was a series of racial murders in the early and mid-1970s. The murders in 1972 at the Fountain Valley Country Club (since renamed) were widely publicized, but many incidents occurred, including murders of white residents and visitors, such as Cheryl Barr, a friend of this writer, who had gone to St. Croix to do social work for the poorest communities of the island. Since the 1970s, overt conflict has been vigorously repressed because of its threat to the tourism-based prosperity of the islands. Black Virgin Islanders, dependent on tourism as much as whites, have readily endorsed the law-and-order measures. Racial tension, however, is unabated and is visible to any attentive observer of everyday interaction—particularly on St. Croix. In the aftermath of Hurricane Hugo in 1989, the looting and violence on St. Croix bore some resemblance to the central Los Angeles riots of 1993.

Conflict over Land. Because the original inhabitants were wiped out early on, none of the groups now resident in the islands have a claim to indigenous ownership of the land, as instead is the case in American Samoa and Guam. In these latter territories, the traditional right of the local people (Samoan and "Chamorro") is established in legislation governing the ownership of communal land, which is restricted to "any person having [more] than one-half native blood." Custodial rights to land are vested in the traditional chiefs, and land alienation is severely restricted.

Under the Danes, blacks and coloreds were permitted to own land, and several availed themselves of this privilege. Without institutional protections, however, the superior economic power of white continentals and the large influx of the 1960s and 1970s inevitably led to rapid land alienation on a vast scale. By 1990, it can be estimated that, although accounting for less than one-fifth of the officially registered population, whites owned three-fifths of the land—including, of course, the choicest locations and scenic sites.

Land sales to whites have been a major source of resentment and tensions, as has the practice of whites to isolate themselves in racial enclaves from which local blacks are barred. In particular, the issue of ownership of beach-front property and access to public beaches has been extremely contentious. The process was largely completed by the end of the 1960s. Local author Gladwin Ellis wrote: "Almost before the local people realized what had happened, nearly all of the beach front land on St. Croix was in the hand of continentals. Many who had owned land running to the beach, sold their property, without realizing that they had also sold their birthright. . . . For the first time, 'keep off' and 'no trespassing' signs appeared."[10]

A local realtor pointed up the economics of land alienation.

Wholesale values, meaning a couple of hundred acres or more in size, continued to increase from 25% to 50% a year . . . prices in wholesale lots are now upwards of six to seven thousand dollars an acre. There may be a few large parcels under that price, but one cannot expect that to last many more months. The unusual, fine lots on the tops of hills or with beach front are commanding very spectacular prices. The lot that recently sold for $10,000.00 is now going for anywhere from $25,000 to $30,000 . . . this could be for one acre.[11]

The reference dates to the 1960s, but the pattern of price increases has not moderated since then—rather the reverse. From real estate information collected in early 1995, a good-sized lot of hilltop (seaview) or beachfront land in St. Thomas sold for anywhere from $50,000 to $500,000. It is, of course, pretty difficult for a local to buy such a lot or for the local owner to resist selling it. The economics of land alienation are easily understandable, inevitable in their effect, and unrelated to racial motives. The outcome of land alienation, however, is an objective contributor to racial resentment—as the land is transferred not only to wealthier hands but, inevitably, to white hands.

Land alienation, thus, is a major source of tension, intertwined as it is with social status, and a sense of territorial belonging. Although Virgin Islanders have attempted to define who is a "native Virgin Islander" in cultural terms, the federal government has prevented this definition from being used in a restrictive sense, to limit ownership of land, or to introduce preferential treatment for the benefit of the predominantly black islanders. Washington has been clearly more attuned to maintaining "equal protection" in the face of enormous disparities in purchasing power, than to preventing de facto dispossession of local blacks by white continentals with the tension and conflict that ensues. In any case, the issue is now moot—as most of the worthwhile land has already changed hands.

Population Pressure. The single most important factor of land alienation and real estate price increases, as elsewhere, has been rapid population

Table 7.3
Population of the U.S. Virgin Islands, 1917–1995

1917	26,051
1930	22,012
1940	24,889
1950	26,665
1960	32,108
1970	62,468
1980	96,660
1990	101,809
1995	105,000[a]

[a] Latest available figures from U.S. Census Bureau, Population Statistics.
Source: U.S. Census, Washington, D.C.: Department of Commerce.

growth combined with the small size of the islands. A combination of the beauty of the islands, the convenience of living under the American flag, and the desire to share in the economic prosperity of the islands, has attracted an increasing number of well-to-do American "continentals" and of poor "aliens." The population of the U.S. Virgin Islands was only 22,000 in 1933 (down from an estimated 26,000 at the time of purchase in 1917),[12] of whom 91 percent were black and mixed-race and a mere 2,000 white (mostly associated with the colonial administration, plus a handful of Danes). Population increased by just one-third over the following twenty-seven years. But in the subsequent twenty years, between 1960 and 1980, the U.S. Census shows the population of the Virgin Islands *tripling*, from 32,100 in 1960 to 62,468 in 1970 and 96,660 in 1980—mostly from immigration, with the proportion of whites rising to almost 20 percent. The fastest rapid spurts occurred in the 1960s (with an average annual growth of 8 percent). The influx slowed down considerably after the Fountain Valley murders in 1972 and other racial incidents, and the 1980s witnessed only a slight further increase to 101,809 in 1990 (almost evenly split between St. Croix and St. Thomas/St. John)—clearly indicating near-saturation of the territory. As of 1995, population is estimated at about 105,000. (Table 7.3 shows these trends.) With most of St. John set aside as a National Park, as well as the mountainous hinterland of St. Thomas, the resulting average population density of about 800 per square mile appears to be as much as the Virgin Islands can support without destroying what remains of their natural beauty and tourist appeal.

In addition to the pressures on land and land prices, the small size of the islands has meant that people of different cultural and racial backgrounds mingle in close proximity to one another. Tensions between the different groups are exacerbated by contact and competition for scarce public goods. The influx of white American residents is particularly resented, even though there is a grudging recognition that they are the source of local economic prosperity. And tourism, for all its advantages, generates more mixed feelings than in other tourist destinations, because the small size of the islands (four cruise liners in port at the same time disembark more passengers into Charlotte Amalie than the entire population of the town) precludes the establishment of "buffer zones" between tourist areas and residents' living space. The "size factor" also has consequences for the particular island pattern of political dependence and greatly influences attitudes toward changes in constitutional status, as discussed in the next section. Finally, market size limitations and the absence of raw materials—both related to small economic size—heighten the islands' economic dependence. The awareness of economic and political dependence reinforces resentment, although never enough to fuel a credible independence movement.

POLITICAL DEVELOPMENTS UNDER AMERICAN RULE

Military Administration, 1917–1931

Whereas (see chapter 5) much of the political struggle in Puerto Rico before and after the American presence was a quantum jump in political autonomy from both the Spanish and American administration, the more modest goal of political activity in the U.S. Virgin Islands in the early period was to get rid of the military administration. As mentioned previously, the military (and particularly the U.S. Navy) was at the time among the most racist of American institutions. The then-strictly segregated U.S. armed forces relied completely upon white southerners to administer the territories. Most of these officers naturally brought their antiblack and antimiscegenation attitudes with them. Accustomed to the Danish pattern of race relations, the Virgin Islanders were shocked and bitterly resented these attitudes and the ensuing racial discrimination.

Delegation after delegation of islanders went to Washington to seek replacement of naval government by a civilian administration. Islanders were particularly keen on an independent judiciary in accordance with the American system, rather than permitting the ranking naval officer to veto the decisions of local courts. The islanders also demanded U.S. citizenship and the voting franchise, instead of being regarded as "Virgin Islanders," who could not be naturalized.[13] Other requests included the adoption of an "organic act"; the stabilization of the currency; the erection of technical schools; the establishment of workmen's compensation; and civil service protection. The immediate goal was realized in 1931, with the transfer of authority from the U.S. Navy to the Department of the Interior and the extension of many legal protections to the Virgin Islands. Paradoxically, one of the first U.S. laws extended to the Virgin Islands was Prohibition, which killed production of the world-famous bay rum of the Virgin Islands—the major industry on St. Thomas—and caused the loss of thousands of dollars to local manufacturers.

The 1936 Organic Act

The Virgin Islands were, and are, an unincorporated territory of the United States. As previewed in chapter 3, that the Virgin Islands are "unincorporated" does not mean that they are an "unorganized" territory. With the Organic Act of the Virgin Islands passed by the Congress of the United States in 1936 and revised in 1954, the islands became "organized." The islanders were granted universal suffrage to begin on January 1, 1938, or, depending on the municipality, subsequent to January 1, 1937. The act continued the system of joint municipal councils, which would henceforth be designated as the Legislative Assembly of the Virgin Islands. An appointed governor would assume executive power and would work under the supervision of the Secretary of the Interior. The act also established a judicial branch and enumerated certain civil rights.[14]

The 1952–1953 Hearings and the 1954 Revised Organic Act

Frequent visits were made to the islands by congressional delegations—usually during the winter months. The casual impressions gathered by the white congressmen during these visits, through the lenses of their prejudices and invariably from white residents of the islands, formed the main empirical (!) basis for decisions on the evolution of political status. The most important set of hearings took place in January 1952, in the Virgin Islands, by the Subcommittee on Territories and Insular Affairs. Under consideration were five issues: (1) election of the governor; (2) establishment of the post of resident commissioner; (3) return of the revenue collected on Virgin Islands rum sold in the United States; (4) the establishment of a unicameral legislature; and (5) clarification of the citizenship status of Virgin Islanders living abroad at the time citizenship was given to residents. These, as described by Alva C. McFarlane, chairman of the Legislative Assembly, consisted of "a great number of men without a country [who] reside in Cuba, Haiti, Panama and Santo Domingo" and who wanted to have their citizenship status defined so that they might return home (quoted in *St. Thomas Daily News,* January 3, 1952, p. 1). Not all agreed on the rights of islanders to elect their governor, although there was support for immediate provision of a resident commissioner. Opposition to the elected governor provision stemmed mainly from the predominantly white business community.

The debate on this issue offered wonderful illustrations of the interaction of racial attitudes with viewpoints about political status. Here is a sample. A St. Thomas hotel owner, Sally Milgram, went straight to the basics of American racism, when she observed that the people of the islands were not ready for any form of self-government and proceeded to justify this view on the basis of her difficulty in finding "reliable" employees.

Alvaro deLugo (A relative of Ron deLugo, the islands' delegate to Congress until 1994) supported this view in tones reminiscent of Booker T. Washington's Atlanta Compromise speech of 1895:

I believe [the voter] must have a high degree of education or the equivalent and intellectual ability of a high order . . . [that] the governor must be of balanced judgement with foresight and demonstrated progressive thinking . . . outstandingly big and a leader. I further believe we should have a sufficiently large pool of such men to choose from and not only one or two. . . . I do not believe the position should be open to the chances and accident of a wild shot. (Quoted in *St. Thomas Daily News*, January 5, 1952, p. 1.)

Congressman Morris Poulson was plainer: "I am violently opposed to their election of a governor. The majority of the people in the islands are not ready for this as yet. . . . Everybody wants to get on the government payroll and nobody wants to work and I am against it and will bet my last cent that this legislation will not pass."[15]

The nemesis of political advancement for the flag territories was the rabidly racist Senator Hugh Butler (who had also opposed statehood for Hawaii, because of "communist influences"—see chapter 3). In November 1953, Butler visited the islands and opened new hearings. As in 1952, the St. Croix Chamber of Commerce opposed many of the political advancement provisions, although they did support the return of the taxes collected. In addition, the Hotel Association of the Virgin Islands opposed the elective governor provision. The spokesperson for the Hotel Association was Alton Adams, a Negro, in the mold of the accommodationist local leadership that is integral to the policy of pragmatic materialism: "our experience to date has convinced the members of our association that such procedure is not entirely advisable at this time; in fact, we doubt if a majority of the residents of these islands favor the election of the governor for reasons best known to them."[16]

The belief that the islanders were incapable of self-determination was also the theme of Harry E. Taylor, former administrator for St. Croix during the administration of Paul Pearson (father of columnist Drew Pearson):

The clamor here ... is for more self-government and not for more efficient self-government. What they have been doing with what they've got is disgraceful and more change of form will accomplish little until they grow up, accept the responsibilities of self-government and evidence moral and mental capacities ... and that goes for the electors as well as the elected. (Quoted in *St. Thomas Daily News*, November 20, 1953, p. 1.)

Finally, there was the view of Senator Butler: "We have been guilty of 'too much too soon' with respect to the Virgin Islands: too much money appropriated for them without wise planning, too much responsibility thrust upon the people in the way of unwarranted imitation of the elaborate system of government we have evolved in the mainland without adequate preparation."[17]

The Butler committee insisted that there be "minority" representation in the legislature. In the context of the predominantly nonwhite population of the Virgin Islands, this referred to whites. This was not unique in American colonial policy, as the evidence from Hawaii illustrated. The Revised Organic Act, however, was passed, and contained the following key provision in addition to establishing a unicameral legislature. For the first time the islands were legally defined as an "unincorporated territory," the significance of which is summarized by James A. Bough: "[which] was to follow the establish[ed] pattern of relationship between the United States and its possessions and to satisfy the opponents of statehood in the Congress that the Virgin Islands, not being even an "incorporated" territory was more than one step away from that cherished constitutional right of statehood" (Bough and Macridis, 1970, p. 123). On the fiscal side the act called for the return of the internal revenue taxes on a dollar-for-dollar matching basis. Expenditures would be approved by the secretary of the Interior.

In adopting the Revised Organic Act, Congress made it clear that although it was providing a detailed framework of government for the islands this was not to be taken as an indication that it had destined the territory for statehood. Therefore, Congress expressly declared that the Virgin Islands were an "unincorporated territory of the United States of America."[18] Reasonably enough, the act required the government to conform to the due process clause, the equal protection clause and the other constitutional safeguards. Less reasonably, the act restricted the authority of the Virgin Islands' government to issue revenue bonds to raise money for public projects and to create new government departments without the approval of the secretary of the Interior. (The issue of an elected governor was not resolved until passage of PL 90–496 of 1968—see below.)

Recent Developments and Current Political Status

As the territory has become increasingly self-governing, federal administration has generally been marked by a significant increase in the number of federal agencies involved in programs and decision-making; and a shift in the Department of Interior's role from direct administration to provision of assistance, limited oversight and advocacy. The trend is to a more decentralized approach, which has resulted in an assistant secretary of the Interior for Territorial and International Affairs and, more recently, a move to eliminate the Office of Territorial and International Affairs (OTIA) altogether.

As the result of PL 90–496 of August 1968, which amended the 1954 Organic Act, the islanders now elect a governor together with the lieutenant governor. At the same time, in a clear expression of ambivalence about local autonomy, the bill also provided for a government comptroller to serve for a period of ten years, working directly with the secretary of the Interior (by whom he was appointed), and required to notify the governor of "any failure to collect money due and of expenditures of funds or uses of property which are irregular."[19]

In 1976, Congress granted the islands the right to draft their own constitution, subject to the approval of Congress and the president. Despite repeated attempts through successive constitutional conventions, no consensus has been reached so far. A constitution permitting a degree of autonomy was drawn up in 1978 and rejected in a March 1979 referendum by the voters. Subsequent provisions for greater autonomy were also rejected in 1981. Following a conference at the University of the Virgin Islands in February 1988, a decision was made to conduct a referendum on political status in November 1989. This was postponed because of Hurricane Hugo. A referendum was held in 1993 with only 10,710 or 31.4 percent of the eligible 39,038 voters participating, which was below the 50 percent plus one needed.

The political status of the Virgin Islands thus remains essentially as set through the 1954 legislation and under 1968 legislation (and, earlier, through the Insular Cases—see chapter 3): "As a Federal authority, the Virgin Islands are an unincorporated territory, subject to the power of Congress which is empowered to make suitable rules and regulations to govern the territory, pursuant to Article 4, Section 3, of the U.S. Constitution."[20] As such, constitutional protections are not extended automatically. Among other things, the three separate and coordinate branches of the government of the Virgin Islands are not constitutionally mandated, but simply authorized by Congress. As an "organized territory," however, the provisions of the U.S. Code 1471 prohibiting the passage of special laws, are fully applicable to the islands.

Political Leadership. Much more than in neighboring Puerto Rico, political leadership in the U.S. Virgin Islands has been heavily influenced by the factor of pragmatic materialism and the economic dominance of the whites. As a result, white continentals play a far greater leading role in island politics than in Puerto Rico—where they are economically influential but politically invisible. Leading white continentals include the stateside-born

Ron deLugo, who served as the Virgin Islands nonvoting delegate in the U.S. Congress for twenty-six years (1968–1994). Although representing a majority black constituency in the U.S. Congress, deLugo, who is white, was not a member of the congressional Black Caucus. Upon his retirement, he was succeeded by Victor O. Frazer, who is black and a member of the Black Caucus.

Other white continentals have held the offices of lieutenant governor and of governor. Black and white political leadership represent a variety of views, all which are basically pragmatic and moderate. These include the late Rothschild Francis, who advocated self-government for the Virgin Islands and full citizenship rights; Alton August Adams, the first black conductor of the U.S. Navy Band, who served as a liaison between the naval administration and the people of the Virgin Islands and later as mouthpiece for the Hotel Association in opposing direct election of the governor; Lionel Valdemar Roberts, chairman of the Organic Act Commission of 1936; the late governors Cyril E. King, founder of the Independent Citizens Movement, and Melvin H. Evans, the first black elected governor of the islands and a registered Republican.

A polarity exists between the mainstream accommodationist leadership and a fluid "militant" group. The mainstream politicians recognize the constraints of a predominantly black polity functioning within a white-dominated system but offer no long-term vision for the black majority. The "militants" are generally younger and more strident critics of American racism and its manifestations in the islands, but offer no realistic short-term alternative programs. Thus, the leading role of white politicians in a black-majority society may appear paradoxical under the circumstances, but is easily understood within the pragmatic materialism paradigm offered in this book.

Political Status Options

It is to be expected that the political response to pragmatic materialism is manifested in different ways in the different American possessions. Attitudes toward political status in the Virgin Islands are in strong contrast to political attitudes in Puerto Rico (and Guam) for example.[21] Political status change is not a burning issue in the Virgin Islands, nor is it intertwined with cultural identity as in neighboring Puerto Rico.

The rejection of proposals for greater autonomy, a general disinterest in radical status change, and the election and reelection of a white politician as the islands' emissary to Congress highlights the pragmatic political outlook of the islanders on the status issue and in their dealings with Washington. Again reminiscent of the politics of Booker T. Washington, Virgin Islanders continually reject radical status change, while opting for the continuation of the economic benefits that association with the United States brings. This is in no way a criticism of their choice, considering how many and varied those economic benefits are—Social Security, Medicare, Medicaid, social welfare, health, education, veterans' benefits, food stamps, surplus-food programs, hospitals, sewage-treatment plants, freshwater mains, housing. It is, however, an explanation and reminder of its costs as well as its benefits.

The late Governor Paiewonsky identified seven status options:

1. Full independence
2. Full statehood
3. Unincorporated territory (status quo)
4. Incorporated territory—with automatic application of the Constitution
5. Free association—the Virgin Islands would be free to determine their own affairs, except foreign affairs, including adoption of a constitution, without congressional approval
6. Compact of federal relations—the Virgin Islands would have the maximum degree of internal self-government in association with the United States
7. Commonwealth—a status to be negotiated between the Virgin Islands and the United States Congress

Governor Paiewonsky considered the question of political status "of paramount importance to the people of the Virgin Islands," but proceeded to advocate negotiating an "agreement with the United States as a result of a dialogue with the Congress and the executive branch ... aimed at creating a closer and more meaningful relationship with the United States with the purpose of securing additional rights and benefits"[22]—in other words, a little more of the same.

It is highly unlikely that the islanders will seek full autonomy (let alone independence), because they are attuned to increasingly xenophobic attitudes in the U.S. Congress and because they have no wish to jeopardize the material benefits of association with the United States. Nor is statehood a realistic possibility—both because of the islands' small size and because of their racial mix. What is left, then, is the prospect of marginal adjustments in the direction of "a little more"—in effect the same direction as advocated by Paiewonsky.

NOTES

Some of the material in this chapter originally appeared in McFerson, *Plural Society*, 1979.

1. This section is based on Albert A. Campbell, *St. Thomas Negroes* (Evanston, Ill.: American Psychological Association, 1946), unless otherwise indicated.
2. Luther Harris Evans, *The Virgin Islands: From Naval Base to New Deal* (Ann Arbor, Mich.: J. W. Edwards, 1945), p. 45. Prior to World War 1, American interest

in the Caribbean has been to a great extent determined by the 1904 Roosevelt Corollary to the Monroe Doctrine, which held that the United States had the right to intervene to prevent "chronic bankruptcy" of Western Hemisphere states that might entangle them politically with European powers.

3. *Virgin Islands of the United States* (Washington, D.C.: Navy Department, 1917), p. 5.

4. Luther H. Evans, "Unrest in the Virgin Islands," *Foreign Policy Reports* 11, no. 2 (March 1945), p. 16.

5. Arnold H. Leibowitz, *Defining Status: A Territorial Analysis of U.S. Territorial Relations*. (Leiden, Netherlands: Nijhoff, 1989), p. 235. This section is based on this source.

6. See, respectively, *Rogers v. Larson* (1977) and *Virgin Islands v. Blumenthal* (1980).

7. The experience of Governor Hastie, in particular, illustrates the transfer of white racism to the islands. Hastie's appointment was bitterly contested by white southerners living in the islands and by Dixiecrats in Washington led by Senator James O. Eastland (D.–Miss.) and Senator Allen Ellender (D.–La.). They claimed that a Negro governor would ruin the island's tourism and even that the appointment would "retard" the islands because Hastie had been affiliated with organizations with "communistic leanings." (*Hartford Times*, May 1946, p. 1). The organization in question was the National Association for the Advancement of Colored People! The coalition, however, was unsuccessful, and Hastie was confirmed as "America's first Negro Governor" in 1946. Leslie F. Huntt, a white continental, emerged as the leader of anti-Hastie forces in the territory. Among other indignities, even after his appointment, Hastie was barred from membership in the all-white St. Thomas Tennis Club, even though complimentary memberships were routinely issued to appointed American officials.

8. This has most recently been mentioned in the hearings of the House Subcommittee on Native American and Insular Affairs of the Committee on Resources, *Impact of Contract with America on the Territories*, 104th Cong., 1st Sess., on H.R. 602, "A Bill to Reform the Laws Concerning Territories and Possessions," January 31, 1995.

9. Paiewonsky, 1990, pp. 194–96. Among the examples cited was the rather typical case of Mississippi-born Herman Moore, a black judge, upon arriving in the islands to assume his post in the early sixties. He had obtained telephone reservations at the Buccaneer Hotel, but when he turned up and the management saw that he was black, he was told that a mistake had been made, and there was no room available.

10. Gladwin Ellis, 1970, p. 58.
11. Quoted in Ellis, 1970, ibid.
12. Leibowitz, 1989, p. 287.
13. As an article in the *St. Thomas Daily News* of December 1934 argued:

The idea which at first appeared fantastic, has caught the imagination of those seeking reward for their labors during the late political campaign. Why shouldn't such a change be made? The total population of the islands is 22,012. Of these, 20,002 are colored people. There are only about 2000 whites in the entire islands yet they are the ruling class forming a privileged minority with their governmental prerequisites and the low cost of living, who exist like lords. Just think what a remarkable experiment in the ability of Negroes to conduct a colonial government could be made in the Virgin Islands!

14. A 1948 referendum asked if the islanders "favor the election of the Governor by the people of the Virgin Islands?" to which 463 responded yes, and 1,530 voted no. In 1948 there were 5,528 voters, of whom 3,236 voted. The same referendum asked the islanders: "Do you favor a Resident Commissioner from the Virgin Islands in the Congress of the United States?" to which 2,194 voted yes and only 286 voted no. The results suggest the pragmatic outlook: A resident commissioner in Washington would be in a stronger position to persuade his congressional colleagues to extend social welfare benefits to the islands than would an elected governor sitting in the Virgin Islands.

15. Quoted in the *St. Thomas Daily News*, Anniversary Edition, August 1, 1970, p. 23D

16. Quoted in Valdemar A. Hill Sr., *A Golden Jubilee* (St. Thomas: Private printing, 1971), p. 149.

17. Quoted in ibid., p. 154.

18. *Territorial Court of the Virgin Islands v. Richards*, D.C.V.I. (1987), affirmed (1988), certiorari denied (1988).

19. St. Thomas League of Women Voters, "Structures and Functions of Government," undated, p. 2.

20. *Government of the Virgin Islands v. Rijos* (1968).

21. In 1995 Guam launched an as of yet unsuccessful movement to change its status from an unincorporated territory to a Commonwealth.

22. Paiewonsky, 1990, pp. 467–68.

8 Back to the Future?

As noted at the outset, the possible positions on the role of race in society can be summarized in the statements: (1) "only race matters"; (2) "race matters"; (3) "race doesn't matter." One cannot conclude that race doesn't matter from a demonstration that other factors have been at work. It would be an equal non sequitur if—having demonstrated that race was a major influence on American territorial expansion—we were to argue here that it was the *only* influence. Economics, geography, population pressure, national security—and a heavy dose of happenstance—all played their role in territorial expansion throughout North America and the overseas colonies. But a history of those periods and of their politics would be very partial and misleading if it didn't include the American racial tradition among its most important factors. This is the added dimension provided in this book.

Because of the tragic events of the post–cold war period—genocide in Bosnia and, on an incomprehensible scale, in Rwanda; Zulu-Xhosa tensions in the new South Africa; mutual paranoia between Albanians and Macedonians; the alarming rise in ethnic violence in Western Europe, and so forth—the lesson of the crucial importance of race and ethnicity might finally have sunk in. W. E. B. Du Bois' prediction—that the race question was going to be the dominant question of the twentieth century—has been proven beyond any doubt. Unless we learn from the experience of the twentieth century, the question of race will remain dominant through the twenty-first.

Since the civil rights movement in the 1960s, there is evidence of greater flexibility in the American racial tradition, with a sharp increase in black participation in professional fields, a shrinkage in the white-black income gap in those fields, and a loosening of de facto residential segregation. We have seen how a flexible tradition is characterized by two key elements: (1) the existence of several racial groups and thus the possibility to "graduate" to a higher-status group; and (2) the coexistence with racial ancestry of other criteria of social stratification—such as culture, phenotype, and economic class. The American racial tradition has not become more flexible in respect to the first element. The racial classification is still basically bipolar, and the official taxonomy does not include a mixed-race group. In respect to the second element, however, there is substantial evidence of increased flexibility: African Americans of significant educational achievements or income levels are in effect being placed into an intermediate social group. Their status, although still, and inevitably, tinged with racial considerations, has been raised upwards. Indeed, a high-achievement educated black today—*on average*—has higher social status than a poor uneducated white. This overlapping between racial groups is characteristic of a flexible racial tradition.

But the current social climate is fluid and dangerously unstable, and political exploitation of racial hostilities and fears is unquestionably higher today than at any time in the last generation. Let's then go back to history to get a glimpse of a possible future. A historic opportunity to change the American racial tradition for the better was tragically missed after the Civil War. With vigorous and consistent political, judicial, and intellectual leadership, the constitutional and legal revolution could have been accompanied, in time, by sufficient change in informal racial attitudes to turn it into a social revolution. However, those who would lead the change could not, and those who could (including the Supreme Court and the new barons of the American Industrial Revolution) would not. Consequently, as immigrants arrived in larger and larger numbers from the late 1880s, they found in place rigid schemes of racial domination and exclusion. As all immigrants do, they conformed to the social consensus, and thus became the engine for reproducing those racial schemes for future generations. Had they found a more liberal, more rational, racial tradition, they would undoubtedly have conformed with *it*, compounding the initial change in a positive direction. How different would America be today?

Although the American racial tradition remains in the main a rigid one, the increased flexibility introduced since the 1960s is real and more sustainable than that introduced after the Civil War or in the early 1950s—more sustainable because a genuine change in informal attitudes of tens of millions of people has accompanied the legislative and executive changes in the formal rules. As of mid-1997, however, it is easy to find evidence either of further evolution or of a return to earlier rigid exclusionary schemes. In such historically fluid situations, much will depend—as it did in the early days of the new United States of America and during Reconstruction—on the actions of a few key individuals in a position to shape policy and mass images. Let us hope that, this time, the Patrick Henrys and John Marshall Harlans, and William Jefferson Clintons of America will prevail over the John Marshalls and Woodrow Wilsons.[1] If the opportunity is again missed, the future of American racial and social relations may well be as bleak as its past.

The short-lived American empire came into being by accident, but was ruled by a system—the same system of racial attitudes and stereotypes (benevolent or malignant) that applied to racial minorities in the continental United States. The political prospects of the remnants of that empire—Puerto Rico, the Virgin Islands, Guam, American Samoa, the Northern Marianas—will still be influenced by racial considerations. Because of those considerations (among other factors, to be sure) I do not believe that statehood is in the cards for any of them. With the alternative of independence ruled out by small size and, even more, by the fear of losing the material benefits of association with the United States, the likeliest prospect is for more of the same. Years from now, these territories will still be in the state of political limbo that they entered a hundred years ago and which was accurately predicted for them by the minority opinion in the Insular Cases.

In preparation for the year 2000 census, the Clinton administration has proposed that a multiracial and multiethnic classification be added. Individuals claiming membership in more than one racial group will be allowed to choose more than one racial category in a self-identification process. The proposal suggests that the government is moving closer to officially recognizing the complexity of racial classification, rather than continuing the bipolar classifications only in rigid black or white terms. This is further indication of the increased recent flexibility of the American racial tradition. It remains to be seen, of course, what the actual policy ramifications will be, including those for the overseas territories. Whether and how fast social practice will catch up to increased flexibility of official racial classifications is the key question.

NOTE

1. In an address at the University of California at San Diego, President Clinton initiated an effort, a national dialogue, to lead America in a "great and unprecedented conversation about race": "Will we become not two, but many Americas, separate, unequal and isolated? Or will we draw strength from all our people and our ancient faith in equality and human dignity to become the world's first truly multiracial democracy? That is the unfinished work of our times, to lift the burden of race and redeem the promise of America" (quoted in the *New York Times*, July 5, 1997, p. 16).

References

Abbott, Edith, ed. 1924, 1969. *Immigration: Select Documents and Case Records.* Chicago: The University of Chicago Press. Reprint: New York: Arno Press.
Adam, Heribert. 1971. *Modernizing Racial Domination.* Berkeley: University of California Press.
The Alien Worker and His Family. 1967. St. Thomas: College of the Virgin Islands.
Anderson, Richard L., reporter. *Virgin Islands Reports.* 1991, 1993. Vol. 1. *Containing Opinions of Courts of Record, and Others, Relating to the Virgin Islands, 1917–1939.* Oxford, N.H.: Equity Publishing Corp.
Andic, Fuad, and Thomas Mathews, eds. 1971. *The Caribbean in Transition.* Rio Piedras, Puerto Rico: Institute of Caribbean Studies.
———. 1966. *Politics and Economics in the Caribbean.* Rio Piedras: Institute of Caribbean Studies.
Andrews, George Reid. 1991. *Blacks & Whites in Sao Paulo, Brazil, 1888–1988.* Madison: University of Wisconsin Press.
Apter, David. 1965. *The Politics of Modernization.* Chicago: The University of Chicago Press.
Baca, Lawrence. 1978, 1990. "The Legal Status of American Indians." In *Handbook of North American Indians,* ed. Wilcomb B. Washburn. Washington, D.C.: Smithsonian Institution.
Bagley, Christopher. 1973. *The Dutch Plural Society: A Comparative Study in Race Relations.* London: Oxford University Press.
Baker, Ray Stannard. 1964. *Following the Color Line: American Negro Citizenship in the Progressive Era.* New York: Harper and Row.
Banton, Michael. 1983. *Race and Ethnic Competition.* Cambridge: Cambridge University Press.
———. 1988. *Racial Consciousness.* London: Longman.

Barclay, William, Krishna Kumar, and Ruth P. Simms. 1976. *Racial Conflict, Discrimination and Power.* New York: AMS Press.
Bell, Roger. 1984. *Last Among Equals: Hawaiian Statehood and American Politics.* Honolulu: University of Hawaii Press.
Bennett, Lerone. 1969. *Before the Mayflower: A History of Black America.* Chicago: Johnson Publishing Co.
Berbusse, Edward J. 1966. *The United States in Puerto Rico, 1898–1900.* Chapel Hill: University of North Carolina Press.
Berreman, Gerald D. 1972. "Caste, Race and Other Invidious Distinctions in Social Stratification." *Race* 13, no. 4.
Beteille, A. 1971. "Race, Caste and Ethnic Identity." *International Encyclopedia of Social Sciences* 23, no. 4.
Beider, Robert E. 1980. "Scientific Attitudes Toward Indian Mixed-Bloods in Early 19th Century America." *Journal of Ethnic Studies* 8, no. 2.
"Black Americans." 1975. *Directory of Data Sources on Racial and Ethnic Minorities.* Washington, D.C.: U.S. Department of Labor, Bureau of Labor Statistics.
Blalock, H. M., Jr. 1967. *Toward a Theory of Minority Group Relations.* New York: Capricorn Books.
Blanshard, Paul. 1947. *Democracy and Empire in the Caribbean: A Contemporary Review.* New York: Macmillan.
Bloomfield, Richard J. 1985. *Puerto Rico: The Search for a National Policy.* Boulder, Colo.: Westview Press.
Blum, John M. et al. 1963, 1968. *The National Experience: A History of the United States.* New York: Harcourt, Brace and World, Inc.
Bough, James A., and Roy Macridis, eds. 1970. *The Virgin Islands: America's Caribbean Outpost.* Wakefield, Mass.: Williams.
Bradford, Philips Verner, and Harvey Blume. 1992. *Ota Benga: The Pygmy in the Zoo.* New York: Dell Publishing.
Braithwaite, Lloyd. 1974. "Social Stratification and Cultural Pluralism." In *Peoples and Cultures of the Caribbean,* edited by Michael Horowitz. New York: Praeger.
Briefing on Puerto Rico Political Status by the General Accounting Office. 1991. Washington, D.C.: U.S. General Printing Office.
Bull, Bartle. 1988. *Safari: A Chronicle of Adventure.* New York: Penguin.
Burns, Alan Cuthbert. 1949. *Colonial Civil Servant.* London: Allen and Unwin.
Cabranes, Jose A. 1979. "Citizenship and the American Empire: Notes on the Legislative History of the United States Citizenship of Puerto Ricans." *University of Pennsylvania Law Review* 127:316.
Campbell, Albert A. 1943. "Notes on the Jewish Community of St. Thomas, U.S. Virgin Islands." *Jewish Social Studies.*
———. 1946. *St. Thomas Negroes.* Evanston, Ill.: American Psychological Association.
Canegata, D. C. 1968. *St. Croix at the Twentieth Century.* New York: Carlton Press.
Carr, Raymond. 1984. *Puerto Rico: A Colonial Experiment.* New York: Twentieth Century Fund, Inc.
Carrión Morales, Arturo. 1983. *Puerto Rico: A Political and Cultural History.* Chapters by Maria Teresa Babin et al. New York: W. W. Norton; Nashville: American Association for State and Local History.

Cashmore, Ernest. 1984, 1988. *Dictionary of Race and Ethnic Relations*. London: Routledge.
Census Reform, Early Outreach and Decisions Needed on Race and Ethnic Questions. 1993. Washington, D.C.: GAO.
Central America and the Caribbean: The Great Contemporary Issues. 1980. New York: The New York Times and Arno Press.
Civil Affairs of Porto Rico. 1899. Washington, D.C.: War Department.
Civil Rights Issues Facing Asian Americans in the 1990s. 1992. A Report of the U.S. Commission on Civil Rights. Washington, D.C.: U.S. Commission on Civil Rights.
Cohen, Felix S. 1942, 1982. *Handbook of Federal Indian Law*. Charlottesville, Va.: Michie/Bobbs-Merrill.
Commanger, Henry Steele. 1940. *Documents of American History*. New York: F. S. Crofts & Co.
Constantino, Renato. 1966. *The Filipinos in the Philippines and Other Essays*. Quezon City, Philippines: Malaya Books.
Cordasco, Francesco, and Eugene Bucchioni. 1973. *The Puerto Rican Experience: A Sociological Sourcebook*. Totowa, N.J.: Rowman and Littlefield.
Corwin, A. F. 1975. "Afro-Brazilians: Myths and Realities." In *Slavery and Race Relations in Latin America*, edited by Robert Brent Toplin. Westport, Conn.: Greenwood Press.
Coser, Lewis. 1956. *The Functions of Social Conflict*. New York: Free Press.
Creque, Darwin D. 1968. *The U.S. Virgins and the Eastern Caribbean*. Philadelphia: Whitmore.
de Crevecoeur, J. Hector St. John. 1782, 1968. *Letters from an American Farmer*. Gloucester, Mass.: P. Smith.
Crowley, Daniel. 1973. "Cultural Assimilation in a Multiracial Society." In *Consequences of Class and Color*, edited by David Lowenthal and Lambrus Comitas. New York: Doubleday.
Dalton, Robert H. 1960. *Education and Social Change*. St. Thomas: Department of Public Health, Division of Mental Health.
Daniels, Roger. 1988. *Asian America: Chinese and Japanese in the United States Since 1850*. Seattle: University of Washington Press.
Davis, James F. 1991. *Who is Black?* University Park: The Pennsylvania State University Press.
DeConde, Alexander. 1992. *Ethnicity, Race and American Foreign Policy: A History*. Boston: Northeastern University Press.
Degler, Carl N. 1971. *Neither Black Nor White: Slavery and Race Relations in Brazil and the United States*. New York: Macmillan.
deLugo, Ron. 1973. "Statement to the People of the Virgin Islands on Water Island." *St. Thomas Daily News*, August 1, 1973.
DeSmith, Stanley A. 1970. *Microstates and Micronesia: Problems of America's Pacific Islands and Other Minute Territories*. New York: New York University Press.
Dookhan, Isaac. 1972. *A Pre-Emancipation History of the West Indies*. London: Collins.
Dovidio, John F., and Samuel L. Gaertner, eds. 1986. *Prejudice, Discrimination and Racism*. Orlando, Fla.: Academic Press.

DuBois, W. E. B. 1896, 1970. *The Suppression of the African Slave Trade to the United States of America.* New York: Longmans, Green and Co.

DuPuy, William Atherton. 1952. *Hawaii and Its Race Problem.* Washington, D.C.: U.S. Department of the Interior.

Dyer, Thomas G. 1980. *Theodore Roosevelt and the Idea of Race.* Baton Rouge: Louisiana State University Press.

Ellis, Gladwin. 1970. *Living in the Changing Caribbean.* New York: Macmillan.

Ely, Melvin Patrick. 1991. *The Adventures of Amos 'n' Andy: A Social History of an American Phenomenon.* New York: The Free Press.

Emerson, Rupert. 1949. *America's Pacific Dependencies: A Survey of American Colonial Policies and of Administration and Progress Toward Self-Rule in Alaska, Hawaii, Guam, Samoa and the Trust Territory.* New York: American Institute of Pacific Relations.

Enloe, Cynthia. 1973. *Ethnic Conflict and Political Development.* Boston: Little, Brown and Company.

Evans, Luther Harris. 1945. *The Virgin Islands: From Naval Base to New Deal.* Ann Arbor, Mich.: J. W. Edwards.

Falk, Pamela S. 1986. *The Political Status of Puerto Rico.* Lexington, Ky.: D.C. Heath and Company.

Fanon, Frantz. 1963. *Wretched of the Earth.* Translated by Constance Farrington. New York: Grove Press.

———. 1967. *Black Skin, White Mask.* Translated by Charles Lam Markmann. New York: Grove Press.

Farr, Kenneth R. 1973. *Historical Dictionary of Puerto Rico and the U.S. Virgin Islands.* Metuchen, N.J.: The Scarecrow Press, Inc.

Feagin, Joe R., and Melvin P. Sikes. 1994. *Living with Racism: The Black Middle-Class Experience.* Boston: Beacon Press.

Federal Policies Regarding the U.S. Insular Areas. 1986. Oversight Hearing Before the Committee on Interior and Insular Affairs. 99th Congress. Washington, D.C.: G.P.O.

Fernandes, Florestan. 1969. *The Negro in Brazilian Society.* New York: Columbia University Press.

Fernandez, Ronald. 1992. *The Disenchanted Islands: Puerto Rico and the United States in the Twentieth Century.* New York: Praeger.

Fieldhouse, D. K. 1965. *The Colonial Empires: From the Eighteenth Century.* New York: Dell Publishing Company.

Flores, Juan. 1993. *Divided Borders: Essays on Puerto Rican Identity.* Houston: Arte Publico Press.

Follett, Helen. 1956. *Stick of Fire.* New York: Macmillan.

Foner, Eric, and John A. Garraty, eds. 1991. *The Reader's Companion to American History.* Boston: Houghton Mifflin Co.

Foner, Philip S., and Daniel Rosenberg. 1993. *Racism, Dissent, and Asian Americans from 1850 to the Present: A Documentary History.* Westport, Conn.: Greenwood Press.

Forbes, Jack D. 1993. *Africans and Native Americans.* Urbana: The University of Illinois Press.

Foster, William Z. 1954, 1970. *The Negro People in American History.* New York: International Publishers.

Frederickson, George M. 1981. *White Supremacy: A Comparative Study in American and South African History.* New York: Oxford University Press.
Fuchs, Lawrence H. 1990. *The American Kaleidoscope: Race, Ethnicity, and the Civic Culture.* Hanover, N.H.: University Press of New England.
Furnivall, J. S. 1948. *Colonial Policy and Practice: A Comparative Study of Burma and Netherlands India.* London: Cambridge University Press.
General Accounting Office. 1985. *Issues Affecting U.S. Territory and Insular Policy.* Washington, D.C.: GAO.
Genovese, Eugene D. 1974. *Roll, Jordan Roll: The World the Slaves Made.* New York: Vintage.
Ginzberg, Eli, and Alfred S. Eichner. 1964. *The Troublesome Presence: American Democracy and the Negro.* New York: New American Library.
Gist, N. P., and R. D. Wright. 1973. *Marginality and Identity.* Leiden, Netherlands: E. J. Brill.
Gleeck, Lewis E., Jr. 1984. *General History of the Philippines: The American Half-Century (1898–1946).* Part V, Vol. I. Manila, Philippines: Historical Conservation Society.
Gonzalez, Jose Louis. 1995. "The Four-Storeyed House: Africans in the Forging of Puerto Rico's National Identity." *Slavery and Beyond: The African Impact on Latin America and the Caribbean,* edited by Darien J. Davis. Wilmington, Del.: Jaguar Books on Latin America.
Gossett, Thomas G. 1963. *Race: The History of an Idea in America.* New York: Schocken Books.
Goveia, Elsa. 1965. *Slave Society in the British Leeward Islands.* Rio Piedras: Institute of Caribbean Studies.
Gray, Captain J. A. C. 1960. *Amerika Samoa: A History of American Samoa and Its United States Naval Administration.* Annapolis, Md.: U.S. Naval Institute.
Gross, Emma R. 1989. *Contemporary Federal Policy Toward American Indians.* Westport, Conn.: Greenwood Press.
Gruening, Ernest. 1973. *Many Battles: The Autobiography of Ernest Gruening.* New York: Liveright.
Guild, Jane Purcell. 1936. *Black Laws of Virginia.* Richmond: Whittet and Shepperson.
Haizlip, Shirley. 1994. *The Sweeter the Juice.* New York: Simon & Schuster.
Hall, Kermit L., William M. Weicek, and Paul Finkelman. 1991. *American Legal History: Cases and Materials.* New York: Oxford University Press.
Hall, Neville A. T. 1992. *Slave Society in the Danish West Indies,* edited by B. W. Higman. Baltimore: The Johns Hopkins University Press.
Handlin, Oscar. 1957. *Race and Nationality in American Life.* Garden City, N.Y.: Doubleday Anchor.
Haney Lopez, Ian F. 1996. *White by Law: The Legal Construction of Race.* New York: New York University Press.
Hanson, Earl Parker. 1960. *Puerto Rico: Land of Wonders.* New York: Alfred A. Knopf.
Harlan, Louis R. 1966. "Booker T. Washington and the White Man's Burden." *American Historical Review.*
———. 1972. *Booker T. Washington: The Making of a Black Leader, 1856–1901.* New York: Oxford University Press.

Harlan, Louis R. et al., eds. 1975. *The Booker T. Washington Papers*. Vol. 4, *1895–1898*. Urbana: University of Illinois Press.
Hart, Thomas J. 1958–59. "Trends in Mate Selection in a Tri-Racial Isolate." *Social Forces* 37.
Hawaiian Native Educational Assistance Act. 1978. Washington, D.C.: Senate Select Committee on Indian Affairs, S.857.
Healy, David. 1970. *U.S. Expansionism: The Imperialist Urge in the 1890s*. Madison: University of Wisconsin Press.
Heine, Carl. 1974. *Micronesia at the Crossroads: A Reappraisal of the Micronesian Political Dilemma*. Honolulu: The University Press of Hawaii.
Hellwig, David J. 1992. *African-American Reflections on Brazil's Racial Paradise*. Philadelphia: Temple University Press.
Henriques, Fernando. 1975. *Children of Conflict: A Study of Interracial Sex and Marriage*. New York: E. P. Dutton.
Higginbotham, A. Leon, Jr. 1978. *In the Matter of Color. Race and the American Legal Process: The Colonial Period*. New York: Oxford University Press.
Hill, Valdemar A. 1971. *A Golden Jubilee*. St. Thomas: Private printing.
———. 1971. *Rise to Recognition*. St. Thomas: Private printing.
Hoetink, Harrimus. 1973. *Slavery and Race Relations in the Americas: An Inquiry Into Their Nature and Nexus*. New York: Harper Torchbooks.
Hoffer, Peter Charles, ed. 1988. *Indians and Europeans: Selected Articles on Indian-White Relations in Colonial North America*. New York: Garland.
Hollister, Frederick J. 1967. "Skin Color and Life Chances of Puerto Ricans." *Caribbean Studies* 9, no. 3.
Hopkins, Elizabeth. 1966. "Racial Minorities in British East Africa." In *The Transformation of East Africa: Studies in Political Anthropology*, edited by Stanley Diamond and Fred G. Burke. New York: Basic Books.
Horsman, Reginald. 1981. *Race and Manifest Destiny*. Cambridge: Harvard University Press.
Hughes, Langston. 1958. *The Langston Hughes Reader*. New York: George Braziller.
———. 1961. *The Best of Simple*. New York: Hill and Wang.
Hultgren, Mary Lou and Paulette Fairbanks Molin, eds. 1989. *To Lead and to Serve: American Indian Education at Hampton Institute, 1878–1923*. Virginia Foundation for the Humanities.
Issues Affecting U.S. Territory and Insular Policy. 1985. (Report by the U.S. General Accounting Office.) Washington, D.C.: GAO.
Jarvis, Antonio J. 1944. *The Virgin Islands and Their People*. Philadelphia: Dorrance.
Jennings, Francis. 1976. *The Invasion of America: Indians, Colonialism, and the Cant of Conquest*. New York: W. W. Norton and Company.
Johns, Stephanie Bernardo. 1981. *The Ethnic Almanac*. Garden City, N.Y.: Doubleday.
Johnson, James Weldon. 1933, 1990. *Along the Way: The Autobiography of James Weldon Johnson*. New York: Penguin Books.
Johnson, Roberta Ann. 1980. *Puerto Rico, Commonwealth or Colony?* New York: Praeger.
Johnston, Harry H. 1910. *The Negro in the New World*. New York: Macmillan.
Jordan; Winthrop. 1968. *White Over Black: American Attitudes Toward the Negro, 1550–1812*. Chapel Hill: University of North Carolina Press.

———. 1974. *The White Man's Burden: Historical Origins of Racism in the United States*. New York: Oxford University Press.
July, Robert. 1970. *A History of the African People*. New York: Scribners.
Kanza, Thomas R. 1972. *Conflict in the Congo: The Rise and Fall of Lumumba*. Translated from the French. Harmondsworth, Eng.: Penguin Books.
Katznelson, I. 1973. *Black Men, White Cities*. Chicago: The University of Chicago Press.
Kennedy, Randall. 1997. *Race, Crime, and the Law*. New York: Pantheon Books.
Kim, Hyung-Chan, ed. 1992. *Asian Americans and the Supreme Court: A Documentary History*. Westport, Conn.: Greenwood Press.
Klein, Herbert S. 1967, 1989. *Slavery in the Americas: A Comparative Study of Virginia and Cuba*. Chicago: The University of Chicago Press. Reprint, Chicago: First Elephant Paperback.
Lai, H. M. 1980. "Chinese." *Harvard Encyclopedia of American Ethnic Groups*. Cambridge, Mass.: Belknap Press.
Laws of Puerto Rico: Annotated. 1982 Ed. Historical Documents, Federal Relations, Constitution, Title 1. Oxford, N.H.: Equity Publishing Corp.
Leab, Daniel J. 1975. *From Sambo to Superspade: The Black Experience in Motion Pictures*. Boston: Houghton Mifflin Company.
Leibowitz, Arnold H. 1989. *Defining Status: A Territorial Analysis of U.S. Territorial Relations*. Leiden, Netherlands: Nijhoff.
Lewis, Gordon K. 1963. *Puerto Rico: Freedom and Power in the Caribbean*. New York: Harper Torchbooks.
———. 1968. "An Introductory Note to the Study of the Virgin Islands." *Caribbean Studies*.
———. 1971. "The U.S. Virgin Islands: Prototype of the Caribbean Tourist Economy." In *Politics and Economics in the Caribbean*, edited by Fuad Andic and Thomas Mathews. Rio Piedras: Institute of Caribbean Studies.
———. 1972. *The Virgin Islands*. Evanston,: Ill.: Northwestern University Press.
Lewisohn, Florence. 1964. *St. Croix Under Seven Flags*. Hollywood, Fl.: Dukane.
———. 1973. *A Romantic History of St. Croix*. Hollywood, Fla.: Dukane.
Loewen, James W. 1971. *The Mississippi Chinese: Between Black and White*. Cambridge, Mass.: Harvard University Press.
Lofgren, Charles A. 1987. *The Plessy Case: A Legal Historical Interpretation*. New York: Oxford University Press.
Logan, Rayford W. 1954, 1965. *The Betrayal of the Negro: From Rutherford B. Hayes to Woodrow Wilson*. New York: Collier Books.
Lopez, Adelberto, and James Petras, eds. 1974. *Puerto Rico and Puerto Ricans: Studies in History and Society*. New York: John Wiley and Sons.
Low, W. Augustus, and Virgil A. Clift, eds. 1981, 1984. *Encyclopedia of Black America*. New York: McGraw-Hill. Reprint: New York: Da Capo.
Lyman, Stanford M. 1992. *Militarism, Imperialism, and Racial Accommodation: An Analysis of the Early Writings of Robert E. Park*. Fayetteville: University of Arkansas Press.
Maclean, Frances. 1992. "They Didn't Speak Our Language; We Didn't Speak Theirs," *Smithsonian*, January.
Mangione, Jerre, and Ben Morreale, 1992. *LaStoria: Five Centuries of the Italian American Experience*. New York: HarperPerennial.

Mathews, Thomas G. 1974. "The Question of Color in Puerto Rico." In *Slavery and Race Relations in Latin America*, edited by Robert Brent Toplin. Westport, Conn.: Greenwood Press.

May, Glen Anthony. 1980. *Social Engineering in the Philippines: The Aims, Execution, and Impact of American Colonial Policy, 1900–1913*. Westport, Conn.: Greenwood Press.

McFerson, Hazel M. 1979a. "Plural Society in the U.S. Virgin Islands." *Plural Societies* 10, no. 1.

———. 1979b. "Racial Tradition and Comparative Political Analysis." *Ethnic and Racial Studies* 2, no. 4 (October).

———. 1982. "Part-Black Americans in the South Pacific." *Phylon* LXII, no. 2.

———. 1996. "Rethinking Ethnic Conflict." *American Behavioral Scientist* 40, no. 1.

Melendez, Edgardo. 1988. *Puerto Rico's Statehood Movement*. Westport, Conn.: Greenwood Press.

Meller, Norman. 1985. *Constitutionalism in Micronesia*. Honolulu: Brigham Young University, The Institute for Polynesian Studies.

Merk, Frederick. 1963. *Manifest Destiny and Mission in American History*. New York: Vintage.

Miller, Stuart Creighton. 1982. *"Benevolent Assimilation": The American Conquest of the Philippines, 1899–1903*. New Haven: Yale University Press.

Mills, Candy. 1992. "More Than Meets the Eye." *Interrace*, May/June.

Morales Carrion, Arturo, et al. 1983. *Puerto Rico: A Political and Cultural History*. New York: W. W. Norton.

Morris, Edmund. 1979. *The Rise of Theodore Roosevelt*. New York: Coward, McCann & Geoghegan, Inc.

Myrdal, Gunnar. 1944. *An American Dilemma*. New York: Harper and Brothers Publishers.

Nash, Nathaniel C. 1993. "Montevideo Journal: Uruguay Is on Notice: Blacks Want Recognition." *New York Times*, May 7.

North, Douglass C. 1989. *Institutions, Institutional Change and Economic Performance*. Cambridge: Cambridge University Press.

Oldham, J. H. 1926. *Christianity and the Race Problem*. Chautauqua, N.Y.: The Chautauqua Press.

Omi, Michael, and Howard Winant. 1986. *Racial Formation in the United States: From the 1960s to the 1980s*. New York: Routledge & Kegan Paul.

Paiewonsky, Ralph M. 1990. *Memoirs of a Governor: A Man for the People*. New York: New York University Press.

Paquin, Lyonel. 1971. *A Candid Look at the American Virgin Islands*. St. Thomas: Private Printing.

Parry, Ellwood. 1974. *The Image of the Indian and the Black Man in American Art, 1950–1900*. New York: George Braziller.

Patterson, Orlando. 1967. *The Sociology of Slavery*. London: MacGibbon and Kee.

Perkins, Whitney. 1962. *Denial of Empire: The United States and Its Dependencies*. Cambridge, Mass.: Harvard University Press.

Pitt, David. 1970. *Traditional and Economic Progress in Samoa: A Case Study of the Role of Traditional Social Institutions in Economic Development*. Oxford: Clarendon Press.

Pratt, Julius W. 1958. *Expansionists of 1898: The Acquisition of Hawaii and the Spanish Islands.* Gloucester, Mass.: Peter Smith.
Proceedings of the Asiatic Exclusion League, 1907–1913. 1977. New York: Arno Press.
Proceso Plebiscitario, 1989–1991. 1992. Volume 1. *Correspondencia del liderato politico y documentos legislativos.* Washington, D.C.: Puerto Rico Federal Affairs Administration.
Proudfoot, Mary. 1954. *Great Britain and the United States in the Caribbean: A Comparative Study in Methods of Development.* London: Faber and Faber.
Puerto Rico: A People Challenging Colonialism. 1976. Washington, D.C.: EPICA Task Force.
Rand, Christopher. 1958. *The Puerto Ricans.* New York: Oxford University Press.
Rappaport, Jacques, Ernest Muteba, and Joseph Therattil. 1971. *Small States and Territories: Status and Problems.* New York: Arno Press.
Reed, Stephen Winsor. 1943. *The Making of Modern New Guinea.* Philadelphia: The American Philosophical Society.
Report of the United States: Puerto Rico Commission on the Status of Puerto Rico. 1966. Washington, D.C.: Government Printing Office.
Reports by the New Zealand Government to the U.N. General Assembly of the U.N. on the Administration of Western Samoa, 1940 to 1959.
Reuter, Edward Byron. 1918, 1970. *The Mulatto in the United States.* Boston: Richard G. Badger. Reprint: Johnson Reprint Corporation.
Rich, Paul B. 1986. *Race and Empire in British Politics.* Cambridge: Cambridge University Press.
Roberts, Sam. 1995. "Greening of the Black Middle Class." *New York Times,* June 18.
Rodriguez, Clara E. 1989. *Puerto Ricans: Born in the U.S.A.* Winchester, Mass.: Unwin Hyman, Inc.
Roff, Sue Rabbit. 1991. *Overreaching in Paradise: United States Policy in Palau Since 1945.* Juneau, Alaska: Denali Press.
Roosevelt, Theodore. 1913, 1985. *An Autobiography.* New York: Macmillan. Reprint: New York: Da Capo.
———. 1918. "The Children of the Crucible." In *America at War,* ed. Albert B. Hart. New York: G. H. Doran Co.
Roosevelt, Theodore, Jr. 1937, 1970. *Colonial Policies of the United States.* New York: Doubleday, Doran and Co. Reprint: Arno Press and The New York Times.
Root, Maria P. 1992. *Racially Mixed People in America.* New York: Sage.
Sater, William F. 1974. "The Black Experience in Chile." In *Slavery and Race Relations in Latin America,* edited by Robert Brent Toplin. Westport, Conn.: Greenwood Press.
Scales-Trent, Judy. 1995. *Notes of a White Black Woman.* University Park: Pennsylvania State University Press.
Schermerhorn, R. A. 1970. *Comparative Ethnic Relations.* New York: Random House.
Schiavo-Campo, Salvatore. 1994. *Institutional Change and the Public Sector in Transitional Economies.* DP 241. Washington, D.C.: World Bank.
Schirmer, Daniel B., and Stephen R. Shalom. 1987. *The Philippines Reader: A History*

of Colonialism, Neocolonialism, Dictatorship and Resistance. Boston: South End Press.
Schmidt, Hans. 1971. *The U.S. Occupation of Haiti, 1915–1934.* New Brunswick, N.J.: Rutgers University Press.
Schwartz, Barry N., and Robert Disch. 1970. *White Racism: Its History, Pathology and Practice.* New York: Dell Publishing Company.
Senior, Clarence. 1952. *Strangers and Neighbors: The Story of Our Puerto Rican Citizens.* New York: Anti-Defamation League of B'i B'rith.
Sheppard, Jill. 1977. *The Redlegs of Barbados.* Millwood, N.Y.: Kraus-Thompson Organization Ltd.
Sickles, Robert J. 1972. *Race, Marriage and the Law.* Albuquerque: University of New Mexico Press.
Sider, Gerald M. 1993. *Lumbee Indian Histories: Race, Ethnicity, and Indian Identity in the Southern United States.* Cambridge: Cambridge University Press.
Sinkler, George. 1972. *The Racial Attitudes of American Presidents.* New York: Doubleday Anchor.
Siu, Paul C. P. 1987. *The Chinese Laundryman: A Study of Social Isolation,* edited by John Kuo Wei Tchen. New York: New York University Press.
Smith, David J. 1993. *The Eugenic Assault on America: Scenes in Red, White and Black.* Fairfax, Va.: George Mason University Press.
Smith, James. 1841. *The Winter of 1840 in St. Croix.* Private publication.
Smith Michael G. 1965. *The Plural Society in the British West Indies.* Berkeley, University of California Press.
Solaun, M., and S. Kronus. 1973. *Discrimination Without Violence: Miscegenation and Racial Conflict in Latin America.* New York: Wiley-Interscience.
Sollors, Werner. 1986. *Beyond Ethnicity: Consent and Descent in American Culture.* New York: Oxford University Press.
Spicer, Edward H. 1980. "Federal Policy Toward American Indians." In *Harvard Encyclopedia of American Ethnic Groups,* edited by Stephen Thernstrom. Cambridge, Mass.: Harvard University Press.
Spingarn, Lawrence. 1957. "Slavery in the Danish West Indies." *The American-Scandinavian Review* (Spring), pp. 35–43.
St. Thomas Daily News. Various editions.
Statistical Policy Directive 15. 1974. *Race and Ethnic Standards for Federal Statistics and Administrative Reporting.* Washington, D.C.: Office of Management and Budget.
Steinberg, Stephen. 1981, 1989. *The Ethnic Myth: Race, Ethnicity, and Class in America.* New York: Atheneum. Reprint: Boston: Beacon Press.
Steward, Julian et. al. 1956, 1972. *The People of Puerto Rico: A Study in Social Anthropology.* Urbana: University of Illinois Press.
Stone, John. 1985. *Racial Conflict in Contemporary Society.* Cambridge, Mass.: Harvard University Press.
Stowe, Harriet Beecher, 1852, 1966. *Uncle Tom's Cabin.* New York: G. Brazille.
Takaki, Ronald. 1989. *Strangers from a Different Shore: A History of Asian Americans.* New York: Penguin.
Tansil, Charles Callan. 1935. *The Purchase of the Danish West Indies.* Gloucester, Mass.: Peter Smith.
Taylor, Charles Edwin. 1888. *Leaflets from the Danish West Indies.* London: William Dawson.

Thompson, Robert K. 1968. "Pan-Indianism." In *The American Indian Today*, edited by S. Levine and N. O. Lurie. Deland, Fl.: Everett Edwards.
Thybony, Scott. 1991. "Against All Odds: Black Seminoles Win Their Freedom from Florida to Texas." *Smithsonian*, April.
Tocqueville, Alexis de. 1848, 1966. *Democracy in America*. Translated by George T. Lawrence and edited by J. P. Mayer. New York: Harper and Row.
Toplin, Robert Brent, ed. 1974. *Slavery and Race Relations in Latin America*. Westport, Conn.: Greenwood Press.
Tumin, Melvin, with Arnold S. Feldman. 1961. *Social Class and Social Change in Puerto Rico*. Indianapolis: The Bobbs-Merrill Co.
Tumin, Melvin. 1969. *Comparative Perspectives on Race Relations*. Boston: Little, Brown.
U.S. House Committee on Interior and Insular Affairs. 1986. *Federal Policies Regarding the U.S. Insular Areas. Oversight Hearings*. 99th Congress, 2nd sess., April 10.
———. 1991. *Virgin Islands Reunification Act—Water Island, Hearings*. 101st Congress, 2nd sess., May 3.
U.S. House Subcommittee. 1952. *A Bill to Elect the Governor, Hearings*. Washington, D.C.: Government Printing Office.
U.S. House Subcommittee on Interior and Insular Affairs. 1992. *Puerto Rico Self-Determination Act, Hearings*. 101st Congress, 2nd sess.
U.S. House Subcommittee on Native American and Insular Affairs. 1995. *Impact of Contract with America on the Territories, Hearing*. 104th Cong., 2nd sess., January 31.
U.S. Senate Committee on Territories and Insular Affairs. 1930. *Independence for the Philippine Islands, Hearings*. 71st Cong., 2nd sess.
U.S. Senate Select Committee on Indian Affairs. 1978. *Hawaiian Native Educational Assistance Act*. 95th Congress, 2nd sess., S.857, May 16.
Van Cleve, Ruth. 1974. *The Office of Territorial Affairs*. New York: Praeger.
Van den Berghe, Pierre. 1967. *Race and Racism*. New York: Wiley.
———. 1970. *Race and Ethnicity*. New York: Random House.
Vaughan, Alden T. 1988. "From White Man to Redskin." In *Indians and Europeans: Selected Articles on Indian-White Relations in Colonial North America*, edited by Peter Charles Hoffer. New York: Garland.
Virgin Islands Code. Annotated, Vol. 1, Title 1 through 3. 1994. Salem, N.H.: Butterworth Legal Publishers.
Virgin Islands Digest: Coverning Opinions of Local and Federal Courts from 1917 to Date. Vol. 1. Oxford, N.H.: Butterworth Legal Publishers.
Virgin Islands of the United States. 1917. Washington, D.C.: Navy Department.
Vobejda, Barbara. 1991. "More Americans Declaring Indian Identity." *Washington Post*, February 11, p. 1.
———. 1991. "Categorizing the Nation's Millions of 'Other Race.'" *Washington Post*, April 29, p. A9.
von Albertini, Rudolph. 1971. *Decolonization: The Administration and Future of the Colonies, 1919–1960*. Translated from the German by Francisca Garvie. Garden City, N.Y.: Doubleday.
Wagenheim, Kal. 1970. *Puerto Rico: A Profile*. New York: Praeger.
———. 1973. *The Puerto Ricans: A Documentary History*. New York: Praeger.

Weinstein, Edwin A. 1962. *Cultural Aspects of Delusion: A Psychiatric Study of the Virgin Islands.* New York: Free Press.

Weisman, Alan. 1990. "An Island in Limbo: State, Nation or Commonwealth? Puerto Ricans Hotly Debate Their Future." *New York Times,* February 18.

Wells, Henry. 1969. *The Modernization of Puerto Rico: A Political Study of Changing Values and Institutions.* Cambridge, Mass.: Harvard University Press.

Westergaard, Waldemar. 1917. *The Danish West Indies Under Company Rule, 1671–1754.* New York: Macmillan.

Weston, Rubin Francis. 1972. *Racism in U.S. Imperialism.* Columbia: South Carolina University Press.

White, John. 1985, 1990. *Black Leadership in America: From Booker T. Washington to Jesse Jackson.* London: Longman.

Williams, Eric. 1942, 1969. *The Negro in the Caribbean.* New York: Negro Universities Press.

———. 1945. "Race Relations in Puerto Rico and the Virgin Islands." *Foreign Affairs* 2, January.

———. 1960. "Race Relations in Caribbean Society." In *Caribbean Studies: A Symposium,* edited by Vera Rubin. Seattle: University of Washington Press.

Williams, Gregory. 1995. *Life on the Color Line: The True Story of a White Boy Who Discovered He Was Black.* New York: Dutton.

Williams, Vernon J., Jr. 1989. *From a Caste to a Minority: Changing Attitudes of American Sociologists Toward Afro-Americans, 1896–1945.* Westport, Conn.: Greenwood Press.

Williamson, Joel. 1980. *New People: Miscegenation and Mulattoes in the United States.* New York: Free Press.

Williamson, Oliver E. 1985. *Economic Institutions of Capitalism: Firms, Markets and Relational Contracting.* New York: Free Press.

Willoughby, William Franklin. 1905. *Territories and Dependencies of the United States: Their Government and Administration.* New York: The Century Co.

Wilson, William J. 1975. *The Declining Significance of Race: Blacks and Changing American Institutions.* Chicago: University of Chicago Press.

Wilson, Woodrow. 1901. "Reconstruction in the Southern States." *Atlantic Monthly* (January). Quoted in Rayford W. Logan, *The Betrayal of the Negro.* 1965; London: Macmillan Ltd., 1969.

World Factbook. 1995. Washington, D.C.: Central Intelligence Agency, 1995.

Index

Abbott, Edith, 37, 40
Abbott v. Hicks (1892), 62
Adams, Alton August, 160, 163
Adams, Heribert, 16
Adams, John Quincy, 27
Africans: African Americans, 16–17, 23; neoconservatives, 21; cultural assimilation and exclusion, 30; and Native Americans, 30; status of, 30; English attitudes toward, 32; early definitions of, 57; and Native American ancestry, 57, 75, 76, 80; and citizenship, 58; middle-class and "greening of," 72; and African American connection in U.S. Virgin Islands, 152, 165
Alaska and statehood, 84
Albizu Campos, Pedro, 126, 131, 132
Alexander, Archie, 152
American case law: racial definition of Native Americans, 53; purpose of, 55; racial definition of African Americans, 57; racial construction (*see Dred Scott* case); and slavery, 58–59; post-Reconstruction period, 61. *See also Plessy v. Ferguson*
American colonial policy: and race, 13–15; evolution, 23; and American case law, 51; "divine mission," 88; legacy of American Revolution on, 99; characteristics of, 100; compared to European colonialism, 100–104, 112; the role of ideology, 101–2; administrative aspects, 105; racial ideology of, 105–9. *See also* Pragmatic materialism; Washington, Booker T.
American colonial possessions, 88, 169; euphemisms for, 99
American racial tradition: administrative structure of, 111–12; role of military in, 111. *See also* Racial tradition
American Samoa. *See* Samoa, American
American territorial expansion: periods of, 2, 79, 80; continental expansion, 81; and link to American racial tradition, 113–15
Anderson v. Millikin et al., 61
Anglo-Saxonism: and Native Americans, 25; white supremacy and citizenship, 52; and "Manifest Destiny," 82, 87
Apter, David, 5
Armstrong, Samuel Chapman: and Booker T. Washington, 28, 105–6;

Reconstruction era policies and Negroes, 28; Hampton Normal and Agricultural Institute, 29; and Native Americans, 29, 106
Articles of Confederation and Native Americans, 53
Asians, 24, 33, 34, 40; and the American legal system, 65–67; impact on U.S. overseas territories, 65; and Naturalization Act (1790), 65; in Hawaii, 85. *See also* Chamorros (Guam); Chinese; Filipinos; Japanese
Assimilation: in America, 23; myth of, 24; and Native Americans, 27, 28, 83; "coercive" and colonized Irish, 28; role of education (*see* Hampton Normal and Agricultural Institute); and nationality, 52; in French colonialism, 102; in Portuguese colonialism, 102; in American colonialism, 104; in European colonialism, 104. *See also* de Crevecoeur, J. Hector St. John (Crevecoeur de Jean, Michel Guillaume)
Atlanta Compromise, 109, 160

Baca, Lawrence, 53, 56
Bagley, Christopher, 6
Baldorioty de Castro, Roman, 119
Bennett, Lerone, 69
Beveridge, Alfred J., 40–41
Beveridge, Andrew A., 72, 87
Bieder, Robert E., 55
Birth of a Nation, The, 33
Black Caucus (U.S. Congress), 163
Blalock, H. M., Jr., 10
Boarding schools. *See* Education, Native American and boarding schools
Boesak, Allan, 18
Bogardus, Emory S., 41, 48 n.21
Bough, James A., 100, 161
Brazile, Leon M., 70
British colonialism: perceptions of race, 103; race and status differences of colonies, 104
Bucchioni, Eugene, 126, 127
Bureau of Indian Affairs, 54
Burgess, John W., 87

Bush, George Herbert Walker, 21 n.13
Butler, Hugh, 160, 161

Cabranes, Jose A., 68, 123
Calero-Toledo v. Pearson Yacht Leasing Co., 138n.13
California: anti-Chinese legislation (federal and state), 36–38; violence against, 36–37
Campbell, Albert A., 141
Canny, Nicholas P., 28
Caribbean Basic Economic Recovery Act, 148
Carlisle Indian Industrial School, 29
Carrión Morales, Arturo, 125
Cashmore, Ernest, 103
Celso Barbosa, José, 121, 125, 131
Chamorros (Guam): racism against, 47 n.20; seeking reparations, 48 n.20, 91, 155
Cherokee Nation, and white missionaries, 74 n.2. *See also* Marshall, Chief Justice John; Native Americans
Chinese: as inassimilable, 3, 7, 34; antimiscegenation laws against, 35, 38; perceived as economic threat and Chinese Exclusion Act, 35, 36; prostitutes, 35; racism toward, 35–38; compared to blacks, 36, 38, 39, 65; sociosexual relations with African Americans, 38–40; in Mississippi Delta, 39; socioracial status of, and changes in, 39–40, 65; anti-immigrant statutes and civil rights activism, 46, 65; racial tradition (*see* Racial tradition); and miscegenation, 70
Chinese-American Citizens Alliance (CACA), 46 n.17
Civil Rights Act: of 1866, 59; of 1964, 64
Clansman, The, 33
Class and culture, 6, 7, 17
Classifications, bureaucratic, of race: and racial groups, 45; American case law and racial purpose, 51; arbitrary socioracial classification, 52; and legal construction of, 53; of mixed-race

INDEX

people, 64. *See also* Office of Management and Budget (OMB)
Cleveland, Grover, 83
Clinton, William Jefferson, 169 n.1
Coase, Ronald, 72, 77 n.26
Cohen, Felix S., 55, 56
Commanger, Henry Steele, 51
Common law and race, 51
Commonwealth status, 3; in Puerto Rico, 133–35
Concepcion de Gracia, Gilberto, 132
Conflict: racial, 5, 7, 8, 16; in flexible racial traditions, 11; in rigid racial traditions, 16; result of American colonial policy, 114; in Puerto Rioco, 125; in U.S. Virgin Islands 154–58
Congress, U.S.: and Native Americans, 27, 53–55; and citizenship of overseas territorial inhabitants, 67; statehood ordinance, 80, 90; congressional supremacy and creation of "Indian Territory," 82–83; annexation of Hawaii, 85; discretion of, toward territories, 94; and Insular Cases, 95; and territorial status, 96; and colonial administration, 113; Puerto Ricans attack on, 126; and status of Puerto Rico, 128–29; administration of U.S. Virgin Islands, 147–49, 162; Subcommittee on Territories and Insular Affairs, 159; and Virgin Islands statehood, 161
Constantino, Renato, 40
Constitution, U.S., 53, 63; as colorblind, 64; and Puerto Rico political status, 129
Cordasco, Francesco, 126, 127
de Crevecoeur, J. Hector St. John (Crevecoeur de Jean, Michel Guillaume), 23, 52, 53, 58, 66
Cuba (as American possession), 88; mixed-race people and annexation, 92; U.S. racism toward, 113

Daniels, Roger, 38
Danish Antilles, 88 (*see* Virgin Islands, of United States); African Americans in, 152; land ownership in, 155

Darwinism, 87
Davis, James F., 41
Dawes Severalty Act (General Allotment Act, 1887), 54; and "blood quantum," code, 54, 55; sociracial status and allocation of land, 54; Congress and, 75 n.3; and "civilized" tribes, 83; termination of Indian Territory, 83
de Castro, Morris, 153
DeConde, Alexander, 100, 113
Deficiency Act (1904) and Chinese, 37
Degler, Carl, 6
deLugo, Ron, 163
Dennis, Rutledge, 46
Disch, Robert, 32
Division of Territories and Island Possessions, U.S., 112
Dookhan, Isaac, 141
Drake, Francis, 24
Dred Scott, case, 37, 57, 58
Du Bois, William Edward Burghardt, 32, 167
Dyer, Thomas G., 88, 108, 109

Economic cooperation, 18
Education, Native American and boarding schools, 29
Ellis, Gladwin, 155
Ely, Melvin Patrick, 33
Emerson, Rupert, 100
Enloe, Cynthia, 16
European ancestry, 24
Evans, Melvin H., 163
Examining Board of Engineers, Architects and Surveyors v. Flores de Otero, 138 n.13
Exclusion: and Native Americans, 24; racial attitudes of, 24; policies toward colonized Irish, 28; Chinese Exclusion Act, 35, 36. *See also* Chinese

Faleomavaega, Eni F. H., 48 n.2
Fanon, Frantz, 103
Farrakhan, Louis, 18
Fernandes, Florestan, 12, 124
Ferré, Luis A., 125
Fieldhouse, D. K., 96

Fifteenth Amendment, 35
Fiji Islands, 46 n.10
Filipinos, 40–41; and "Benevolent Assimilation," 40; compared to Negroes, 40; racism toward, 40–41, 48–49; and *Pajaro* Resolutions, 48; and statehood (*see Toyota v. United States* [1924]); as inassimilable, 67; and naturalization, 67; and intermarriage with whites, 70, 77; views of Theodore Roosevelt on, 109; racial classification and purpose, 122; racial mixture of, 123
Finkelman, Paul, 59, 60
Fiske, John, 87
"Flag territories," 1; and race, 2, 80; and statehood, 90–91, 93–94; race-mixing and annexation, 92. *See also* Territorial acquisitions
Fletcher, Arthur A., 16
Foner, Philip S., 63, 81
Foraker Act, 128
Foster, William Z., 30
Fountain Valley Country Club murders, 155, 157
Fourteenth Amendment and citizenship, 35, 59, 60, 62, 63
Francis, Rothschild, 163
Frazer, Victor O., 163
Freedmen's Bureau (Bureau of Refugees, Freedmen and Abandoned Lands), 105
Freeman, Edward A., 103
Furnivall, J. S., 5, 23

Garraty, John A., 63, 81
Garvey, Marcus, 18
Geary Act, 35. *See also* Chinese
General Allotment Act (1887). *See* Dawes Severalty Act
Genovese, Eugene D., 64
Georgia, Cherokees and land alienation in (1829), 54, 74
Godoy, Hernan, 43
Gonzales, Antonió, 125
Gonzalez, Jose Louis, 123
Gonzalez v. Williams, 128
Gordon, Walter A., 152

Gossett, Thomas G., 25, 27
Green, Rayna, 29, 30
Griffith, D. W., 33
Grito de Lares. See Spanish
Guam: Organic Act and American citizenship, 48 n.20; American territory, 88; trends in government, 89; population and language, 91; current status of, 166 n.21
Guild, Jane Purcell, 57

Haiti, American occupation of, 101
Haizlip, Shirlee Taylor, 42
Hall, Kermit L., 59, 60
Hall v. DeCuir, 60. *See also Plessy v. Ferguson*
Hampton Normal and Agricultural Institute, 29; African American education, 29; Native American Program and education, 29, 30, 106; the "Wigwam," 29, 106; and Samuel Chapman Armstrong, 106; and territorial education, 106; and U.S. Virgin Islands, 146, 147
Handbook of Federal Indian Law, 56
Haney Lopez, Ian F., 65, 71
Hanson, Parker Earl, 126
Harlan, John Marshall, 46, 74
Harlan, Louis R., 116, 137
Harrison, Benjamin, 86
Hastie, William E., 152, 165
Hawaii: race and annexation, 2, 79; racial composition of, and evolution to statehood, 84–87, 161; statehood, and evolution to, 84; Committee of Safety, 85; representative government, 85; arrival of American troops, 86; and U.S. Senate, 86, 88
Heegaard, Anna, 145
Hemins, Sally, 145
Henriques, Fernando, 26
Henry, Patrick, 26, 68, 74
Hernández Colón, Rafael, 125
Higginbotham, A. Leon, Jr., 69
Higham, John, 52
Hispanics, racial classification of, 42, 49
Hoetink, Harrimus, 32
Hollister, Frederick J., 137 n.8

INDEX

Holmes, Oliver Wendell, 51, 64
Hoover, Herbert, 146
Hopkins, Elizabeth, 10
Horsman, Reginald, 100
Hostos, de Eugenio Mario, 131
Howard, O. O., 105, 115 n.4
Howard University and territorial education, 105
Hughes, Langston, 127; fictional character Jess B. Simple and Puerto Ricans, 127–28
Hultgren, Mary Lou, 29, 30

Images and stereotyping: of African Americans, 32, 33, 34; of Native Americans, 32
Independence of Puerto Rico, 135–36
Indian Citizenship Act (1924), 55; and land, 83–84
Indian Claims Commission Act, 55
Indian Intercourse Act (1834), 84
Indian Removal Act (1830), 55
Indian Reorganization Act (IRA), 30, 55; definition of Indians, 56
Indian Territory and land alienation, 75; creation of, 82
Innis, Roy, 152
Institutionalized inequality and power (slavery, colonialism), 6, 8
Insular Areas. *See* Territorial acquisitions
Insular Cases, The, 92, 129. *See also* Puerto Rico, Commonwealth of
Interior Department, U.S., and colonial administration, 112
Interracial marriage (prohibitions against), 42; as a crime, 70; and Fourteenth Amendment, 70
Inuit (Greenland), 75
Ireland, 24
Irish, colonized (English policy toward) and similar policy toward Native Americans, 28; cultural assimilation of, 28; "wild," 28; immigrants and anti-Chinese sentiment, 35; British perceptions of, 103
Italy, 24

Japanese: as inassimilable, 34; Occupation of Guam, 47; and legal challenges to racism, 65–68; racial classification of, 65–66; as nonwhite, 67
Jefferson, Thomas, 68, 145
Jennings, Francis, 25, 28, 45
Jibaro, 134
Johns, Stephanie Bernardo, 35
Johnson, Jack, 33
Johnson, James Weldon, 77 n.23
Johnston, Harry H., 141, 142
Johnston, Hugh, 57, 76 n.9
Jones, J. Raymond, 152
Jones Act (1916, 1917), 122, 128
July, Robert, 103

Kaamehameha, King, III, 85
Kanza, Thomas, 104
Katznelson, Ira, 5–6
Kennedy, Randall, 33
Kim Ark Wong v. United States (1898), 47 n.17
King, Cyril E., 163
Kingsley, Charles, 103
Kipling, Rudyard, 97 n.4, 108
Klein, Herbert S., 30
Ku Klux Klan. *See* Griffith, D. W.

Lai, H. M., 46
Lanterns on the Levee (Percy), 39
Law. *See* American case law
Leadership, colonial, 18
Leibowitz, Arnold H., 80, 109, 165
Letters from an American Farmer (de Crevecoeur), 23, 52
Lewis, Gordon, 145, 151
Lewisohn, Florence, 141, 142, 145
Liliuokalani, Queen "Lydia," 85
Loewen, James W., 38–40
Lofgren, Charles A., 61, 62
Logan, Rayford W., 34, 116
Louisiana: "Creoles of color," 61–62; Separate Car Act, 62
Louisiana, racial classifications, 41
Loving v. Virginia (1967), 70

Macridis, Roy, 100
McFarlane, Alva C., 159
McKinley, William, 100, 110–11

Malcolm X, 12
Manifest Destiny: and John L. O'Sullivan, 81–82; and race, 81; and contiguous territories, 82; Hawaii, 85; and racial tradition, 87
Marianas, Northern, 88, 89, 97 n.7; trends in government, 89; population and language, 91
Mari Brás, Juan, 125
Marriage and race. *See* Miscegenation
Marshall, John, 27, 52, 54, 74
Marshall Islands, 88, 89; population and language, 91
Martinez Berrios, Ruben A., 125, 136, 138 n.15
Massachusetts Bay Colony, 25
Mathews, Thomas G., 121, 127
"Melting pot," American, 24
Mexico, war with and territorial acquisition, 2; mixed-race population, 92
Micronesia, Federated State of, 88, 89; population and language of, 91
Middle-men minorities, characteristics of, 10
Milan, Gabriel, 153
Miller, Loren, 63
Miller, Stuart Creighton, 40
Miscegenation, 17; antimiscegenation doctrine, 25, 42, 68; interracial marriage, 25; and Filipinos, 48 (*see* Rigid racial tradition); and Thomas Jefferson, 68; persistence in America, 71; and sexual fears, 77; in Hawaii, 86. *See also* Africans; Asians; Mixed-race people; Native Americans
Missionaries (American) in Hawaii, 85
The Mississippi Chinese: Between Black and White (Loewen), 38
Missouri Compromise and slavery, 58
Mixed-race people: terms in United States, 42, 43; classifications of, 43–44; "tragic mulatto" syndrome, 49; and annexation of territories, 92–94. *See also* Rigid racial tradition
Model Asians/"Model minority." *See* Chinese; Japanese
Modernization theory and race, 7, 8
Molin, Paulette Fairbanks, 29, 30

Monroe, James, 27
Monroe Doctrine, 90
Moore, Herman, 154
Morton v. Mancari (1974), 54
Mulatto, historical evolution of term, 57; as white, 61–63; in Louisiana, 62; as concubines (New Orleans), 64
Muñoz Marin, Luis, 125, 129, 131, 133
Muñoz Rivera, Luis, 131
Myrdal, Gunnar, 68, 76 n.17

Naim v. Naim (1955), 70
Native Americans: conquest myth, 24; European views of, 24, 28; "redskins," 24, 45; children of, 25–26; marriage with Europeans, and debate on, 25; with white women, 26; and land alienation, 27, 28, 55; and power, 27; comparison to Africans, 28; cultural assimilation of, 28; as U.S. government policy, 28; and Booker T. Washington, 29; as "half-Negro" mongrels, 29; Hampton Normal and Agricultural Institute, 29; and *Plessy v. Ferguson*, 29; and Samuel Chapman Armstrong, 29; and white education, 29; de Tocqueville on "half-castes," 30; and Gen. Philip Sheridan, 45; definitions of, 53, 56; and Chief Justice John Marshall, 54; federally recognized, 54; reservation land allotments (*see* Dawes Severalty Act); suppression of, 79; and "manifest destiny," 82; "civilized tribes" and termination of Indian Territory, 83
Native Sons of the Gold State (Chinese), 46 n.17
Naturalization Act of 1790, 35, 65
Navy, U.S., and colonial administration, 112
Negro: The Southerner's Problem, The (Page) 33
Negroes as legal "persons," 60. *See also* Africans, African Americans
Nicaragua, American occupation of, 101

North, Douglass C., 72, 77 n.26
Northern Marianas. *See* Marianas, Northern
Northwest Ordinance (1787): and Native Americans, 27, 80; establishment of federal authority, 80; territorial incorporation, 80, 81; and Thomas Jefferson (1784), 80; role of U.S. Congress, 81

Office of Management and Budget (OMB) and racial classifications, 44; Statistical Policy Directive 15, 44, 49 n.28
Office of Territorial Affairs, 113
Oldham, J. H., 34
Oliphant v. Suquamish Tribe of Indians (1978), 53
Organic Act: in Hawaii, 86; Puerto Rico, 128; U.S. Virgin Islands, 148, 154, 159. *See also* Individual territories
Overseas territories, American: comparison to Native Americans, 28, 83; and *Ozawa v. United States* (1922) and citizenship in, 65–67; and manifest destiny, 87; and race, 87; "white man's burden" in, 87; compared to contiguous territories, 90
Ozawa v. United States (1922), 65–67

Pacific Trust Territories, 88
Page, Thomas Nelson, 33
Paiewonsky, Ralph M., 153, 154
Palau, 88, 89, 97 n.7; population and language, 91
Panama Canal, 80
Paquin, Lyonel, 153
Paris, Treaty of, 79, 90, 92
Parry, Ellwood, 46 n.11
Partido Democratico Popular, 132, 134
Partido Independentista Puertorriqueno, 132, 135
"Path dependence," 72
Patterson, Orlando, 32
Peary, Robert, 75 n.2
People v. Hall (Chinese), 37
Percy, William Alexander, 39

Perez v. Lippold (1948), 70
Philippines: Tydings-McDuffie Act (1934), 40; U.S. colonization of, 40; as American territory, 67; statehood of, 68; and American (racial) aims in, 88; African Americans and desertion to, 92; and racial mixing, 92; antiannexation sentiment, 93; American colonial reluctance toward, 100, 111; independence of, 118; resident commissioner in, 118; Jones Act (1916), 122
Platt Amendment and Cuba, 90
Plessy, Homer, 43, 61; and Chinese socioracial status, 40
Plessy v. Ferguson (1896), 3, 61–64, 73, 126
Plural society, 5, 7, 24
Pocahontas: and John Rolfe, 25, 26; and King James I, 26; symbolism of, 26; and Virginia State Bureau of Vital Statistics, 30
Popular Democratic Party, 132
Poulson, Morris, 160
"Power hematology" of African ancestry, 42
Pragmatic materialism: as centerpiece of American colonialism, 99, 105–13; and Atlanta Compromise, 109; assessment of, 114; and Commonwealth status, 134; in Puerto Rico, 136; in U.S. Virgin Islands, 147–49, 151, 160, 163–64. *See also* Washington, Booker T.
Pratt, Richard Henry, and Native Americans, 29
Puerto Ricans: views of Theodore Roosevelt on, 109; downward leveling of mixed-race socioracial status, 114; as "rainbow people," 118, 122; as Negroes, 122, 123, 124; as whites, 122, 123, 124; denial of African ancestry and purpose, 124; pathology of normality, 124; elimination of racial classifications in, 125; flexible racial tradition, 125; "limpieza de sangre" in, 126; Negroes in, 126–27; white bias in, 126; socioracial status of

"dark" Puerto Ricans, 127; in the United States, 127
Puerto Rico, Commonwealth of: racial formation in, 66, 88, 89; trends in government, 89; population and language, 91; insular case law, 95; pragmatic materialism and colonial policy, 110, 111; demographics of, 117; as Commonwealth, and compared to Alaska and Hawaii, 118; government structure, 118; resident commissioner, 118; American occupation, 119; race and society under American rule, 121–23; Booker T. Washington on, 122; Jones Act (1917), 122, 128; Negro politicians, 125; "white" politicians, 125, 126; "mixed-race politicians" in, 126; Organic Act and citizenship, 128; political developments, 128–31; Public Law 600, 128, 132; ambiguity of political status, 129–31; Commonwealth status, 129–31; 1993 plebiscite and status alternatives, 129–32; and Bush administration, 130, 133, 138; independence issue, 131; Nationalist Party and Blair House attack, 131–32; "Operation Bootstrap," 131; statehood, 131, 132; cultural nationalists, 132
Puerto Rico Department of Consumer Affairs v. Isla Petroleum, 138 n.13

Race and European colonialism, 102–4
Race and immigration: naturalization and racial restrictions, 71; white-person prerequisite cases, 71. *See also* Naturalization Act of 1790
"Race enforcers": at Denny's Restaurant, 73; and Josephine Baker, 73; Lester Maddox, 73
Racial classification: in bureaucratic practice, and U.S. Census, 43; and Fourteenth amendment, 66; racial formation of nonwhites, 66; "common knowledge rationale," 71
Racial separation. *See Plessy v. Ferguson*
Racial tradition: concept and characteristics, 7–17; and socioracial status, 7–8; colonialism and power, 8; mixed-race ancestry, 8, 9, 10, 11; flexible racial tradition, characteristics of, 9–14, 103, 168; lower-class Europeans, 11; "mulatto escape hatch," 11; Spanish, 12; leadership in, 13; sociosexual relationships (concubinage, marriage), children of, 13; in Danish Antilles, 14, 149; raising status of, 14; in western Samoa, 14; and Native Americans, 29, 30, 56; formal and informal aspects, 72–74, 168; and the "new institutional economics," 72; and white immigrants, 74; influence on colonial policy, 100–102; exported to overseas territories, 113; American ignorance of racial nuances in, 114; in U.S. Virgin Islands, 149–51; increasing movement toward, 167
Racism, and American colonialism, 136; in U.S. Virgin Islands, 154
Racism, and American colonial military administration, 113, 114, 158
Raleigh, Walter, 24
Ramos Antonini, Ernesto, 126
re Ah Yup v. Sawyer (1878), 67
Reconstruction, failure of, 73, 168
Reports of the United States Immigration Commission, 37
Reports of the United States Industrial Commission, 37
Reservations and Native Americans, comparison to "Bantustans," 82
Reuter, Edward Byron, 120
Rice v. Gong Lum (1925), 39
Rigid racial tradition, American: hypo-descent, and "one drop" rule, 15, 24, 30, 41, 42, 57; characteristics of, 15–17; genotype and racial classification, 15; in Nazi Germany and South Africa, 15; sociosocial status of mixed-race people, 15–16, 49; Americans, 16; "genes prisoners" in, 16; "passing," 16; political consequences of, 16, 17–18; status incongruity, 16, 17; subordinate races and caste, African

Americans, 16–17; leadership in, 17; mixed marriages, 17; styles of, 18; of Asians, 34, 40; Chinese in, 38–40; centerpiece of, 68; increasing flexibility of, 72, 74; in U.S. Virgin Islands, 149, 150–51, 154
Roberts, Lionel Valdema, 163
Roberts v. The City of Boston (1849), 61
Rodriguez, Clara E., 118
Rohrback, D. W., 48n.21
Romero Barceló, Carlus, 125, 133
Roosevelt, Theodore, 105; anti-Asian legislation, 38; and Anglo-Saxon assimilation, 52; and Nordic myths of civilization, 88, 108; and American colonial policy, 107–8; and Booker T. Washington, 107; and Lamarckian theories, 108; attitudes toward African Americans, 109, 116; racial views of, 109
Roosevelt, Theodore, Jr.: governor of Puerto Rico and the Philippines, 116 n.9; racial views, 116
Roosevelt Corollary and Latin America, 90, 165 n.2
Rosselló, Pedro, 125
Roxbury, Mass., Chinese in, 47
Ruggles, Steven, 72

St. Croix Chamber of Commerce, 160
St. Thomas Daily News, 159, 160, 161, 165 n.13
Samoa, American, 88–89; trends in government, 89; population and language, 91; nationals in, 97 n.11
Sanchez Villella, Roberto, 125
Scalia, Anton, 21 n.13
Schermerhorn, R. A., 6
Schirmer, Daniel B., 41, 49, 100
Schwartz, Barry N., 32
Shalom, Stephen R., 41, 49, 100
Shawnees and statehood, 83
Sheridan, General Philip, 24, 45n.2
Sickles, Robert J., 55
Slaughterhouse cases, 60
Slavery, 6; American, Brazilian, Danish Antilles, Spanish justifications for, 32
Smith, David J., 30

Smith, M. G., 144
Socioracial status, 7
Sollors, Werner, 26
South Africa (predemocratic): racial tradition of, 16; interracial sex, 42
Souther v. Commonwealth (1851), 59
Spanish: colonialism of Puerto Rico, 118–19; colonial structure of, 118–19; Charter of Autonomy, 119, 128; *Grito de Lares*, 119; race and society in, 119–21; Black Code, 120–21; changing race relations in, 120; slavery, 120–21; socioracial hierarchy in, 120; Negroes, 121
Spanish, American War (1898): defeat and acquisition of territories, 1; and Hawaii, 86; and colonial acquisitions, 88
Spanish language in Puerto Rico, 133
Spicer, Edward H., 29
"Squaw" (as derogatory term), 45 n.3
Stanhope, Dorothy, 92
Statehood (of overseas territories): conditions for, 80, 81; and "civilized tribes," 83; and Indian Territory, 83; and white majority territories, 84; precedent of Louisiana and Florida, 86; resident commissioner and, 118; for Puerto Rico, 133, 136. *See also Toyota v. United States* (1924)
State v. Mann (1869), 58
Status, political: evolution of territories, 2; race and statehood, 3, 114–15; primacy of English for, 80; status limbo, 95; status options (Puerto Rico), 132–35
Steinberg, Stephen, 54
Steward, Julian H., 120–21
Stone, John, 5
Stowe, Harriet Beecher, 32
Strong, Josiah, 87
Sutherland, George Justice (1922), 66

Taft, Chief Justice William Howard, 40
Takaki, Ronald, 35, 36, 40, 65, 67, 69
Taney, Justice Roger Brooke and Chinese, 37; and *Dred Scott* case, 58
Taylor, Charles Edwin, 144

Tecumseh. *See* Shawnees and statehood
Territorial acquisitions: acquisition of Trust Territories of the Pacific Islands (1947), 1, 79, 88; contiguous and overseas, 1; Danish Antilles (1917 purchase), 1; Eastern Samoa acquisition by Treaty of Berlin (1899), 1; racial status of inhabitants, 65; racial formation of population, 66; restrictive naturalization laws against, 71; "dissimilar" populations of, 80; and Spanish American War, 1898 (Cuba, Puerto Rico, Philippines, Guam), 88. *See also* Virgin Islands, of United States
Territorial status: incorporated and unincorporated territories, definitions of, 94–95; status uncertainty, 95; second-class status, 100
Teutonic nations and civilization, 87–88
Thirteenth Amendment, 61, 63
Thomas, Clarence, 21 n.13
Thurmond, Strom, 21 n.13
Tochoway (Comanche), 45 n.2. *See also* Sheridan, General Philip
Tocqueville, Alexis de, 30
Toyota v. United States (1924), 67
Trail of Tears, 74 n.1
Transportation law and race, in post-Reconstruction period, 61. *See also* Hall v. DeCuir; Plessy v. Ferguson
Tribe, Lawrence, 130
Tugwell, Rexford Guy, 134
Twa ("pygmies"), 75 n.2
Tydings, Senator Millard, 135

Uncle Tom's Cabin (Stowe), 33, 46 n.13
Underwood, Congressman Robert A. (Guam), 47 n.20
"Unincorporated" territory, 3; disadvantages of (Puerto Rico), 128–29
United States, as "accidental" imperialist, 88; as reluctant imperialist, 99, 100
United States Department of the Interior, 159, 161, 162

United States Supreme Court and territorial status, 94
United States v. Gue Lim (1900), 46 n.17
Up from Slavery (Washington), 29

Van Cleve, Ruth, 100, 109, 148
van den Berghe, Pierre, 32
Virginia: Code and racial classification of whites and Indians, 55; Act of 1705 (Indians and "coloreds" defined), 57; and antimiscegenation statutes, 69; status of mixed-race children, 69
Virginia Act to Preserve Racial Integrity (1924), 70
Virginia Legislature and Native Americans, 26
Virginia State Bureau of Vital Statistics and Native Americans, 30
Virgin Islands, of United States: trends in government, 89; population and language, 91; as "unincorporated" territory, 95–96; pragmatic materialism and colonial policy, 110; U.S. Navy stewardship of, 114, 140; demographics, 139; Danish acquisition and colonialism, 140–41; political status of, 140; plantation society and slavery in, 141–42; flexible racial tradition, 142–45; socioracial status of mulattoes, 142–43; American purchase of, 144–45; sociosexual components of, 144–45; economic conditions in, 146; economic development, 147–49, 158–59; pragmatic materialism, 147; socioracial structure, 149–54; blacks in, 150–52; African Americans in, 152; Puerto Ricans in, 152–53; Caribbean immigrants, 153; whites in, 153–55; land ownership in, 154–56; white racism in, 154–55, 160–61, 165; political developments, 158–64; size and politics, 158; Interior Department administration of, 159; 1952 congressional hearings in, 159; as unincorporated territory, 159, 161; Re-

INDEX

vised Organic Act (1954), 161; 1993 referendum, 162; political leadership in, 162–63; political status options, 163–64; pragmatic materialism, 163; 1948 referendum, 166
von Scholten, Governor, 142, 145

War Department, U.S.: and colonial administration, 112; racial survey in Puerto Rico, 125
Warren, Chief Justice Earl, 70
Washington, Booker T., 18; and Native Americans, 28; and Tuskegee Institute, 106; as influence on American colonial policy, 107, 109; political philosophy, 107; and pragmatic materialism and "Atlanta Compromise," 107; and Theodore Roosevelt, 107; and southern Italian immigrants, 115–16 n.6; impact on African colonial policies, 116; and Negroes in Puerto Rico, 122
Weicek, William M., 59, 60
Weisman, Alan, 109
Westergaard, Waldemar, 142
Weston, Rubin, 100

White, Walter, 20 n.6, 49 n.22
"White man's burden," 87, 97, 101
"White man's territories" and Native Americans, 82
Whites and Native American ancestry, 56, 75
White settlers and Native Americans: attitudes of, 83; clashes between, 83; in Oklahoma territory, 84; settlement policies, 84; in Hawaii, 85; in Texas, 92
Whites only citizenship. *See* Naturalization Act of 1790
White women, punishment of, for intermarriage, 77
Wilkins, Roy, 18
Williams, Armstrong, 21n.13
Williamson, Oliver, 72, 77n.26
Williams v. Lee (1959), 53
Willoughby, William Franklin, 2, 79, 83, 93, 94, 110–11
Wilson, Woodrow: racism of, 34, 74; and U.S. Virgin Islands, 146
Wong Wing v. United States (1896), 66

Yick Wo v. Hopkins (1886), 66

About the Author

HAZEL M. MCFERSON is Assistant Professor in the Department of Public and International Affairs and Associate at the Institute for Conflict Analysis and Resolution at George Mason University.